# Molecular Architecture
## in Cell Physiology

PRENTICE-HALL INTERNATIONAL, INC., *London*
PRENTICE-HALL OF AUSTRALIA, PTY., LTD., *Sydney*
PRENTICE-HALL OF CANADA, LTD., *Toronto*
PRENTICE-HALL OF INDIA (PRIVATE) LTD., *New Delhi*
PRENTICE-HALL OF JAPAN, INC., *Tokyo*

# Molecular Architecture
# in Cell Physiology

A symposium held under the auspices of
*The Society of General Physiologists*
at its annual meeting at
The Marine Biological Laboratory
Woods Hole, Massachusetts, September 8–11, 1964

Teru Hayashi,
Andrew G. Szent-Györgyi,
*Editors*

Prentice-Hall, Inc.
*Englewood Cliffs, New Jersey*

Library of Congress Catalog Card Number 66–23369
Printed in the United States of America
59964C

# *Preface*

The annual meeting of the Society of General Physiologists was held September 8–11, 1964, at the Marine Biological Laboratory, Woods Hole, Massachusetts. The papers presented at the featured symposium have been collected into this volume, the eleventh annual volume of the Society. This series of volumes has been characterized by excellence in the review of current information, and in pointing out the direction and emphasis of future problems and experimentation. We, the editors, hope that the present volume is in full keeping with this tradition.

The symposium was planned in the firm belief that modern biological investigation has carried our understanding of cell processes to the point where the traditional "unity of structure and function" concept of the cell biologist must be extended to the molecular level. Problems in the understanding of specificity in protein synthesis, genetic coding in cellular development, crystal configuration in the packing of cell components, and other processes fundamental in cellular physiology must have their bases in the topography and energetics of molecular structure. This symposium and this volume is an attempt to present the thinking and information available at several levels in the organized state of matter of importance to biologists. No attempt was made to gather together all available information; rather, the attempt was to bring in scientists from different fields to make for a coverage in breadth.

The symposium consisted of four sessions, and the order of the speakers made for a natural grouping consisting of Basic Chemical Theory, Molecular Architecture of Proteins, Molecular Architecture and Cell Information, and Molecular Architecture and Biological Structures. In the third session, Dr. Giulio Cantoni was unable to attend, but his contribution is included in this volume.

The editors wish to thank the officers and administration of the Marine Biological Laboratory for their kind help and cooperation in making this symposium and the annual meeting an extremely enjoyable one for all the participants. Thanks are also extended to Dr. Seymour S. Cohen and Dr. Allan Hodge for their able chairmanship of sessions III and IV. Grateful acknowledgment is also made to Mrs. Sally Hayashi, whose skill and indefatigable efforts made the final editing of this volume possible. We thank all the authors, not only for their participation and contributions, but also for their patience in the face of the considerable delay in the final publication. Finally, we wish to express our appreciation to the National Institutes of Health, whose support of the symposium contributed so greatly to its success and made this volume possible.

Teru Hayashi
A. G. Szent-Györgyi

# Contents

vii

Contents

# Basic
# Chemical Theory

# The Dynamics
## of Macromolecular Systems[1]

**A. Katchalsky and A. Oplatka**

*Polymer Department*
*and*

**A. Litan**

*Department of Chemical Physics*
*The Weizmann Institute of Science*
*Rehovoth, Israel*

## 1. Introduction

Recent developments in molecular biology have profoundly changed our views on the structure of biocolloids. The picture which has emerged is one of organized macromolecules whose structures contain a wealth of functional information. In the light of present-day knowledge, it is difficult to maintain the older view that saw the cell constituents as a mixture of morphogenetic coacervates, associating and dissociating in a random manner. Electron microscopy indicates not only that cellular function is based on an orderly array of membrane elements, but that the very structure of biocolloids lends itself to formation of higher and more intricate molecular patterns in two and three dimensions.

The beauty of the static patterns revealed in crystalline biopolymers by X-ray analysis should not, however, obscure the more realistic picture of biological macromolecules in their natural milieu. Here the biocolloids

[1] The research reported in this paper has been sponsored by the Office of Scientific Research, OAR, through the European Office of Aerospace Research, United States Air Force.

3

undergo continuous change, both with respect to the internal arrangements of their chain elements and in their over-all molecular shape. Changes of biological interest are not generally those induced by thermal fluctuations, analyzed in detail by the students of rubber elasticity, but rather are those changes of a directed, vectorial, nature. There are strong indications that the macromolecular components of biochemical processes expand and contract, "melt" and "crystallize," during metabolic interactions. It is known that the activity of intracellular organelles, such as the mitochondrion, is accompanied by volume changes that can be attributed to mechanical forces developed during the chemical processes. This coupling between chemical change and mechanical performance in isothermal and isobaric systems has been termed *mechanochemical* conversion (Engelhardt, 1946; Katchalsky, 1951). Since the shape dynamics of biopolymers might involve mechanochemical transformations, we shall devote the first part of this paper to certain physicochemical aspects of mechanochemical processes.

As pointed out by Volkenstein (1962), the intimate relationship between chemical reaction and mechanical shape changes may have a profound cybernetic significance. To obtain a reversible mechanochemical conversion, the working system should be able to develop long-range interactions capable of bringing about observable changes in the dimensions of the system. By the same token, a change in dimension should modify the reactivity of the working system, thereby changing the extent of chemical reaction. Macromolecules are very suitable devices for fulfilling coupling requirements, since a reagent interacting with several groups on the polymeric chain may cause a cooperative change, such as melting, which would then be propagated along the macromolecule, or, if the reagent changes the degree of ionization of the biopolymer, a long-range force may develop, which, on transmittance along the macromolecular chain, could bring about contraction or expansion. Conversely, application of a mechanical force should influence the reactivity by altering the distances between the groups involved in the chemical transformation. From a cybernetic point of view, this means that biocolloidal systems are endowed with an elementary feedback mechanism, for local chemical reaction with a macromolecule provides the signal for dimensional change, while a change in dimension controls and modifies the extent of chemical interaction.

Mechanochemical coupling applies both to equilibrium and to rate processes. One of the major interests of the physiologist is the coupling between metabolic rates and the mobility of organs, cells, and cell constituents. From a theoretical point of view, however, equilibrium coupling is easier to handle and is necessary to any discussion of rate processes.

The first part of this paper will be devoted to a thermodynamic analysis of mechanochemical equilibria; the second part will describe metastable states, which, like equilibrium states, are time-independent.

Many studies have been made on simpler macroscopic models based primarily on the contraction and expansion of polyelectrolyte fibers and gels (Engelhardt, 1946; Katchalsky, 1951; Katchalsky *et al.*, 1960; Kuhn, 1960). These latter materials were, by and large, amorphous and their molecules randomly coiled. Here we shall restrict our attention to collagen fibers as a mechanochemical model and whose behavior is closer to the dynamics of cellular macromolecules. The existence of reproducible metastable states will be demonstrated on the basis of the remarkable hysteresis phenomena observed in solutions of RNA and complexes of polyriboadenylic acid and polyribouridylic acid.

## 2. General Thermodynamic Considerations

**2.1.** Equilibrium thermodynamics deals with memoryless systems and requires minimal information about the object under consideration. It is therefore invaluable in providing a set of general statements about the reversible behavior of any system. The Gibbs equation relates the change in the inner energy $dU$ to the changes in the magnitude of the extensive properties by

$$dU = TdS - pdV + fdl + \sum_i \mu_i dn_i \tag{1}$$

where $T$, $S$, $p$, and $V$ have their usual meaning. A mechanochemical system is open to exchange of matter with the surroundings, so that Eq. (1) includes the change in number of moles, $dn_i$, of the $i^{\text{th}}$ component, the chemical potential of which is $\mu_i$. Since a mechanical performance may accompany the chemical process, Eq. (1) also includes the force $f$ and the change in dimension $dl$.

If a cyclic process is carried out under isothermal and isobaric conditions (i.e., at constant $p$ and $T$), we may write

$$\oint dU = T\oint dS - p\oint dV + \oint fdl + \oint \sum_i \mu_i dn_i \tag{2}$$

At the end of a cycle, all state parameters return to their initial values, so that $\oint dU = \oint dS = \oint dV = 0$, and hence

$$-\oint fdl = \oint \sum_i \mu_i dn_i = \sum_i \oint \mu_i dn_i \tag{3}$$

The term $-\oint fdl = W$ is the total work obtained in a mechanochemical cycle, while $\sum_i \oint \mu_i dn_i$ is the total chemical "investment" accompanying the conversion. Equation (3) is therefore a statement about the total convertibility of chemical energy into mechanical work for reversible equilibrium cycles.

It should be noted that if all the chemical potentials remain constant throughout the cycle, then

$$\sum_i \mu_i \oint dn_i = 0$$

for the $n_i$'s are also functions of the state, and each cyclic integral $\oint dn_i = 0$. Thus any mechanochemical transformation is based on the existence of non-vanishing gradients of chemical potentials for at least some of the components undergoing reaction with the macromolecular system. This requirement is similar to Kelvin's formulation of the second law of thermodynamics, which states that a thermal engine produces positive work only if there exists a temperature gradient that is the driving force in the conversion of thermal energy into mechanical performance.

**2.2.** The simplest case to be considered is that in which the polymeric system is open to only one mobile component. It is helpful to analyze an elementary work cycle which may serve for the characterization of a point in a mechanochemical field. In an elementary cycle, the parameters change by differential amounts, so that the range of chemical potentials of the mobile component involved in the process is $\mu$ to $(\mu + d\mu)$. The work and the chemical change may be represented on a mechanical $f$-$l$ plane and on a chemical $\mu$-$n$ plane as shown in Fig. 1a, b. The mechanical work obtained in the conversion is given by

$$W_{\text{mech}} = [(\partial f/\partial l)_n - (\partial f/\partial l)_\mu]dl_1 dl_2 \tag{4}$$

while the chemical counterpart is given by the rectangle of Fig. 1b

$$W_{\text{chem}} = -(\partial \mu/\partial l)_n(\partial n/\partial l)_\mu dl_1 dl_2 \tag{5}$$

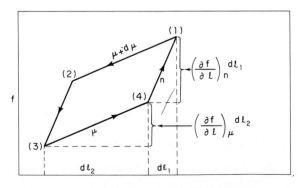

**Fig. 1a.** An elementary mechanochemical cycle ($f$ vs. $l$).

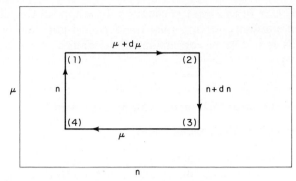

**Fig. 1b.** An elementary mechanochemical cycle ($\mu$ vs. $n$).

Since by the rules of differentiation $-(\partial\mu/\partial l)_n = (\partial\mu/\partial n)_l(\partial n/\partial l)_\mu$, we may write

$$W_{\text{chem}} = (\partial\mu/\partial n)_l(\partial n/\partial l)_\mu^2 dl_1 dl_2 \tag{6}$$

Now, by Eq. (3), the area covered by the mechanical projection of the cycle is equal to that of the chemical projection, so that

$$(\partial f/\partial l)_n - (\partial f/\partial l)_\mu = (\partial\mu/\partial n)_l(\partial n/\partial l)_\mu^2 > 0 \tag{7}$$

Equation (7) shows that the difference between the coefficient of the dependence of force on length at constant amount of reagent $(\partial f/\partial l)_n$ and the coefficient $(\partial f/\partial l)_\mu$, i.e., the force-length dependence for a system maintaining equilibrium with a bath ($\mu$ constant), is positive. This results from the fact that $(\partial\mu/\partial n)_l$ must be positive for any stable thermodynamic system, while $(\partial n/\partial l)_\mu^2$ is, of course, positive irrespective of the sign of $(\partial n/\partial l)_\mu$. Indeed, in order to obtain conversion of chemical into mechanical energy, $(\partial n/\partial l)_\mu$ should differ from zero; i.e., the absorption of reactant ($n$) into the macromolecular system from a bath of constant chemical potential should change with change in length ($l$).

**2.3.** It is also of interest to indicate the thermodynamic requirements for the conversion of mechanical work into chemical energy. For this purpose, consider the differential $d(U + pV - TS - fl) = dU + d(pV - TS - fl)$. By Eq. (1),

$$d(U + pV - TS - fl) = Vdp - SdT - ldf + \mu dn \tag{8}$$

Since this is a total differential,

$$-(\partial l/\partial n)_f = (\partial\mu/\partial f)_n \tag{9}$$

Let the reagent under consideration be a contractile reagent, so that its accumulation in the fiber ($dn > 0$) causes a diminution in length ($dl < 0$) and hence $-(\partial l/\partial n)_f > 0$. By Eq. (9), this means that for a contractile reagent $(\partial\mu/\partial f)_n > 0$; i.e., by increasing the force applied to a closed system $(df > 0$ and $n$ constant), we may raise the chemical potential of the reagent $(d\mu > 0)$. This is a case of conversion of mechanical work into potential chemical energy.

## 3. On the Interaction of Macromolecular Systems with

## Binary Solutions. The Enrichment Factor

**3.1.** For a fuller study of the behavior of a macromolecular system interacting with a binary mixture of solute, s, and solvent (say water, w) it is useful to construct a thermodynamic potential of the form

$$\psi \equiv U + pV - TS - n_s\mu_s - n_w\mu_w \tag{10}$$

which, upon differentiation and introduction of the Gibbs equation, gives for constant temperature, pressure, and number of moles of polymer,

$$d\psi = fdl - n_s d\mu_s - n_w d\mu_w \tag{11}$$

We shall now consider the case in which the system maintains equilibrium with an external bath so that $\mu_s$ and $\mu_w$ have the same value in the fiber and in the external solution. For the external solution (o) we may write the Gibbs-Duhem equation for constant $p$ and $T$:

$$n_s^o d\mu_s + n_w^o d\mu_w = 0 \tag{12}$$

or

$$d\mu_w = -(n_s^o/n_w^o)d\mu_s \tag{13}$$

where $n_s^o/n_w^o$ is the molar ratio of solute to solvent in the bath. Introducing $d\mu_w$ from Eq. (13) into Eq. (11), we obtain

$$d\psi = fdl - [n_s - (n_s^o/n_w^o)n_w]d\mu_s = fdl - \epsilon d\mu_s \tag{14}$$

The factor $\epsilon \equiv n_s - (n_s^o/n_w^o)n_w$ measures the relative accumulation of the solute in the fiber as compared to its external concentration. We shall call it the enrichment factor of solute in the macromolecular fiber. The value of $\epsilon$ per monomeric unit may be regarded as an indicator of the extent of binding of the reactant by the macromolecules.[2]

---

[2] The enrichment factor may be translated into more familiar terms as follows. Let the volume of the fiber phase be $V$ and that of the external solution $V_o$. Then the accumulation of solute and water in the macromolecular system may be described by conventional distribution coefficients $K_s$ and $K_w$: $K_s = (n_s/V)/(n_s^o/V_o)$ and $K_w = (n_w/V)/(n_w^o/V_o)$. Denoting the external concentration as $c_s^o = n_s^o/V_o$, we obtain

$$\epsilon/V = c_s^o(K_s - K_w) \tag{15}$$

Since $d\psi$ is a total differential, we may derive from Eq. (14) the relation between enrichment and dimensional change

$$(\partial\epsilon/\partial l)_{\mu_s} = -(\partial f/\partial\mu_s)_l = (\partial f/\partial l)_{\mu_s}(\partial l/\partial\mu_s)_f \qquad (16)$$

The significance of this equation is seen as follows. Let the solute be a contractile reagent; i.e., $(\partial l/\partial\mu_s)_f < 0$. Since, from stability considerations, $(\partial f/\partial l)_{\mu_s}$ can never be negative, Eq. (16) states that in this case $(\partial\epsilon/\partial l)_{\mu_s} < 0$, which means that stretching the fiber in a bath of constant composition must be accompanied by a decrease in the ratio $n_s/n_w$ in the fiber. Investment of mechanical work thus leads to a change in chemical composition. The existence of such effects was demonstrated experimentally by Kuhn et al. (1960) on polyelectrolyte fibers.

Inverse mechanochemistry may be utilized for the enrichment and separation of valuable reagents and for the purification of solvents. The solution under consideration is divided into two baths and a suitable fiber made to contract in one of them. The contracted fiber is now transferred from this bath into the other, where it is stretched mechanically. This cycle is repeated many times in order to amplify the effect. By stretching, we reduce the enrichment factor of the contractile reagent in the fiber, which is equivalent to increasing that factor for the surrounding solution. The opposite will happen in the bath where relaxation takes place. The net result will be the dilution of one solution and the concentration of the other.

## 4. "Chemical Melting"

**4.1.** We shall now consider, as a concrete example of thermodynamic treatment, the mechanochemical behavior of collagen fibers in LiBr solutions.[3] Figure 2 represents the length of the fiber as a function of the molar salt concentration $c_s$ in the surrounding aqueous medium, for various stretching forces. These curves are reversible, the loose fibers having been pretreated with water and with concentrated LiBr solution, alternately.

It will be observed that at zero force, the collagen may contract by as much as 40% of its initial length upon increasing the salt concentration. According to Eq. (16), the stretching of a contracted fiber in a contractile medium should produce a decrease in the enrichment factor $\epsilon$. The changes in $\epsilon$, due to changes in length, were evaluated for collagen fibers by integrating Eq. (16), using $(\partial f/\partial\mu_s)_l$ values derived from the experimental curves of Fig. 2. We define $\Delta\epsilon$ as the increase in $\epsilon$ on reducing the force from the maximum

---

[3] Collagen fibers from sheep submucosa, chrome-formaldehyde tanned. We are indebted to Dr. M. Levy of this laboratory for having kindly permitted the use of his data prior to publication.

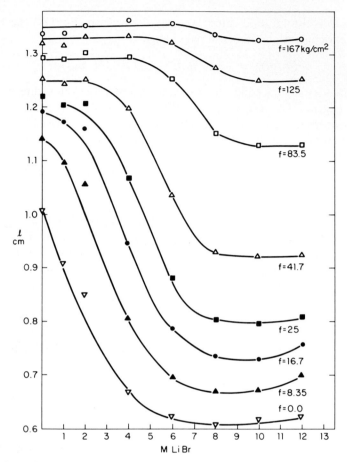

**Fig. 2.** Length $l$ of collagen fibers, under various loads $f$, at equilibrium with aqueous LiBr solutions of molar concentration $M$. (From the measurements of M. Levy.)

value used (167 kg/cm² of dry collagen) to a value $f$, keeping the concentration of salt constant in the external bath. Figure 3 gives $\Delta\epsilon$ as a function of the force for various constant concentrations.

Figure 3 demonstrates the way in which an applied mechanical force affects the reactivity of a macromolecular system, or, in our specific case, the dependence on force of collagen ability to bind LiBr molecules.

It is evident that if the value of $\epsilon$, as a function of $c_s$ is known along the $l$-$c$ curve under maximal force (or along any other $l$-$c$ curve), then $\epsilon$ at any state could be evaluated, with the use of Eq. (16). Experimentally, it is easiest to determine $\epsilon$ for the fiber under zero force. This could be carried out either by a direct analytical determination of the salt and water contents of the fiber, or by the following procedure. Let $N_s$ and $N_w$ be the total amounts (in moles)

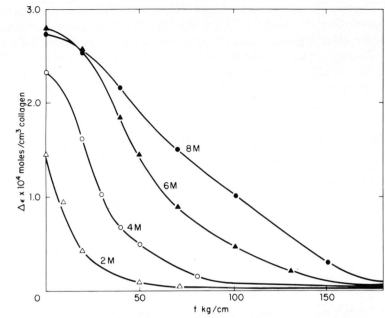

**Fig. 3.** $\Delta\epsilon$ as a function of $f$, for various constant molar concentrations $M$. (From the measurements of M. Levy.)

of salt and water, respectively, in the system comprising both the fiber and the external solution. Then

$$n_s = N_s - n_s^o \quad \text{and} \quad n_w = N_w - n_w^o$$

Substituting these expressions in that of $\epsilon$ (see Eq. [14]), we obtain

$$\epsilon = N_s - (n_s^o/n_w^o)N_w$$

The value of $\epsilon$ can thus be derived from the composition of the total system and the salt concentration in the equilibrium liquid.

**4.2.** X-ray analysis (Santhanam, 1959) reveals that the contraction of collagen fibers is accompanied by a breakdown or "melting" of their crystalline structure. It was further found that upon stretching a contracted collagen fiber at constant salt (KCNS) concentration, the typical diffraction pattern of the crystalline structure reappears (A. Yonath, W. Traub, J. Yonath, A. Oplatka, and A. Katchalsky, unpublished results).

A first-order phase transition is characterized by a discontinuity in the plot of an extensive parameter of the system considered (e.g., volume, entropy, length) against an intensive property such as pressure, temperature, stretching force, or chemical potential. From Fig. 2 it is evident that the chemical melting of a collagen fiber is not a typical first-order phase transition.[4] The continuous decrease in length might be attributed to the existence of crystalline domains in the collagen fiber that differ in size and chemical composition (Harrington and von Hippel, 1961), and it would be expected that the different crystallites would melt at different salt concentrations. The experimental continuous curve is, therefore, regarded as the result of a smoothing-out of many small discontinuities, each of the small jumps corresponding to a genuine sharp phase transition. It is therefore of interest to consider first an ideal fiber exhibiting a *single* phase transition. In this case, the length at a given stretching force should decrease discontinuously when the salt concentration exceeds the "melting concentration," whatever the applied force. The thermodynamic treatment outlined below resembles that of Flory (1956) for a similar thermoelastic system.

If $p$, $T$, $f$, $\mu_s$, and $\mu_w$ are held constant, then at a melting point

$$\mu_p^a = \mu_p^c \tag{17}$$

where $\mu_p^a$ and $\mu_p^c$ denote the chemical potentials of a monomeric residue in the amorphous (a) and crystalline (c) phases, respectively. In the treatment that follows, the values of $p$ and $T$ are held constant throughout, and $f$ and $\mu_s$ are chosen as the free variables; by Eq. (13) it is clear that $\mu_w$ then becomes a dependent variable. Changes in $f$ and $\mu_s$ which preserve Eq. (17) are characterized by

$$d(\mu_p^a - \mu_p^c) = 0$$

or, alternatively, by

$$\left(\frac{\partial(\mu_p^a - \mu_p^c)}{\partial f}\right)_{\mu_s} df + \left(\frac{\partial(\mu_p^a - \mu_p^c)}{\partial \mu_s}\right)_f d\mu_s = 0 \tag{18}$$

In order to elucidate the meaning of the coefficients of $df$ and $d\mu_s$, let us consider the thermodynamic potential

$$\phi \equiv U - TS + pV - fl - \mu_s n_s - \mu_w n_w \tag{19}$$

For a given phase, say the amorphous one, we have (at constant $p$ and $T$)

$$d\phi^a = -l^a df - \epsilon^a d\mu_s + \mu_p^a dn_p^a \tag{20}$$

from which the following relations follow:

$$\bar{l}^a \equiv (\partial l^a/\partial n_p^a)_{f,\mu_s} = -(\partial \mu_p^a/\partial f)_{\mu_s, n_p^a} \tag{21}$$

and

$$\bar{\epsilon}^a \equiv (\partial \epsilon^a/\partial n_p^a)_{f,\mu_s} = -(\partial \mu_p^a/\partial \mu_s)_{f, n_p^a} \tag{22}$$

where $\bar{l}^a$ and $\bar{\epsilon}^a$ are the partial length and partial enrichment factor in the amorphous phase, respectively. Similar relations can be obtained for $\bar{l}^c$ and

---

[4] Phase transitions of a crystal brought about by changes in the activity of some chemical species in its surroundings are known, e.g., various salt hydrates at equilibrium with water vapor.

$\bar{\epsilon}^c$ of the crystalline phase. Since the intensive parameters $\mu_p^a$ and $\mu_p^c$ do not depend on $n_p^a$ and $n_p^c$, Eq. (18) can now be rewritten as (see Eqs. [21] and [22])

$$(\bar{l}^a - \bar{l}^c)df + (\bar{\epsilon}^a - \bar{\epsilon}^c)d\mu_s = 0$$

or

$$(\partial\mu_s/\partial f)_{\text{"melting"}} = -\Delta\bar{l}/\Delta\bar{\epsilon} \tag{23}$$

where $\Delta$ denotes a difference between the values in the amorphous and crystalline states. Equation (23) can be written in a more useful form by making use of the conventional expression $\mu_s = \mu_s^o(p, T) + RT\ln a_s$ or $(d\mu_s)_{p,T} = (RT/a_s)da_s$, where $a_s$ is the salt activity in the surrounding solution.

$$(\partial a_s/\partial f)_{\text{"melting"}} = -\left(a_s \frac{\Delta\bar{l}}{RT\Delta\bar{\epsilon}}\right)_{\text{"melting"}} \tag{24}$$

Let the ideal fiber considered resemble the real collagen fiber in that its "melting" is enhanced, both by an increase in salt concentration at constant stretching force and by a decrease in the force at constant salt concentration. Thermodynamically, these properties imply that

$$\left(\frac{\partial(\mu_p^a - \mu_p^c)}{\partial\mu_s}\right)_f < 0 \tag{25}$$

and that

$$\left(\frac{\partial(\mu_p^a - \mu_p^c)}{\partial f}\right)_{\mu_s} > 0 \tag{26}$$

namely, that

$$\bar{\epsilon}^a - \bar{\epsilon}^c > 0 \tag{27}$$

and that

$$\bar{l}^a - \bar{l}^c < 0 \tag{28}$$

Substituting these inequalities into Eq. (24), we obtain

$$(\partial a_s/\partial f)_{\text{"melting"}} > 0 \tag{29}$$

Indeed, the curves in Fig. 2 that correspond to larger forces are shifted toward higher salt concentrations.


## 5. Hysteresis and Macromolecular Memory

**5.1.** The previous paragraphs dealt with reversible phenomena in which the state functions of a system were single-valued functions of the state variables. There exist, however, systems which exhibit time-independent hysteresis phenomena, i.e., systems whose properties depend on their previous history. A closed, reproducible loop is obtained when the value of some property is plotted against a state variable, the latter changing first in one, and then in the opposite direction. Such behavior is observed upon stretching-releasing rubber strips, in magnetization-demagnetization, and in adsorption-desorption cycles (Hill, 1949; Enderby, 1955; Everett, 1955; Treloar, 1958; Brown, 1962; Kington and Smith, 1964). It was recognized by some of the physicists of the last century, particularly Boltzmann (1876), that these systems are endowed with a capacity for memorizing processes enacted in the past. There is little doubt that hysteresis phenomena are due to the existence of energy barriers that, in some intervals along the cycle, prevent the system from attaining equilibrium, thus permitting the existence of long-lived metastable states. However, at certain points, abrupt irreversible transitions occur from the metastable to the more stable states.

The studies on hysteresis exhibited in macroscopic systems (Hill, 1949; Enderby, 1955; Everett, 1955; Treloar, 1958; Brown, 1962; Kington and Smith, 1964) assume that the behavior may be attributed to the existence of metastable states in microstructures, or domains, of which the system is composed. There is, however, a growing realization that hysteresis may be also exhibited by single macromolecules or macromolecular complexes in solution. The first convincing observations on the existence of memory functions in macromolecular systems were made on synthetic polynucleotides and on RNA solutions. Warner and Breslow (1959) found that if solutions of polyadenylic acid (poly-A) and polyuridylic acid (poly-U) are brought separately to a $p$H of 6.0 and then mixed, a complex of poly-$(A+U)$ is formed that does not break down to its constituent macromolecules until the $p$H is lowered to 4.6. On the other hand, if the two polynucleotides are mixed together at a $p$H of 5.5, no complex is formed. Similar results were obtained by Steiner and Beers (1959b). Recently, Cox (1963) extended these observations and found reproducible hysteresis loops in spectrophotometric titrations of poly-A + poly-U mixtures. It was found that the optical density (O.D.) of the system at any $p$H depends on the history of the titration; i.e., different O.D. values are obtained when one starts with a low $p$H and adds alkali, or when one starts with a high $p$H and adds acid to bring the polynucleotides to the same $p$H (Fig. 4).

Even more intriguing is the reproducible and time-independent hysteresis loop found in RNA from different sources by Cox et al. (1956) and studied more extensively by Cox and Littauer (1963). If the titration of RNA is stopped within the hysteresis loop and the process reversed, the titration curve does not retrace the original path but instead one obtains "scanning curves" (Fig. 5) (Cox, unpublished results) similar to the scanning curves found in the magnetization-demagnetization cycles of ferromagnets. A detailed study of the scanning curves should lead to a deeper insight into the distribution of metastable crystalline domains in the macromolecules (R. A. Cox and A. Katchalsky, in preparation).

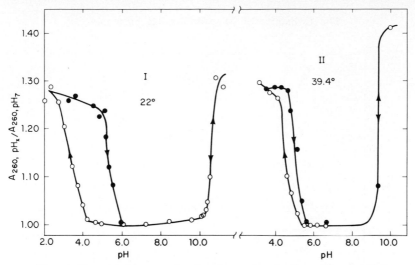

**Fig. 4.** Spectrophotometric titration of poly-(A + U) at 22°C (I) and 39.4°C (II). ○—○: titration with acid or alkali from pH 7; ●—●: titration with alkali or acid from low or high pH values. (From Cox, 1963, *Biochim. Biophys. Acta* 68: 401.)

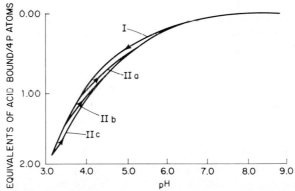

**Fig. 5.** Hysteresis loop (curves I and IIc) with scanning curves (IIa and IIb) of ribosomal RNA from *E. coli* (in 0.1 M NaCl at 0.4°C). (Courtesy, R. A. Cox.)

**5.2.** A formal interpretation of the hysteresis loop observed in the titration of a 1:1 mixture of poly-A and poly-U is based on the "phase diagram" for the system (Cox, 1963) (Fig. 6). The abscissa of the diagram is the pH of the solution, and the ordinate is the "melting temperature" $T_m$, determined from the sharp transition in UV absorption, of the double-helical forms of poly-(A+U) and poly-(A+A). The curve $AOB$ divides the plane of Fig. 6 into an upper part, above $AOB$, in which the complex poly-(A+U) does not exist and a lower part in which the complex is stable for long periods. Similarly the curve $POQ$ divides the plane of the figure into a left-hand side where

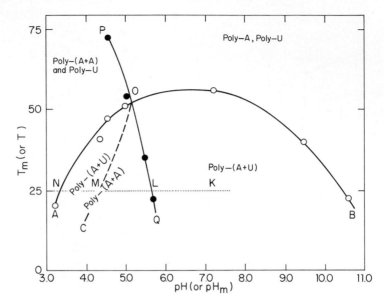

**Fig. 6.** "Phase diagram" for the poly-A, poly-u system. ○—○: equilibrium "melting" curve for poly-$(A+U)$; ●—● equilibrium "melting" curve for poly-$(A+A)$ (Modified from Cox, 1963).

the double-helical poly-$(A+A)$ is stable and a right-hand side where this complex cannot form. In the area $AOQ$, both complexes, poly-$(A+U)$ and poly-$(A+A)$, can exist. In the case of thermodynamic equilibrium, the area $AOQ$ should vanish and shrink to a single line — say $OC$. Thus on the left-hand side of $OC$, in the region $AOC$, the complex poly-$(A+U)$ is metastable, while on the right-hand side of $OC$, i.e., in the region $QOC$, it is the double-helical poly-$(A+A)$ that is metastable. Because of the difficulty of passing from one crystalline form to another, the metastable forms may have very long lifetimes, beyond practical determination.

Let us follow the titration of the mixture, say at 25°C. Starting at $p$H 7, and reducing the $p$H by stepwise addition of acid, we shall proceed along the straight line $KLMN$ (Fig. 6) parallel to the $p$H axis. Dissociation of the complex poly-$(A+U)$ does not occur when the straight line $KLMN$ intersects the equilibrium curve $OC$, but the complex survives a further decrease in $p$H until the melting point $N$, on the metastability curve $AO$, is reached. At this point the complex will be transformed into the thermodynamically stable mixture of poly-$(A+A)$ and poly-U. The back titration from $p$H 3 starts now with poly-$(A+A)$ + poly-U. Here again, the increase in $p$H will not induce a breakdown of poly-$(A+A)$ at the phase equilibrium point $M$, but the double helix will survive a further increase in $pH$ until the metastable melting point $L$ of poly-$(A+A)$ is reached. At this point the stable complex poly-$(A+U)$ is formed.

It is clear that titration in either direction will give different results when passing the range of metastability, for on decreasing the $pH$, we are titrating A groups with the dissociation constant characteristic of the poly-$(A+U)$ complex, whereas on increasing the $pH$, we titrate A groups in poly-$(A+A)$ with a different dissociation constant. Upon raising the temperature, the range of metastability decreases and the area of the hysteresis loop diminishes, until point $O$ is reached, when the loop entirely vanishes.

In the above description, it has been assumed that there exists a $pH$ range ($MN$ in Fig. 6) where poly-$(A+U)$ is metastable, *and* that there is some other range ($ML$) where poly-$(A+A)$ is metastable, the occurrence of these metastable states being the result of energy barriers preventing the transitions to the corresponding stable forms. However, had there been a range of metastability for only *one* of the complexes, say for poly-$(A+U)$, the other complex poly-$(A+A)$ transforming into the former at point $M$, hysteresis would still have been observed, though in a smaller $pH$ range.

**5.3.** The hysteresis phenomenon discussed above will now be analyzed thermodynamically.

The three curves drawn in Fig. 7 represent, *schematically*, the free energy (as a function of $pH$) for a solution containing poly-A and poly-U in a 1:1

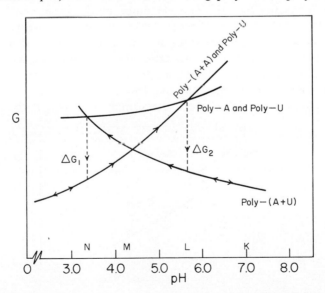

**Fig. 7.** The free energy $G$, as function of $pH$, of a solution containing poly-A and poly-U in a 1:1 nucleotide ratio (schematic).

nucleotide ratio, at three different states of the polymeric chains. At any pH, the thermodynamically stable state is the one possessing the lowest free energy. This representation excludes the coexistence of more than one state within any finite pH interval, which is practically the case when the equilibrium constants for the transformation of one state into another depend strongly on pH. This behavior is to be expected if the polymers have high degrees of polymerization.

Assuming that Fig. 7 has been drawn for a temperature of 25°C, let us use it to follow the change in free energy with pH corresponding to the path *KLMN* in Fig. 6. We start at pH 7 (point *K*) where the polymer is in the form poly-(A+U). Upon lowering the pH, the free energy will change along the curve designated poly-(A+U). Beyond point *M*, the system would possess a lower free energy had the polymer been converted into poly-(A+A) and poly-U. However, the polymer remains in the now metastable form, poly-(A+U), until point *N* is reached, where the curve corresponding to single-stranded poly-A and poly-U is met. No potential barrier exists for the separation into single strands, and the liberated poly-A chains immediately interact to form the stable poly-(A+A). The free energy drops abruptly — the over-all change being $\Delta G_1$. On further lowering the pH, the free energy follows the poly-(A+A) curve. In the back titration, we proceed along the same curve to point *M*, and here again transition to poly-(A+U) does not occur. At point *L*, the complex is broken into single strands, and the free energy drops abruptly, changing by $\Delta G_2$. The pH range of the hysteresis loop is obviously *NL*.

A schematic titration curve for such a system is given in Fig. 8. In the following discussion, extensive properties always refer to one mole of adenylic (or uridylic) residues. The sharp transitions occurring at the points *N* and *L* are accompanied by changes $\Delta n_1$ and $\Delta n_2$ in the number of moles of HCl, respectively (one or both of these terms might be zero). If these transitions

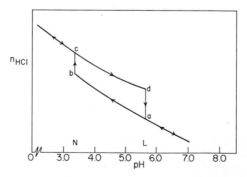

**Fig. 8.** Schematic titration curve of a solution containing poly-A and poly-U in a 1:1 nucleotide ratio. The ordinate gives the number of moles HCl added per mole adenylic residues.

had been reversible, $\Delta G_1$ and $\Delta G_2$ would be given by $\mu_1 \Delta n_1$ and $\mu_2 \Delta n_2$, respectively ($\mu_1$ and $\mu_2$ being the chemical potentials of the acid at $N$ and $L$), but since the changes are abrupt, they are clearly irreversible, and so,

$$\Delta G_1 = \mu_1 \Delta n_1 + \Delta G_{\text{irr.},1}$$
$$\Delta G_2 = \mu_2 \Delta n_2 + \Delta G_{\text{irr.},2}$$

(30)

By the second law of thermodynamics, since the processes take place at constant $p$ and $T$, both $\Delta G_{\text{irr.}}$ terms are negative, or

$$\sum \Delta G_{\text{irr.}} < 0 \tag{31}$$

The total change in free energy for a closed cycle ($a$, $b$, $c$, $d$, Fig. 8) should be zero. With Eqs. (30), it can therefore be written as

$$0 = \oint dG = \int_a^b \mu_{\text{HCl}} dn_{\text{HCl}} + \Delta G_1 + \int_c^d \mu_{\text{HCl}} dn_{\text{HCl}} + \Delta G_2$$

$$= \oint \mu_{\text{HCl}} dn_{\text{HCl}} + \sum \Delta G_{\text{irr.}} \tag{32}$$

or

$$\oint n_{\text{HCl}} d\mu_{\text{HCl}} = -\oint \mu_{\text{HCl}} dn_{\text{HCl}} = \sum \Delta G_{\text{irr.}} \tag{33}$$

Since[5]

$$\oint n_{\text{HCl}} dpH = -(2.303 \, RT)^{-1} \oint n_{\text{HCl}} d\mu_{\text{HCl}} \tag{34}$$

we obtain, from Eqs. (31), (33), and (34), that

$$\oint n_{\text{HCl}} dpH = -(2.303 \, RT)^{-1} \sum \Delta G_{\text{irr.}} > 0 \tag{35}$$

The area of the hysteresis loop is thus proportional to the sum total of the irreversible changes in free energy. The positive sign of this area means that the titration cycle is traversed clockwise.

The terms $\Delta G_{\text{irr.},1}$ and $\Delta G_{\text{irr.},2}$ arise from the abrupt irreversible chemical transformations

(Reaction 1)                    poly-A $\rightarrow \frac{1}{2}$ poly-(A+A)

and

(Reaction 2)        poly-A + poly-U $\rightarrow$ poly-(A+U)

occurring at points $N$ and $L$, respectively. These energy changes are now evaluated in terms of the thermodynamic parameters of the molecular species involved. As $G$ is a state function of the system, $\Delta G_{\text{irr.}}$ for each of the reactions depends only on the initial and final states, and can therefore be calcu-

---

[5] It is assumed that the system contains enough NaCl so that $\mu_{\text{Cl}^-}$ can be taken as constant. Hence, $d\mu_{\text{HCl}} \equiv d\mu_{\text{H}^+} + d\mu_{\text{Cl}^-} = d\mu_{\text{H}^+}$

lated for a reversible path. To simplify this calculation, we assume that the strands of poly-A and of poly-U are monodisperse, both having a degree of polymerization $Z$.

Thus, for Reaction (1), the change in free energy per mole monomeric residues is given by

$$\Delta G_{irr.,1} = \Delta G_{rev.,1} = -(1/Z) \int_{\xi=0}^{1} A_1 d\xi \qquad (36)$$

where $A_1$ is related to the chemical potentials (per mole of polymeric molecules) by

$$A_1 = \mu[\text{poly-A}] - \tfrac{1}{2}\mu[\text{poly-(A+A)}] \qquad (37)$$

and $\xi$ is the fractional degree of advancement of the reaction. For a solution that is sufficiently dilute with respect to the polymer, the dependence of the chemical potentials on $\xi$ is given by the ideal relations

$$\mu[\text{poly-A}] = \mu^{\circ}[\text{poly-A}] + RTln[(1 - \xi)c_p/Z] \qquad (38)$$

$$\mu[\text{poly-(A+A)}] = \mu^{\circ}[\text{poly-(A+A)}] + RTln[\xi c_p/2Z] \qquad (39)$$

where $c_p$ is the total concentration of A nucleotides. Introducing Eqs. (38) and (39) into Eq. (37), substituting the resulting expression for $A_1$ into Eq. (36), and carrying out the integration, we obtain

$$\Delta G_{irr.,1} = -[(A_1^{\circ}/Z) + (RT/2Z)ln(2c_p/eZ)] \qquad (40)$$

where

$$A_1^{\circ} = \mu^{\circ}[\text{poly-A}] - \tfrac{1}{2}\mu^{\circ}[\text{poly-(A+A)}] \qquad (41)$$

is related to the equilibrium constant, $K_1$, of Reaction (1), by

$$A_1^{\circ} = RTlnK_1 \qquad (42)$$

When $Z$ tends to infinity, each of the $\mu^{\circ}$ terms in Eq. (41) becomes proportional to $Z$. Under these conditions, the first term on the right-hand side of Eq. (40) is independent of $Z$, whereas for a given value of $c_p$, the second term approaches zero; i.e.,

$$\Delta G_{irr.,1} \cong -A_1^{\circ}/Z \qquad (43)$$

Similar considerations when applied to Reaction (2) lead to the conclusion that

$$\Delta G_{irr.,2} \cong -A_2^{\circ}/Z \qquad (44)$$

Combining Eqs. (35), (43), and (44), the final conclusion is reached that

$$2.303 \; RT \oint n_{\text{HCl}} dp\text{H} = Z^{-1}(A_1^{\circ} + A_2^{\circ}) \qquad (45)$$

This equation relates the area enclosed by the hysteresis titration loop and the standard affinities of the reactions occurring in the irreversible steps.

This equation may be useful in elucidating the nature of the processes responsible for the hysteresis phenomenon. Thus, for example, in the system discussed above we have assumed that there were *two* irreversible steps, involving Reactions (1) and (2). However, there exists the possibility, mentioned briefly before and which will be discussed in the following subsection, that there is only *one* irreversible step. The latter could be, for instance, the one corresponding to Reaction (1), with the transformation

$$\tfrac{1}{2} \text{ poly-(A+A)} + \text{poly-U} \rightarrow \text{poly-(A+U)}$$

being uninhibited, and occurring at the $pH$ determined from equilibrium thermodynamics. Equation (45) would then be replaced by

$$2.303 \ RT \oint n_{\text{HCl}} dp\text{H} = Z^{-1}\text{A}_1^\circ \tag{46}$$

Hence, if in addition to the titration cycle, we separately have other data on Reactions (1) and (2), Eqs. (45) and (46) can help to decide which of the above alternatives is the correct one.

In the acid titration of RNA, the ionization of adenylic groups is involved (Cox and Littauer, 1963), and the hysteresis observed is explained in terms of double-helical regions of (A+A) and (A+U). It is reasonable to assume that the regions of, say (A+U), are not all of equal length and neither entirely composed of A and U units, but may contain other nucleotides. These may either introduce different kinds of hydrogen-bonded pairs or form closed loops, protruding out of the helical region, thereby affecting its stability. In this case, one might expect that upon lowering the $pH$ the regions of different stabilities would undergo abrupt irreversible changes at different values of $pH$. The hysteresis loop would then contain many "steps," which, owing to their smallness, would be smeared out to give a continuous titration curve. The very fact that scanning curves could be detected is a strong indication that the double-helical regions [of oligo-(A+U) or oligo-(A+A)] are not all identical and vary appreciably in their degree of metastability. The above treatment can be extended to RNA, and it can be shown that Eq. (35) holds true; i.e., the area enclosed by the hysteresis loop is proportional to the sum of the irreversible changes in free energy. Again, each $\Delta G_{\text{irr.}}$ can be related to the standard affinity of the reaction responsible for it. Moreover, if all the molecular transformations of the RNA are *intra*molecular, the $\Delta G_{\text{irr.}}$ terms are independent of the total RNA concentration, in contrast to Eq. (40), which was derived for the poly-A + poly-U system.

The experimental data mentioned (Fig. 5) relate the amount $n_b$ of acid bound to the polymer as a function of $pH$, rather than the total amount $n_{\text{HCl}}$ of acid added. However, as will be presently shown,

$$\oint n_{\text{HCl}} dp\text{H} = \oint n_b dp\text{H} \tag{47}$$

and thus the experimental loop measures the irreversible change in free energy. To prove Eq. (47), we note that $n_{HCl} - n_b$, which by definition is the amount HCl added to the pure solvent in order to attain a given $p$H, is a single-valued function of the $p$H. Hence, for the complete cycle,

$$\oint (n_{HCl} - n_b) dp\text{H} = 0 \qquad (48)$$

from which follows Eq. (47).

From Eqs. (35) and (47) we reach the conclusion that

$$\oint n_b dp\text{H} > 0 \qquad (49)$$

as is borne out by experiment (e.g., see Fig. 5).

In the Appendix of this paper, it is shown that $\sum \Delta G_{irr.}$ is in fact equal to the heat dissipation in the irreversible cycle.

To allow an idea of the energies involved, the following analysis of the data was carried out. From potentiometric titration curves (Cox, unpublished results) of various RNAs at *ca.* 0°C, the value of 2.303 $RT \oint n_b dp\text{H}$ per nucleotide was found to be about 0.18 $RT$ for *Escherichia coli* RNA and 0.20–0.25 $RT$ for rat-liver RNA. By Eqs. (35) and (47) this gives the sum of all irreversible free-energy changes and by Eq. (55) (see Appendix) also the heat dissipated per nucleotide. Since not all the RNA nucleotides are involved in these irreversible transitions, it is clear that these results are merely lower bounds of the values for the nucleotides participating in the transitions.

**5.4.** The interpretation adopted above is based on the assumption that the potential barriers underlying the metastability of polynucleotide complexes arise from the necessity of complete breakdown of the double-helical structure before another and more stable structure can be formed.

There are, however, known cases when this interpretation is not tenable, for there exists apparently the possibility of transition from one ordered form to another by the gradual interaction of small segments. Thus it was shown (Sigler *et al.*, 1962) that the reaction

$$2 \text{ poly-C} + \text{poly-}(A+2\ I) \rightarrow 2 \text{ poly-}(I+C) + \text{poly-A}$$

(where I = inosine and C = cytosine) takes place at a temperature well below the melting point of the less stable form. Similarly the interaction

$$\text{poly-}(A+2\ U) + \text{poly-A} \rightleftharpoons 2 \text{ poly-}(A+U)$$

occurs readily at temperatures lower than the melting points of the reactants (Steiner and Beers, 1959b).

The reason why, in the case of $2 \text{ poly-}(A+U) \rightarrow \text{poly-}(A+A) + 2 \text{ poly-U}$, the melting point of poly-$(A+U)$ has to be reached before the recombination to a new double helix can take place might be the following:

As was shown by Rich *et al.* (1961), the structure of poly-(A+A) is that of two parallel strands, in contradistinction to, say, that of DNA, where the molecular chains run antiparallel. Thus a poly-(A+A) molecule will have difficulties in forming by the twining of a single strand about itself, and two independent chains have to partake in the double-helix formation. Now it might be expected that free "tails" from two different poly-(A+U) molecules might initiate the growth of a poly-(A+A) molecule before the complete melting of the former.   It is, however, known (Steiner and Beers, 1959a) that the double helix of poly-(A+A) is labile in a medium of high ionic strength, and the free poly-A tails of a partially molten poly-(A+U) are indeed surrounded by a dense ionic atmosphere created by the close proximity of charged poly-U tails. Hence, the formation of incipient poly-(A+A) is prevented, and only when the single poly-A strands are fully liberated will double-helix formation become possible.

Further, it is reasonable to assume for an RNA molecule that whole patches of oligo-(A+U) are required to break down into single-stranded regions before a suitable orientation of the RNA chain might take place, enabling the meeting of A-rich parts to form oligo-(A+A) structures.

To sum up, the high energy barriers responsible for the occurrence of hysteresis phenomena in the acid-base titration of poly-A + poly-U and of RNA are assumed to be due to the necessity of breaking many bonds, collectively, before more stable bonds can be formed. If this explanation is correct, then it seems that of all molecules, the polymeric ones are those most likely to have high energy barriers, giving rise to metastable states or to extremely slow processes.

It is intriguing to speculate that controlled changes in the environment of metastable macromolecules may induce reproducible imprints of a memory nature. The distribution of the crystalline parts, both in length and in position, will then carry an informational content different from that of the nucleotide sequence alone and presents a possibility for recording the impact of the surroundings. However, further investigation is required before such a possibility will assume a more concrete form.

## APPENDIX

Let us imagine the following set-up. The solution, located at the bottom of a cylinder, is separated from gaseous HCl by a membrane permeable to HCl only. The pressure of the gas can be changed by means of a piston, and the whole system is maintained at constant temperature. The chemical potential of HCl as measured in the solution is equal to that in the gas. From the first law of thermodynamics, we have for the total (tot.) system

$$dU_{\text{tot.}} = \delta Q_{\text{tot.}} - p_g dv_g = \delta Q_g + \delta Q_{\text{sol.}} - p_g dV_g \qquad (50)$$

# Basic Principles
# of Molecular Architecture

**E. Bright Wilson, Jr.**

*Mallinckrodt Chemical Laboratories*
*Harvard University*
*Cambridge, Massachusetts*

In a short paper one could hardly begin to outline the many rules available concerning molecular architecture, and certainly even greater space would be required to explain away the numerous examples of the ways in which these rules are violated. Instead of this impossible task, which would anyway go over ground very familiar to most of you, I have chosen to discuss a few selected topics which happen to interest me particularly.

First of all, it is obvious that the chemical bond is the most important element in molecular structure and it would be agreeable to be able to say that we really understood it. At various times in the history of chemistry such claims have been made, but they have always been shattered by new experimental discoveries, such as the structures of the boron hydrides, and, within the past two years, the many compounds of the rare gases, particularly xenon (Hyman, 1963). After each of these traumatic experiences, the theoreticians have returned to their drawing boards, modified or extended their theories and sometimes even proclaimed, with more or less truth, that they had known it all along. Now the facts obviously show that our understanding of chemical bonding has either been inadequate or at the very least lacking in the power to convince.

But I believe that progress is being made and that a much more certain and convincing understanding will emerge from the quantum mechanical calculations of greatly improved rigor that are beginning to be made. After all, the computer age only began, in effect, a few years ago.

We probably do understand pretty well ionic binding, such as occurs commonly in inorganic minerals. The attraction of oppositely charged ions has a nice simplicity.

Long ago, Pauling (1939) wrote down a very reasonable set of rules for ionic crystals. These included such ideas as the importance of the ratio of the radii of positive to negative ions in determining the number of large negative ions which will surround a small positive ion. Another rule concerned the tendency for local electroneutrality; i.e., over small regions the total negative charge tends to equal the total positive charge. These and other ideas have continued to be useful and have shown considerable predictive power.

But covalent binding is much more important in biochemistry and is much more subtle. The energy change on combining two atoms is only a minute fraction of the total energy of the electrons in the fields of the nuclei, and the redistribution of electron density has scarcely been detected as yet experimentally. It is no wonder that semirigorous calculations are only just beginning to show theoretically that some molecules ought to exist, whereas qualitative, semiempirical theories often go quite far astray. Unfortunately, bond energy is just about the hardest quantity to calculate reliably.

On the other hand, theorists using computers and fairly rigorous approximations have begun to do very well with the calculation of certain other properties, such as dipole moments for first-row diatomic molecules. Certainly, for such simple molecules, the experimentalists are going to have to start being more careful, because the theorists are beginning to have more courage when their calculations disagree with observations.

One of the current disagreements concerns the sign of the dipole moment in CO. There exists a rather delicate experimental result from microwave spectroscopy which led to the sign $C^-O^+$, whereas recent Hartree-Fock calculations have consistently yielded the opposite polarity. Nesbet (1964) has now challenged the interpretation of the experimental data, which were indeed at best of only marginally sufficient accuracy for this purpose.

With these remarks as a background, it is understandable why theorists have not convincingly explained as yet the considerably smaller energies associated with the potential barriers hindering internal rotation about single bonds. This phenomenon is displayed most simply in ethane, $CH_3$—$CH_3$ (Fig. 1), where one methyl group is not completely free, as once thought, to rotate about the C—C axis, but instead must surmount a barrier 3,000 cal high every 120° (Fig. 2). These barriers are surely important in biochemistry. We now have a certain amount of experimental information about them and something like eight rival theories, none of which as yet has any appreciable predictive power.

Experimentally it seems that, where there is threefold symmetry, the barrier is closely approximated by a cos $3\alpha$ dependence, with higher Fourier components cos $6\alpha$, $9\alpha$, etc., of no real importance. Where the symmetry requires sixfold dependence, as in $CH_3NO_2$, the barrier is negligible. It also is

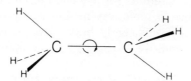

**Fig. 1.** Model for ethane molecule, showing possible internal rotation about C—C bond.

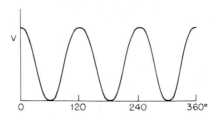

**Fig. 2.** Form of potential energy barrier hindering free rotation in ethane.

very small in molecules with well-separated rotating groups such as dimethyl acetylene, $CH_3$—$C\equiv C$—$CH_3$. In general, the barrier diminishes as the groups are separated more and more, as for example in the series $CH_3CH_3$, $CH_3SiH_3$, $CH_3GeH_3$, $CH_3SnH_3$.

In all compounds so far studied with three atoms attached to each end, the equilibrium conformation is staggered; i.e., the attached atoms act as if they were repelling each other. However, if there is a double bond at one end, as in propylene, $CH_3CH{=}CH_2$, then one H of the $CH_3$ lies in the plane of the double bond and closer to the double bond, as if attracted to it (Fig. 3).

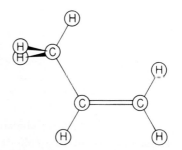

**Fig. 3.** Conformation of methyl group in propylene.

Another noticeable fact is the relatively small effect of substituting F for H on one end. This usually lowers the barrier somewhat, except in ethane itself. A chlorine replacing a hydrogen usually raises the barrier, but only 10 or 20%.

I shall not try to describe or compare the many theories of barrier forces, as I do not believe that it has been convincingly shown which one is correct, if any. However, I would like to say that simple van der Waals repulsion models are not very much in fashion today, at least not for ethane. Personally, I think it useful to continue for a while longer to regard the origin of barriers as unknown but in some way an intrinsic property of this kind of atomic grouping. Then if sufficiently bulky groups are introduced, effects due to van der Waals repulsive forces, i.e., steric hindrance, will need to be added.

Long ago a striking example of this steric effect was demonstrated by Dauben and Pitzer (1956). From thermodynamic measurements, they showed that while the methyl groups in trans-butene-2

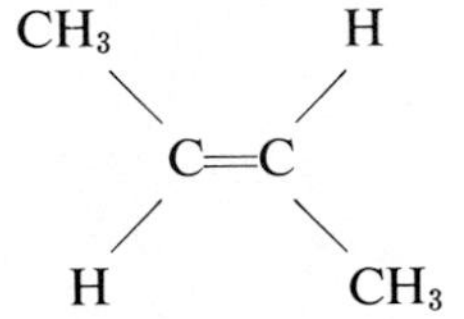

$$
\begin{array}{ccc}
CH_3 & & H \\
\diagdown & & \diagup \\
& C\!=\!C & \\
\diagup & & \diagdown \\
H & & CH_3 \\
\end{array}
$$

had barriers about the same as in propylene

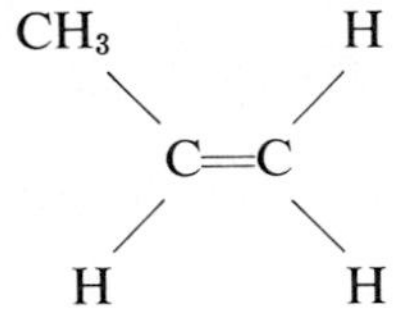

$$
\begin{array}{ccc}
CH_3 & & H \\
\diagdown & & \diagup \\
& C\!=\!C & \\
\diagup & & \diagdown \\
H & & H \\
\end{array}
$$

the barrier in the cis compound

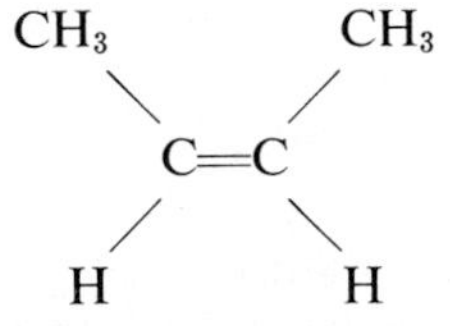

$$
\begin{array}{ccc}
CH_3 & & CH_3 \\
\diagdown & & \diagup \\
& C\!=\!C & \\
\diagup & & \diagdown \\
H & & H \\
\end{array}
$$

was greatly reduced, perhaps to 450 cal.

Beaudet (1964) by microwave spectroscopy showed a similar effect in the cis and trans fluoro- and chloropropylenes (Fig. 4), where the halogen cis to the methyl lowers the methyl barrier from about 2.2 kcal to 1.0 kcal for fluorine and to 0.6 kcal for chlorine.

These effects can be qualitatively explained as due to repulsive forces between the halogen and the nearest hydrogen of the methyl group, acting as a force less strong than the intrinsic barrier force. Note that the barrier potential has its minimum value when one of the methyl hydrogens is closest to the halogen. The steric repulsion will be strongest then and will thus tend to raise the bottoms of the potential curve, thus lowering the barrier.

For the butenes-2, Kistiakowsky and coworkers (1935) showed that the trans form was indeed of lower energy than the cis, in agreement with the steric picture. However, for chloropropylene Mr. David Schmalz is now

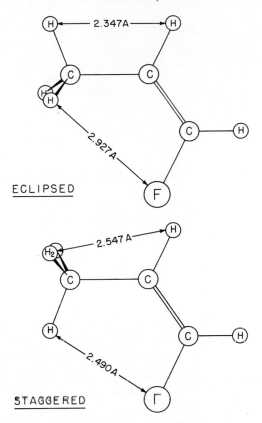

**Fig. 4.** Cis-fluoropropylene. (From Beaudet, 1964, *J. Chem. Phys.* 40: 2705.)

making equilibrium-constant measurements that are showing that the cis
form is the more stable. In fact, it has been found by many experimenters
that for simple cis-trans pairs such as difluoro, dichloro, chlorofluoro, methyl-
chloro, the cis form is the more stable.

How can this be reconciled with a repulsive theory of the barrier lowering
in the cis form? I think it can be, at least qualitatively. In the first place, as
the methyl group is turned so as to bring a hydrogen close to the halogen, the
force may indeed be repulsive and yet the energy can still be below zero
(Fig. 5). Furthermore, it is likely that the methyl group consists of a nearly
spherical charge distribution with small bumps protruding for the hydrogens.
The spherical part will not affect the barrier and may well be attracting the
halogen, while the bumps may provide the required weaker repulsion to lower
the barrier.

We have now studied also the rotational isomerism of a number of compounds by our microwave techniques. They all suggest that attractive forces
are dominant in the cases studied.

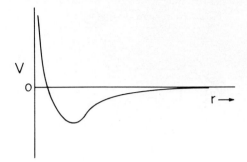

**Fig. 5.** Probable form of nonbonded potential energy function.

Thus Hirota (1962) has examined n-propyl fluoride

$$CH_3 \qquad\qquad F$$
$$CH_2\!\!-\!\!CH_2$$

in considerable detail by microwave spectroscopy and definitely demonstrated the existence of two rotational isomers, trans and gauche, with the latter slightly more stable (Fig. 6). Further, he determined the methyl group barrier for each form separately and found them nearly the same. Perhaps this means that the force between the fluorine and the spherical part of the methyl group is attractive at the pertinent distances whereas the effect of the nonspherical part ("bumps" due to hydrogens) is here negligible, possibly because of the angles involved, which are different from the case of cis-fluoropropylene. The fact that it is the gauche and not the cis form that occurs is to be expected from the barrier force, though at the cis conformation the fluorine-methyl interaction may also have become repulsive and thus have added to the instability. We do not have a very good figure for the energy barrier at the cis position.

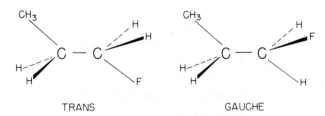

TRANS                              GAUCHE

**Fig. 6.** Rotational isomers in n-propyl fluoride. (From Hirota, 1962, *J. Chem. Phys.* 37: 283.)

Hirota (1965) has also studied 3-fluoropropylene

```
      F
       \
   H—C        H
  /    \      /
 H      C=C
       /    \
      H      H
```

and finds three forms. The more stable form has the fluorine in the plane as shown, again as if attraction were involved (Fig. 7). The other two forms are equivalent and are obtained by rotating the $CH_2F$ group about 120°. Hirota did just about the best job at present possible on the detailed, quantitative structures of these isomers, hoping that nonbonded forces would cause characteristic changes in structure between the isomers, for example changes in C—C—F angles. Unfortunately, the results just do not seem conclusive. At least I am unable to interpret them.

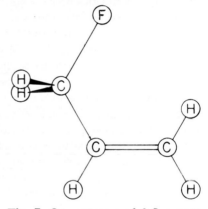

**Fig. 7.** One rotamer of 3-fluoropropylene.

If a large enough group replaces the fluorine, nuclear magnetic resonance results (Bothner-By *et al.*, 1962) indicate that the "gauche" form becomes the more stable. Ultimately, of course, there is just no room for a really large group in the planar position.

We have a few more detailed studies on rotational isomers finished and some in progress. These are putting some boundary conditions on our views about nonbonded forces, and I should be very happy if they led to a nice clean and simple set of rules, but that may be too optimistic.

I would like to end this topic by a strong plea for caution in making and accepting calculations of conformations based on some assumed force law between nonbonded atoms. So many quite different force laws appear in the literature that, by choosing an appropriate one, it is hardly possible to fail to get a result in agreement with experiment, provided that the experimental result is known in advance. Of course, such a calculation may still have value if it truly fits a large mass of data in a consistent manner, and especially if it builds a record of many successful predictions, but I fear we have a way to go before we can even be sure that there exists such a thing as a characteristic force law for nonbonded atoms, independent of the environment.

Finally, I wish to mention a set of observations that suggests the existence of weak attractive forces that could perhaps be of some significance in bio-chemical molecules. It was noted by Burkhard and Dennison (1951) some time ago that the methyl group in methyl alcohol appeared to be slightly tilted (about 1°) away from the O—H hydrogen. This is small enough to be a bit doubtful by itself, but similar tilts have shown up in a number of microwave studies (Hayashi and Pierce, 1961; Levine, 1963) of other molecules, always when there is an atom with an unshared electron pair, as pointed out by Hayashi and Pierce (1961). One is tempted to say that the methyl group (or methylene) is tilted because a hydrogen is attracted by the unshared pair on the nonadjacent atom (Fig. 8). Perhaps this is merely a very weak incipient hydrogen bond, weak because the H is attached to a carbon instead of to a more electronegative element and also because the angles are quite unfavor-able. The amount of energy required is really very small, perhaps only ten small calories, so the phenomenon may not be very important. It also could be ascribed to steric repulsions from the atoms on the other side, but this seems somewhat unlikely, especially in view of the way in which unshared pairs seem to take up more space than bond pairs.

I should like to conclude by asserting that we now have tools of very considerable precision and power for the determination of the quantitative molecular structure of crystals of great complexity and vapor-phase molecules of very limited complexity. Unfortunately, we are not well off at all for the study of quantitative structures in the liquid phase.

These structural tools have supplied data from which have been drawn many empirical regularities, most of which are far from being universal. Some of these have some modest theoretical backing of an approximate sort but still must be accepted or rejected primarily on purely empirical grounds.

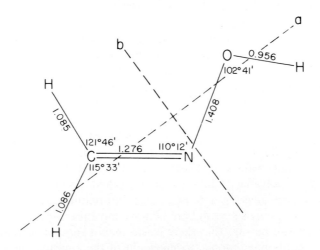

**Fig. 8.** Tilt of methylene group in formadoxime.

I hope and believe that the quantum mechanical derivations will soon be much more rigorous, but right now most of them are little more than verbalizations of experimental generalizations.

In the field of complex biochemical molecules, all the rules gained from the study of small molecules should be useful, and, in fact, indispensable. My only suggestion is that they should always be applied with caution and a certain amount of skepticism.

## REFERENCES

Beaudet, R. A. 1964. *J. Chem. Phys.* 40: 2705.

Bothner-By, A. A., C. Naar-Colin, and H. Gunther. 1962. *J. Am. Chem. Soc.* 84: 2748.

Burkhard, D. G., and D. M. Dennison. 1951. *Phys. Rev.* 84: 408.

Dauben, W. G., and K. S. Pitzer. 1956. In *Steric Effects in Organic Chemistry*, ed. M. S. Newman. New York: John Wiley & Sons, Inc. P. 58.

Hayashi, M., and L. Pierce. 1961. *J. Chem. Phys.* 35: 479.

Hirota, E. 1962. *J. Chem. Phys.* 37: 283.

Hirota, E. 1965. *J. Chem. Phys.* 42: 2071.

Hyman, H. H., ed. 1963. *Noble-Gas Compounds.* Chicago: Univ. of Chicago Press.

Kistiakowsky, G. B., J. R. Ruhoff, H. A. Smith, and W. E. Vaughan. 1935. *J. Am. Chem. Soc.* 57: 876.

Levine, I. N. 1963. *J. Chem. Phys.* 38: 2326.

Nesbet, R. K. 1964. *J. Chem. Phys.* 40: 3619.

Pauling, L. 1939. *Nature of the Chemical Bond.* Ithaca, N. Y.: Cornell Univ. Press.

*Molecular Architecture*

*of Proteins*

# Principles of Protein Structure[1,2]

**Harold A. Scheraga**

*Department of Chemistry*
*Cornell University*
*Ithaca, New York*

## I. Introduction

When the physical chemist considers the problem of protein structure, he accepts the principles deduced from systems of low molecular weight and takes over from these systems the information about bond angles, bond lengths, potential barriers for internal rotation about single bonds, cis-trans isomerism about double bonds, force constants, bond strengths, etc. His problem is to apply these principles to macromolecules, in which many atoms are connected together in long chains, parts of which may come close enough to interact with each other even though they are remotely spaced along the contour length of the chain.

In applying these principles to proteins, the physical chemist is concentrating on two main problems today. In the first, he formulates simple models for polypeptide chains and more complicated ones for polypeptide chains that interact with each other, as in a globular protein, and seeks to determine the relative probability of occurrence of all possible forms in which the model systems may exist; i.e., he seeks information about the stability of the various conformations that are accessible to the model. In the second, he starts with

[1] This work was supported by research grants (AI–01473 and HE–01662) from the National Institutes of Health and by a research grant (GB–2238) from the National Science Foundation.

[2] Since the presentation of this paper in September, 1964, much progress has been made in the areas discussed in this paper. The reader is referred to the more recent literature for further details.

the covalent structure (amino acid sequence and positions of disulfide bonds) of a protein and, recognizing that the three-dimensional structure will be a distribution over many conformations, he tries to determine the conformation of the most probable form; i.e., he is searching for the "structure" of the protein. Unlike the crystallographer, who answers this question for the molecule in a crystal, the physical chemist is searching for these answers for a protein dissolved in a dilute aqueous solution. Implicit in his approach to this second problem is the hypothesis, stated by Anfinsen (1961) and demonstrated by him for ribonuclease (Epstein *et al.*, 1962) and other proteins, that the amino acid sequence contains the information (or the basis for the ultimate noncovalent interactions) that determines the three-dimensional structure of the protein. Our aim here is to discuss recent developments in the attempt to solve both of these problems.

## II. Nature of Forces Affecting Protein Conformation[3]

The many possible three-dimensional conformations of a given polypeptide chain will be determined by a variety of factors. First of all, there are those that are already detected in each amino acid residue or in a dipeptide. These are the bond lengths, bond angles, bond strengths, hindrance to internal rotation, and excluded volume, all of which will be discussed in more detail in Section VI. Secondly, there are the interactions between groups of atoms distantly separated from each other along the polypeptide chain. This is the information Pauling *et al.* (1951), Corey and Pauling (1953), and Pauling and Corey (1953) used in their proposal of the existence of the $\alpha$-helix, which Kendrew *et al.* (1960) later found in myoglobin. Besides the $\alpha$-helix, several other ordered structures exist, as well as the randomly coiled one.

Many authors (see, e.g., Lifson and Roig, 1961) have presented statistical mechanical treatments for the helix–random-coil system in polyglycine (in a solvent) and for the transition between these two forms, taking into consideration all possible intermediate states. Essentially, the problem of helix formation involves the gain of energy of a hydrogen bond between the NH group of an $i$th residue and the CO group of the $(i+4)$th residue, and the loss of conformational entropy of residues $i + 1$, $i + 2$, and $i + 3$.

Not all interactions between remote groups appear in polyglycine, and more complicated models must be used to discuss these additional interactions. If cystine residues are present, the possibility of disulfide bonds exists; these generally introduce loops in the polypeptide chain and reduce the conformational entropy of the random-coil form, thereby lowering its stability. This accounts for the general observation that proteins with many disulfide bonds are usually more stable than those with fewer covalent cross-

---

[3] A review of the noncovalent bonds in proteins has been published by the author (Scheraga, 1963).

links. Schellman (1955) and Flory (1956) have calculated the influence of disulfide bonds on the conformational entropy where the loops are independent of each other. Poland and Scheraga (1965) have made similar calculations for systems, such as ribonuclease, where the loops are not independent of each other. The lack of independence involves additional constraints, in that the conformations of a given loop are more restricted if it is appropriately connected to another loop.

If the polypeptide chain contains polar side chains, then hydrogen bonds can be formed between donor groups (DH) (e.g., the phenolic OH group of a tyrosyl residue) and acceptor groups (A) (e.g., the carboxylate ion COO$^-$ group of a glutamyl or aspartyl residue). Laskowski and Scheraga (1954), and more recently Némethy et al. (1963), estimated the strengths of such side-chain hydrogen bonds and their influence on various reactions of proteins such as ionization of the polar groups, limited proteolysis, denaturation, and protein association. In the context of this paper, such side-chain hydrogen bonds can influence the relative stability of the various conformations of the backbone. Since the existence of such bonds depends on the pH, i.e., on whether or not the proton is on the right group for hydrogen-bond formation, the influence of pH on the equilibrium (Scheraga, 1960) and kinetics (Laskowski and Scheraga, 1961) of protein denaturation can be calculated.

If the polar side-chain groups are ionizable, then the charge will depend on the pH. This is another source of a pH-dependence of the conformation. For example, polyglutamic acid is in a helical form when the carboxyl groups are uncharged; ionization leads to an electrostatic repulsion which disrupts the helix (Doty et al., 1957).

Many of the side-chain groups, and also the $\alpha$—CH group of the backbone chain, are nonpolar. Interaction between these nonpolar groups in water has been referred to as a hydrophobic bond (Kauzmann, 1959). Nonpolar groups tend to have more ordered water around them than exists in ordinary water (Frank and Evans, 1945; Kauzmann, 1959; Némethy and Scheraga, 1962a). When these groups come into contact, the water-hydrocarbon surface is reduced, leading to a "melting" of some of the ordered water. On this basis, Némethy and Scheraga (1962b) have computed the thermodynamic parameters for the formation of hydrophobic bonds between all possible pairs of nonpolar side chains that occur in proteins; similar calculations were made for interactions between more than two groups at a time (multiple interactions). Subsequently, a series of experimental investigations provided verification of the calculated parameters. As one example, we may cite the influence of pairwise hydrophobic bonds between the nonpolar R-groups in the dimerization of the monocarboxylic acids R—COOH (Schrier et al., 1964). Hydrophobic bonds may exist in the random coil as well as in the helix (Poland and Scheraga, 1965).

Additional small-molecule components besides water, such as urea ("denaturing agents"), can influence the helix–random-coil equilibrium by binding to the exposed groups of the random-coil form and shift the equilibrium in the direction of the random coil. The effect of such binding on the equilibrium has been computed by Schellman (1955) and Peller (1959).

## III. Helix–Random-Coil Equilibrium
## (Two-State Approach)

Having discussed the factors that influence protein conformation, we may now consider the helix–random-coil equilibrium in aqueous solution as a first simple model of protein denaturation. In this initial simple approach, we shall use the two-state assumption, viz., that the backbone exists in only one of two states, helix or random coil, and that there is an equilibrium between these two forms at all temperatures. We may thus write for $\Delta F_{\text{unf}}$, the free energy of unfolding the "native" conformation (Scheraga, 1960, 1962),

$$\Delta F_{\text{unf}} = \Delta F_{\text{b}} + \Delta F_{\text{x}} + \Delta F_{\text{H}} + \Delta F_{\text{elec}} + \Delta F_{\text{H}\phi} + \Delta F_{\text{binding}} \qquad (1)$$

where the free-energy terms on the right-hand side of Eq. (1) arise from the interactions discussed in Section II; i.e., $\Delta F_{\text{b}}$ pertains to the backbone, $\Delta F_{\text{x}}$ to the disulfide cross-links, $\Delta F_{\text{H}}$ to the side-chain hydrogen bonds, $\Delta F_{\text{elec}}$ to the electrostatic interactions, $\Delta F_{\text{H}\phi}$ to the hydrophobic bonds, and $\Delta F_{\text{binding}}$ to the binding of denaturing agents of low molecular weight to the "denatured" conformation. Equation (1) corresponds to the two-state equilibrium represented in Fig. 1.

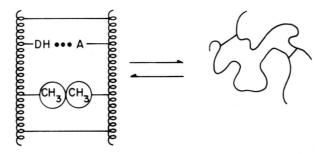

**Fig. 1.** Schematic representation of the interactions that stabilize the conformation of a protein molecule. Equilibrium indicated is between a native protein (left) and a denatured one (right). Backbone of the native protein represented in helical form, that of the denatured one in a randomly coiled form. Solid cross-links represent disulfide bonds; and DH $\cdots$ A and $CH_3$ $\cdots$ $CH_3$ represent side-chain hydrogen and hydrophobic bonds, respectively.

While Eq. (1) provides a basis for discussing protein denaturation, and has been used for this purpose by several authors (Scheraga, 1960, 1962; Tanford, 1962; Brandts and Lumry, 1963; Wetlaufer et al., 1964), it is incorrect in two important aspects. First of all, being based on a two-state assumption, it ignores intermediate states containing varying degrees of the type of noncovalent interactions discussed in Section II. The omission of these intermediate states gives an erroneous view of the transition curve for thermal denaturation. Secondly, Eq. (1) does not contain free-energy terms for mixing of the various species that are present at any temperature, a point discussed by Némethy et al. (1963). While these terms are missing from Eq. (1), they would automatically be included in a correct statistical mechanical theory starting from the partition function.

These two major difficulties have been circumvented 1) for the case of polygycine by several investigators (see, e.g., Lifson and Roig, 1961); 2) for the case of poly-L-alanine, containing hydrophobic bonds in the helix (Bixon et al., 1963); and 3) for more complicated protein-like models involving interactions between helices (Poland and Scheraga, 1965). The simple case of polyglycine and poly-L-alanine will be considered first and then the more complicated models will be discussed.

## IV. Helix–Random-Coil Equilibrium in Polyglycine and Poly-L-Alanine (Simple Case)

An $\alpha$-helix of poly-L-alanine contains a hydrophobic bond between the $\beta$-methyl group on an $i^{\text{th}}$ residue and the $\alpha$—CH group in the backbone of the $(i+3)$ residue (Némethy and Scheraga, 1962b). If one assumes that no hydrophobic bonds exist in the random coil, then one can (Bixon et al., 1963) modify the Lifson–Roig theory for the helix-coil transition in polyglycine to detect the effect of the hydrophobic bond in poly-L-alanine.

With polyglycine, Lifson and Roig (1961) allowed for all intermediate states, as illustrated in Fig. 2, where $h$ refers to a helical state and $c$ to a coil state. A residue is said to be in a helical state when the angles of rotation about its N—C$^\alpha$ and C$^\alpha$—C' bonds are those characteristic of the $\alpha$-helix, within an allowed narrow range of variation; for all other values of these angles, the residue is said to be in a coil state. Figure 2 illustrates one particular conformation for a 15-residue sequence. Lifson and Roig assign conditional probabilities $(u, v, w)$ to these states, depending on whether they are coil states $(u)$ or, if helical states, whether they are at the ends of the helical sequence $(v)$ or in the interior of the helical sequence $(w)$. Taking the coil as a reference state $(u = 1)$, $v$ is essentially a measure of the conformational entropy that is lost when a residue passes from a coil to a helical state, and $w$ is a measure not only of this entropy loss but also of the gain of energy upon

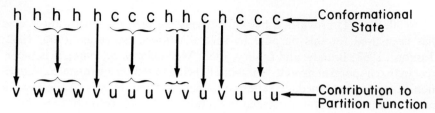

**Fig. 2.** Hypothetical conformational state of a chain of 15 units, each of which can be in a helical (*h*) or coil (*c*) state. The corresponding contribution of this state to the partition function is also shown.

formation of an NH . . . OC hydrogen bond. Figure 2 illustrates the contribution of these conditional probabilities to the partition function for the particular conformation, which is also shown in Fig. 2. The partition function, of course, is a sum over all possible conformational states (of which Fig. 2 is only one) in which a polyglycine chain of a given number of residues can exist. Lifson and Roig evaluated the partition function by a matrix method and deduced an equation for the temperature dependence of $\theta$, the fraction of hydrogen bonds that are present in the system. This equation, of course, contains $v$ and $w$ as parameters, which can be evaluated by application of the theory to experimental data.

Bixon *et al.* (1963) modified this treatment for poly-L-alanine by introducing two additional parameters, $\sigma$ and $\alpha$, the latter being related to the former by the equation

$$\alpha = 1 + v^{1/2}(\sigma - 1) \tag{2}$$

The parameter $\sigma$ is a conditional probability representing a $\beta_i$—$\alpha_{i+3}$ hydrophobic bond in a helical state; essentially, $\sigma w$ replaces $w$ of the polyglycine theory. The parameter $\alpha$ takes account of the fact that a $\beta_i$—$\alpha_{i+3}$ hydrophobic bond can exist if a residue in a coil state is next to a helical sequence. The quantity $\sigma$ is given by

$$\sigma = e^{-\Delta F_{H\phi}/RT} \tag{3}$$

where $\Delta F_{H\phi}$ has been computed, as a function of temperature, by Némethy and Scheraga (1962b). Thus, Bixon *et al.* (1963), using the matrix method of Lifson and Roig (1961), computed the dependence of $\theta$ on $T$. The results for chains of various lengths are shown in Fig. 3. It can be seen that the hydrophobic bond makes the poly-L-alanine helix much more stable than the polyglycine helix. Also, only short chains of poly-L-alanine should melt in the temperature range between 0°C and 100°C.

These results are in agreement with experimental results of Gratzer and Doty (1963), who were unable to melt a poly-L-alanine helix of 175 residues at 95°C in water. Lotan *et al.* (1966) have made shorter poly-L-alanine helices and, in agreement with the predictions of Fig. 3, have been able

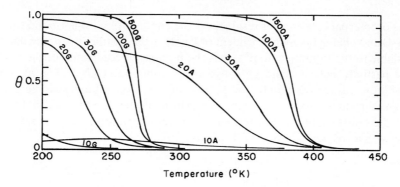

**Fig. 3.** Computed curves for helix–random-coil transition for polyglycine ($G$) and poly-L-alanine ($A$) for the various degrees of polymerization indicated on the curves. (From Bixon *et al.*, 1963, *Biopolymers* 1: 419.)

to melt them below 100°C in water. In all of these experiments the poly-L-alanine chain was rendered water-soluble by incorporating it as the central chain in a block copolymer between two chains of either poly-D,L-glutamic acid or poly-D,L-lysine.

## V. Helix-Coil Equilibrium in More Complicated
## Protein-Like Models

A more rigorous alternative to Eq. (1) was presented recently by Poland and Scheraga (1965), who developed a statistical mechanical theory for the denaturation of several protein-like models. In order to avoid mathematical complexity, the theory was developed for short chains (approximately 20 residues long). However, even though the theory, in its present form, is not applicable to longer chains, several interesting features reminiscent of protein denaturation are already present in the short-chain models.

The theory was developed in stages by formulating models of increasing degrees of complexity until, ultimately, protein-like models were achieved. Model I was simply a polyglycine chain imbedded in a polar medium, i.e., water, but not forming hydrogen bonds with the water. Since it was demonstrated that the probability of an internal break in the helix was negligibly small for a 20-residue chain (i.e., the helices unwind from the ends), the partition function $Z$ for such a system is

$$Z = \Omega^N + \sum_{n=1}^{N-4} \Omega^{N-2-n}(N - 3 - n)(e^{-\epsilon/RT})^n \tag{4}$$

where $N$ is the number of residues in the chain, $n$ is the number of amide hydrogen bonds, $\Omega$ is the effective number of isoenergetic stable conformations of internal rotation per residue, $\epsilon$ is the energy of hydrogen-bond formation ($\Omega$ and $\epsilon$ being taken independent of $T$), $\Omega^N$ is the number of conformations available to the random coil, $\Omega^{N-2-n}$ is the number of conformations available to a partially helical chain of $n$ hydrogen bonds, and $(N - 3 - n)$ is the number of ways in which a helical portion of $n$ hydrogen bonds can be placed on an $N$-residue chain. An exact evaluation of the summation in Eq. (4) (and the omission of a factor $\Omega^N$, which makes the random coil the reference state with a free energy of zero) leads to

$$Z = 1 + \frac{AB}{(B-1)^2} \left\{ B^{N-3} + (N-4) - (N-3)B \right\} \tag{5}$$

where

and

$$\left. \begin{array}{l} A = \Omega^{-2} \\[2mm] B = \dfrac{e^{-\epsilon/RT}}{\Omega} \end{array} \right\} \tag{6}$$

A consequence of Eq. (5) is that the chemical potential of each species is almost linear in $n$ and $T$. If linearity is assumed, then it follows that all species, from $n = 0$ to the maximum value, $N - 4$, are equally probable at the transition temperature. For the actual case, corresponding to Eq. (5), all species are *almost* equally probable at the transition temperature. This is in distinct contrast to the two-state theory, in which only two species exist at the transition temperature, the random coil ($n = 0$) and the perfect helix ($n = N - 4$), and both species are of equal concentration. As a result, the shapes of the transition curves of the two theories will differ. In particular, Poland and Scheraga (1965) have shown that the $\theta$ vs. $T$ curve of the two-state theory is three times steeper at the transition temperature than the corresponding curve derivable from Eq. (5). Thus, the use of a two-state theory to compute $\Delta H$ for an experimental transition curve will involve a 300% error.

The second stage of the theory (Model II) involved the introduction of the possibility that water may bind to those CO and NH groups of the polyglycine chain which are themselves not hydrogen-bonded to each other. Equation (4) was modified to take this effect into account.

$$\begin{aligned} Z = \Omega^N (1 + e^{-\Delta F_{H_2O}/RT})^{2N} \\ + \sum_{n=1}^{N-4} \Omega^{N-2-n}(N-3-n)(1 + e^{-\Delta F_{H_2O}/RT})^{2(N-n)}(e^{-\epsilon/RT})^n \end{aligned} \tag{7}$$

where $2(N - n)$ is the number of CO and NH sites available for water binding, and $\Delta F_{H_2O}$ is the change in free energy to transfer a total of one mole of water from its various energy levels in bulk water to the energy state in which it resides when bound to the protein. If the factor $\Omega^N (1 + e^{-\Delta F_{H_2O}/RT})^{2N}$ is omitted, Eq. (7) may be evaluated to give Eq. (5) with, however, the following definitions for Model II:

$$A = \Omega^{-2}$$

and

$$B = \frac{e^{-\epsilon/RT}}{\Omega(1 + e^{-\Delta F_{H_2O}/RT})^2}$$

(8)

Using the Némethy–Scheraga (1962a) theory for the structure of water, it was possible to demonstrate that $\Delta F_{H_2O} = 0$; i.e., there is no net change in free energy in the process in which water molecules are taken from bulk water and singly bound to the NH and CO groups, this being accompanied by a reshuffling among the various hydrogen-bonded species in the bulk water. With $\Delta F_{H_2O} = 0$, the squared term in the denominator of the expression for $B$ in Eq. (8) is equal to 4. This corresponds to an entropy term arising simply from the number of ways in which bound water may be distributed over the random chain.

With the effect of water thus introduced explicitly, the theory was extended to poly-L-alanine, in which the $\beta_i$—$\alpha_{i+3}$ hydrophobic bond mentioned in Section IV was present in the helical portions and in which a methyl-methyl hydrophobic bond was present in neighboring residues of the random-coil portions of the chain (Model III). It was shown that the random portions would be more likely to have such hydrophobic bonds between neighboring residues, rather than between remote residues along the chain, since there are many ways to place neighbor-neighbor bonds on a chain and neighbor-neighbor bonds restrict the *whole* chain less than do the large loops formed by bonds between remote residues. The partition function for Model III is

$$Z = \Omega^N (1 + e^{-\Delta F_{H_2O}/RT})^{2N} (1 + e^{-\Delta F_{NN}/RT})^{N-1}$$
$$+ \sum_{n=1}^{N-4} \Omega^{N-2-n} (N - 3 - n)(1 + e^{-\Delta F_{H_2O}/RT})^{2(N-n)} (e^{-\Delta F_{H\phi}/RT})^{n-1}$$
$$(1 + e^{-\Delta F_{NN}'/RT})^{N-4-n} (1 + e^{-\Delta F_{NN}'/RT})^2 (e^{-\epsilon/RT})^n \quad (9)$$

where $\Delta F_{NN}$ is the free energy of formation of a neighbor-neighbor hydrophobic bond in the random coil, $\Delta F_{NN}'$ is the corresponding quantity for a residue in a coil state next to a helical sequence, and $\Delta F_{H\phi}$ arises from the $\beta_i$—$\alpha_{i+3}$ hydrophobic bond in the helix. Evaluation of Eq. (9) also leads to Eq. (5), with the omission of the factor

$$\Omega^N (1 + e^{-\Delta F_{H_2O}/RT})^{2N} (1 + e^{-\Delta F_{NN}/RT})^{N-1}$$

and with the following definitions for Model III:

$$A = \frac{(1 + e^{-\Delta F_N/RT})^2}{\Omega^2 (1 + e^{-\Delta F_{NN}/RT})^3 e^{-\Delta F_{H\phi}/RT}}$$

and

$$B = \frac{e^{-\epsilon/RT} e^{-\Delta F_{H\phi}/RT}}{\Omega(1 + e^{-\Delta F_{H_2O}/RT})^2 (1 + e^{-\Delta F_{NN}/RT})}$$

(10)

With Model III as a basis, Poland and Scheraga (1965) then introduced
the possibility that several helical portions of a given chain could interact
with each other either by side-chain hydrogen or hydrophobic bonds. While
an internal break is improbable in a polyglycine helix, this break becomes
possible in a helix if the break will allow two or more helical portions to interact through their side chains. Two models, showing side-chain interactions,
are illustrated in Figs. 4 and 5.

In the model of Fig. 4, the tyrosyl-carboxylate ion hydrogen bonds, and
associated hydrophobic bonds between the R groups, influence the stability

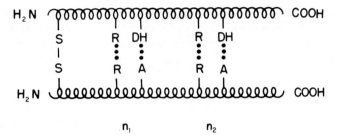

**Fig. 4.** Model in which two helical portions of a protein molecule
interact by side-chain hydrogen and hydrophobic bonds. (From
Poland and Scheraga, 1965, *Biopolymers* 3: 357.)

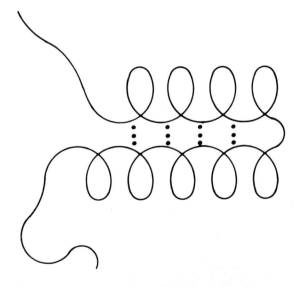

**Fig. 5.** Model in which two helical portions of a protein molecule
interact by side-chain hydrophobic bonds. (From Poland and
Scheraga, 1965, *Biopolymers* 3: 305.)

of the "native" form of this protein-like model. The transition curves for this model are shown in Fig. 6. The values of $\theta_{sc}$ and $\theta_H$, the fractions of side-chain and amide hydrogen bonds, respectively, depend on both $p$H and

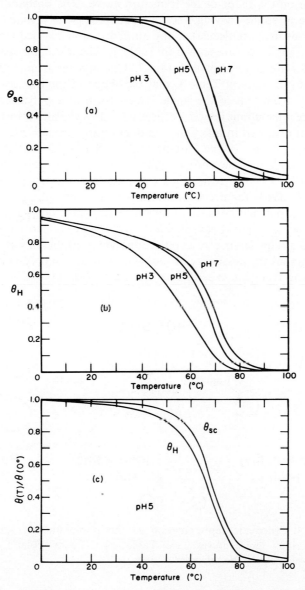

**Fig. 6.** Transition curves at three $p$H's for model in Fig. 4. (From Poland and Scheraga, 1965, *Biopolymers* 3: 357.)

temperature. At, say, $pH$ 5, the $\theta_{sc}$ vs. $T$ and $\theta_H$ vs. $T$ curves parallel each other. Such behavior has been observed by Hermans and Scheraga (1961) for ribonuclease.

In the model of Fig. 5, the side-chain hydrophobic bonds have a considerable influence on the shape of the transition curve. The probabilities $P(n, i)$ of occurrence of species having $i$ helical sequences (with a *total* of $n$ amide hydrogen bonds in the molecule), if any number $i$ of helical sequences can be present in the molecule, are shown in Table 1. The *dominant* species at the various temperatures are shown in Fig. 7. One can see from Fig. 8, which corresponds to the data of Table 1, that the shape of the transition curve is quite different from that of the single helical form of a polyamino acid; in particular, the interactions between helices leads to a sharper transition curve, more like that observed in many protein-denaturation reactions.

With proper choice of the parameters, the flat portion of the curve of Fig. 8 can be made to show both a minimum and a maximum. Such a curve is shown in Fig. 9, which is intended to simulate the situation observed by Fasman *et al.* (1964) for a copolymer of leucine and glutamic acid. Presumably, the copolymer consists of several helical portions interacting with each other by side-chain hydrophobic bonds between leucyl residues, the glutamic acid groups serving to keep the copolymer soluble in water. Further information about the possibility of interacting helices in poly-L-alanine may be forthcoming from the experiments of Lotan *et al.* (1966), mentioned in Section IV.

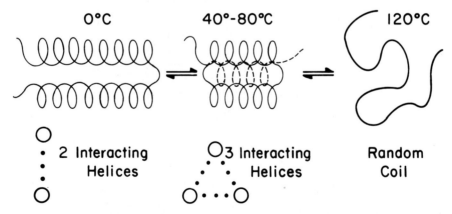

**Fig. 7.** Schematic representation of the predominating species at various temperatures (see Table 1). (From Poland and Scheraga, 1965, *Biopolymers* 3: 305.)

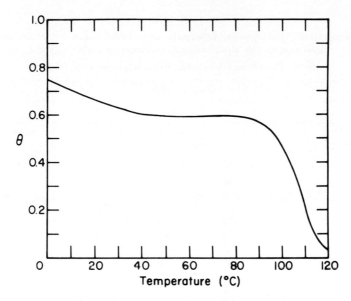

**Fig. 8.** Transition curve obtainable from data of Table 1. (From Poland and Scheraga, 1965, *Biopolymers* 3: 305.)

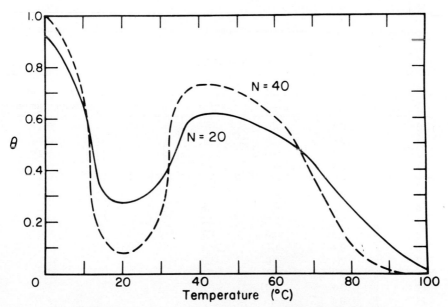

**Fig. 9.** Type of curve obtainable for a molecule of 20 or 40 residues, respectively, containing helices that interact through side-chain hydrophobic bonds.

## TABLE 1

NORMALIZED PROBABILITIES, EXPRESSED AS PERCENT, AS A FUNCTION OF
TEMPERATURE FOR A TWENTY-RESIDUE CHAIN OF POLY-L-ALANINE

(From Poland and Scheraga, 1965, *Biopolymers* 3: 305.)

| | | | | | |
|---|---|---|---|---|---|
| | **T = 0°C** | | | | |
| | $P(n, i) \times 100$ | | | | $P(n) \times 100$ |
| $n$ | $i = 1$ | $i = 2$ | $i = 3$ | $i = 4$ | (Sum over $n$) |
| 0 | 0.1 | | | | 0.1 |
| 1 | 0.0 | | | | 0.0 |
| 2 | 0.1 | 0.0 | | | 0.1 |
| 3 | 0.1 | 0.0 | 0.0 | | 0.1 |
| 4 | 0.2 | 0.0 | 0.0 | 0.0 | 0.2 |
| 5 | 0.3 | 0.0 | 0.0 | 0.0 | 0.3 |
| 6 | 0.4 | 0.1 | 0.1 | 0.0 | 0.6 |
| 7 | 0.6 | 0.2 | 0.4 | 0.1 | 1.3 |
| 8 | 0.9 | 0.6 | 1.3 | | 2.8 |
| 9 | 1.5 | 1.3 | 3.9 | | 6.7 |
| 10 | 2.1 | 3.0 | 8.7 | | 13.9 |
| 11 | 3.1 | 6.3 | | | 9.4 |
| 12 | 4.5 | 12.4 | | | 16.9 |
| 13 | 6.0 | 17.3 | | | 23.3 |
| 14 | 7.8 | | | | 7.8 |
| 15 | 9.0 | | | | 9.0 |
| 16 | 7.6 | | | | 7.6 |

| | | | | | |
|---|---|---|---|---|---|
| | **T = 40°C** | | | | |
| | $P(n, i) \times 100$ | | | | $P(n) \times 100$ |
| $n$ | $i = 1$ | $i = 2$ | $i = 3$ | $i = 4$ | (Sum over $n$) |
| 0 | 0.3 | | | | 0.3 |
| 1 | 0.2 | | | | 0.2 |
| 2 | 0.2 | 0.0 | | | 0.2 |
| 3 | 0.2 | 0.0 | 0.0 | | 0.2 |
| 4 | 0.2 | 0.0 | 0.1 | 0.0 | 0.3 |
| 5 | 0.2 | 0.1 | 0.2 | 0.1 | 0.6 |
| 6 | 0.3 | 0.2 | 0.8 | 0.4 | 1.7 |
| 7 | 0.3 | 0.3 | 2.4 | 1.1 | 4.1 |
| 8 | 0.3 | 0.6 | 7.7 | | 8.6 |
| 9 | 0.3 | 1.1 | 20.8 | | 22.2 |
| 10 | 0.4 | 2.0 | 43.3 | | 45.7 |
| 11 | 0.4 | 3.4 | | | 3.8 |
| 12 | 0.4 | 5.0 | | | 5.4 |
| 13 | 0.4 | 5.5 | | | 5.9 |
| 14 | 0.3 | | | | 0.3 |
| 15 | 0.3 | | | | 0.3 |
| 16 | 0.2 | | | | 0.2 |

$T = 80°C$

| n | $P(n, i) \times 100$ | | | | $P(n) \times 100$ (Sum over $n$) |
|---|---|---|---|---|---|
| | $i = 1$ | $i = 2$ | $i = 3$ | $i = 4$ | |
| 0 | 0.6 | | | | 0.6 |
| 1 | 0.2 | | | | 0.2 |
| 2 | 0.2 | 0.0 | | | 0.2 |
| 3 | 0.1 | 0.0 | 0.0 | | 0.1 |
| 4 | 0.1 | 0.1 | 0.1 | 0.0 | 0.3 |
| 5 | 0.1 | 0.1 | 0.3 | 0.2 | 0.7 |
| 6 | 0.1 | 0.2 | 1.0 | 0.5 | 1.8 |
| 7 | 0.1 | 0.4 | 3.0 | 1.3 | 4.8 |
| 8 | 0.0 | 0.7 | 8.7 | | 9.4 |
| 9 | 0.0 | 1.2 | 22.8 | | 24.0 |
| 10 | 0.0 | 2.1 | 43.0 | | 45.1 |
| 11 | 0.0 | 3.3 | | | 3.3 |
| 12 | 0.0 | 4.6 | | | 4.6 |
| 13 | 0.0 | 4.9 | | | 4.9 |
| 14 | 0.0 | | | | 0.0 |
| 15 | 0.0 | | | | 0.0 |
| 16 | 0.0 | | | | 0.0 |

$T = 120°C$

| n | $P(n, i) \times 100$ | | | | $P(n) \times 100$ (Sum over $n$) |
|---|---|---|---|---|---|
| | $i = 1$ | $i = 2$ | $i = 3$ | $l = 4$ | |
| 0 | 50.5 | | | | 50.5 |
| 1 | 14.0 | | | | 14.0 |
| 2 | 8.3 | 0.5 | | | 8.8 |
| 3 | 4.6 | 0.5 | 0.0 | | 5.1 |
| 4 | 2.6 | 0.5 | 0.0 | 0.0 | 3.1 |
| 5 | 1.5 | 1.0 | 0.0 | 0.0 | 2.5 |
| 6 | 1.0 | 1.0 | 0.5 | 0.0 | 2.5 |
| 7 | 0.5 | 1.0 | 0.5 | 0.0 | 2.0 |
| 8 | 0.5 | 1.0 | 0.5 | | 2.0 |
| 9 | 0.0 | 1.5 | 0.5 | | 2.0 |
| 10 | 0.0 | 1.5 | 0.5 | | 2.0 |
| 11 | 0.0 | 1.5 | | | 1.5 |
| 12 | 0.0 | 1.0 | | | 1.0 |
| 13 | 0.0 | 1.0 | | | 1.0 |
| 14 | 0.0 | | | | 0.0 |
| 15 | 0.0 | | | | 0.0 |
| 16 | 0.0 | | | | 0.0 |

Another important consequence of these models is that ΔH should vary with temperature, having a maximum value near the transition temperature. Some data on protein denaturation (Fig. 10) bear out this prediction.

In summary, the presence of side-chain interactions greatly modifies the denaturation behavior of simple polyamino acid helices. The theory presented in this section describes the features of the transition more accurately than does the two-state theory mentioned in Section III.

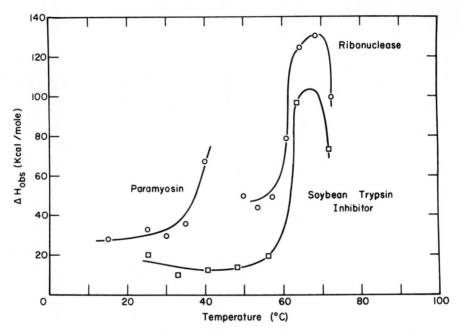

**Fig. 10.** Representative data on the temperature-dependence of ΔH for the denaturation of several proteins. (From Poland and Scheraga, 1965, *Biopolymers* 3: 401.)

## VI. Calculation of Three-Dimensional Structure

Having discussed the problem of the stability of various conformations, we turn now to the larger task of computing the most probable structure that a protein will have as a result of its particular amino acid sequence and the locations of its disulfide bonds. The locations of the disulfide bonds themselves seem to be determined by the amino acid sequence, as demonstrated by Anfinsen and coworkers (Epstein *et al.*, 1962) for ribonuclease, the covalent structure of which is shown in Fig. 11.

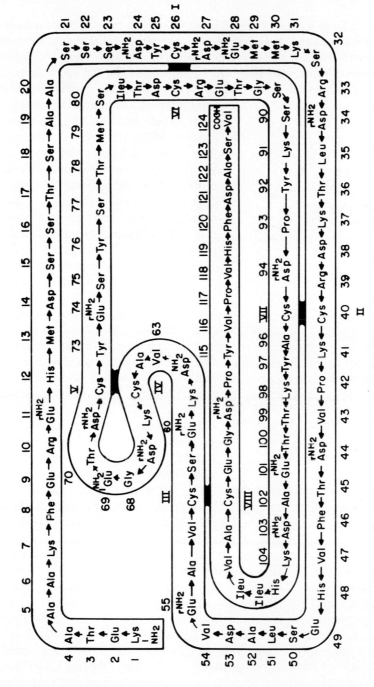

**Fig. 11.** Covalent structure of bovine pancreatic ribonuclease. (Data from Hirs *et al.,* 1960; Spackman *et al.,* 1960; Gross and Witkop, 1962; Potts *et al.,* 1962; Smyth *et al.,* 1962, 1963.)

It is easiest from a computational point of view to break a protein molecule up into several loops and carry out the computation separately for each loop. The methods currently being employed in our laboratory for calculating three-dimensional structure will be illustrated for the small loop of ribonuclease (residues 65 to 72 of Fig. 11). It should be emphasized that only perhaps one or two of the structures thereby calculated will be that of the loop in the ribonuclease molecule. The others can be ruled out only when a similar calculation is carried out for all the other loops of the molecule. For the present, the 65-to-72 loop should be considered as an isolated cyclic octapeptide. Similar calculations are planned and being carried out for other cyclic peptides (gramicidin, tyrocidin, actinomycin, oxytocin, vasopressin, and insulin).

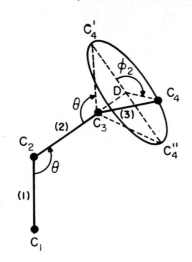

**Fig. 12.** Spatial representation of a simple singly bonded carbon chain. $\theta$ is the fixed valence angle, and $\phi_2$ is the angle of rotation of atom $C_4$ about bond 2. (From Flory, 1953, *Principles of Polymer Chemistry*, Cornell Univ. Press.)

The initial approach of Némethy and Scheraga (1965) was to consider first a cyclic octapeptide containing two cystine and six alanine residues and to focus attention on the rotation about the single bonds of each residue.

Consider first the general problem of internal rotation about single bonds, say, in a chain of carbon atoms (see Fig. 12). If all angles of internal rotation were equally probable, then the number of conformations allowed for a chain of a given number of carbon atoms would be very large. However, for such rotations, all angles are not equally probable. For a simple molecule, like ethane, a periodic potential function for internal rotation exists, shown schematically in Fig. 13. The three minima correspond to the three positions in which the hydrogen atoms of the two methyl groups are staggered with respect to each other, as shown in Fig. 14. The computation of the potential functions for internal rotation for ethane and substituted ethane molecules is still a difficult problem; however, some progress has recently been made (Scott and Scheraga, 1965). As substituents are added to the carbon atoms, the potential functions, though still periodic, become more complicated. For the N—$C^\alpha$ and $C^\alpha$—$C'$ single bonds in proteins, Pauling and Corey (1951) originally assigned sixfold potential functions, recognizing that some of the positions corresponding to minima would not be sterically pos-

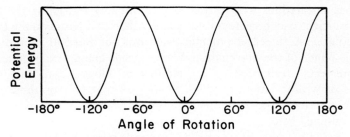

**Fig. 13.** Threefold potential function for the relative rotation of the methyl groups about the C—C bond in ethane. (From Flory, 1953, *Principles of Polymer Chemistry*, Cornell Univ. Press.)

sible. From the work of Mizushima and Shimanouchi (1961) and Scott and Scheraga (1965), the $C^\alpha$—$C'$ bond appears to have a sixfold potential; however, it is not yet clear whether the N—$C^\alpha$ bond should have a sixfold or a threefold potential. Ramachandran *et al.* (1963) showed which conformations were sterically possible for a dipeptide, the question of what is allowed being quite sensitive to the choice of van der Waals radii. Using the Pauling and Corey (1951) criteria for minima in the potential functions, Némethy and Scheraga (1965) assigned a discrete set of stable conformations for the two single bonds of each residue.

Using a matrix method, and a CDC–1604 computer, to generate the octapeptide, each conformation was examined according to the following criteria: 1) no two atoms could approach each other at a distance shorter than the sum of their van der Waals radii and 2) the last cystine residue had to approach the first within a distance and range of orientations to allow formation of the disulfide bond. Approximately $10^6$ nonrandomly selected stable conformations were generated, using the Pauling–Corey conditions for stable minima. Of these, approximately 80 satisfied the above criteria. Since so many conformations were allowed, it was concluded that further

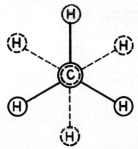

**Fig. 14.** Staggered conformation of ethane. (From Flory, 1953, *Principles of Polymer Chemistry*, Cornell Univ. Press.)

attempts in this direction, without introducing the side chains beyond the $\beta$-carbon, would be fruitless. Therefore, the program was modified to include the side chains at the beginning.

At the same time that the above result for the cyclic alanine-cystine copolymer was obtained, Némethy and Scheraga became aware of the results of Ramachandran *et al.* (1963) for the restrictions in the dipeptide. Therefore, all further calculations were carried out by initially restricting the number of minima in the backbone to a value smaller than that based on the Pauling–Corey criteria. A threefold potential was used for internal rotation about the single bonds of the side chains. When the side chains are included, there is a more severe restriction on the number of allowed conformations. At the time of writing (August, 1964), it appears that two or three possible structures for the 65-to-72 loop in ribonuclease will result, based on the method outlined here.

This method is also being applied in our laboratory to the other cyclic peptides mentioned earlier in this section. When one breaks a protein molecule like ribonuclease into several loops and treats each loop separately, one should calculate several conformations for each loop. Then, when the loops are combined into the parent molecule, presumably some of the conformations of the isolated loops will no longer be allowed, and the most probable structure of the parent molecule will emerge. In this respect, loops can be formed by noncovalent bonds as well as by disulfide bonds. For example, reasonably good evidence is now available to allow one to pair up three tyrosyl residues with three aspartyl residues in ribonuclease (Riehm et al., 1965). Thus, the effective number of loops in ribonuclease is increased, and therefore the number of residues per loop is decreased, thereby simplifying the computational problem.

This first attempt to compute the three-dimensional structure is a crude one. However, it already provides "starting structures" that can be used to compute X-ray diffraction patterns for comparison with experimental data and that can be used for further refinement by methods outlined in the next section.

## VII. Future Directions

It is worthwhile now to consider some of the shortcomings of the method outlined in Section VI and to indicate the direction in which future progress may be expected.

The main difficulty with the aforementioned method is that it confines the backbone chain to the potential minima. Such minima are shallow, and it is too expensive energy-wise for the backbone to rotate away from the minimum position if it can compensate this cost in energy by forming other interactions such as hydrogen and hydrophobic bonds. In fact, the $\alpha$-helix, which involves amide hydrogen bonds, has angles of rotation that do not correspond to minima in the potential function.

An alternative method, under investigation in our laboratory, and used previously by Lifson and Rosen (private communication) for cyclo-alkanes, is based on a principle of minimization of energy. One would start with a trial structure, determined by the method of Section VI and presumably reasonably close to the correct structure. With this structure, one would write an expression for the total energy of the system as a function of all coordinates. This would include all types of interactions of parts of the chain with each other and with the solvent. The computer would be asked to vary the coordinates systematically until a minimum in the energy was reached. Presumably, the conformation corresponding to the energy minimum would be the most probable one for the given protein.

As ingredients in the expression for the total energy, one would have to include the potential functions for internal rotation about single bonds, the energy to distort bond angles and bond distances, the energy to distort the planarity of the amide group, hydrogen-bond energy, dipole interactions, potential functions for interactions between nonbonded atoms, hydrophobic bonds, solvent effects, etc. De Santis *et al.* (1963) have used this approach for synthetic polymers, using only nonbonded interactions. A note in their paper indicates that the same method has been applied to polypeptide structures.

Such a method would enable one to compute the difference in stability between a right- and a left-handed helix (of L-amino acids) in water and to obtain significant information about protein structure. One could also investigate the effect on the structure of substituting a "wrong" amino acid for the correct one; presumably such a substitution can have a profound effect, as in the abnormal hemoglobins (Murayama, 1964).

In conclusion, the time seems to be near at hand when the information provided by the organic chemist (amino acid sequence and positions of disulfide bridges) can be used as a basis to locate, by chemical and physico-chemical means, a few noncovalent interactions between side chains, and to compute the most probable conformation of a protein molecule in aqueous solution.

## REFERENCES

Anfinsen, C. B. 1961. *J. Polymer Sci.* 49: 31.

Bixon, M., H. A. Scheraga, and S. Lifson. 1963. *Biopolymers* 1: 419.

Brandts, J., and R. Lumry. 1963. *J. Phys. Chem.* 67: 1484.

Corey, R. B., and L. Pauling. 1953. *Proc. Roy. Soc. (London) Ser. B* 141: 10.

De Santis, P., E. Giglio, A. M. Liquori, and A. Ripamonti. 1963. *J. Polymer Sci.* A1: 1383.

Doty, P., A. Wada, J. T. Yang, and E. R. Blout. 1957. *J. Polymer Sci.* 23: 851.

Epstein, C. J., R. F. Goldberger, D. M. Young, and C. B. Anfinsen. 1962. *Arch. Biochem. Biophys.* Suppl. 1: 223.

Fasman, G. D., C. Lindblow, and E. Bodenheimer. 1964. *Biochemistry* 3: 155.

Flory, P. J. 1953. *Principles of Polymer Chemistry.* Ithaca, N.Y.: Cornell Univ. Press.

Flory, P. J. 1956. *J. Am. Chem. Soc.* 78: 5222.

Frank, H. S., and M. W. Evans. 1945. *J. Chem. Phys.* 13: 507.

Gratzer, W. B., and P. Doty. 1963. *J. Am. Chem. Soc.* 85: 1193.

Gross, E., and B. Witkop. 1962. *J. Biol. Chem.* 237: 1856.

Hermans, J. Jr., and H. A. Scheraga. 1961. *J. Am. Chem. Soc.* 83: 3283.

Hirs, C. H. W., S. Moore, and W. H. Stein. 1960. *J. Biol. Chem.* 235: 633.

Kauzmann, W. 1959. *Advan. Protein Chem.* 14: 1.

Kendrew, J. C., R. E. Dickerson, B. E. Strandberg, R. G. Hart, and D. R. Davies. 1960. *Nature* 185: 422.

Laskowski, M. Jr., and H. A. Scheraga. 1954. *J. Am. Chem. Soc.* 76: 6305.

Laskowski, M. Jr., and H. A. Scheraga. 1961. *J. Am. Chem. Soc.* 83: 266.

Lifson, S., and A. Roig. 1961. *J. Chem. Phys.* 34: 1963.

Lotan, N., A. Berger, E. Katchalski, R. T. Ingwall, and H. Scheraga. 1966. *Biopolymers.* In press.

Mizushima, S., and T. Shimanouchi. 1961. *Advan. Enzymol.* 23: 1.

Murayama, M. 1964. *Nature* 202: 258.

Némethy, G., and H. A. Scheraga. 1962a. *J. Chem. Phys.* 36: 3382, 3401.

Némethy, G., and H. A. Scheraga. 1962b. *J. Phys. Chem.* 66: 1773.

Némethy, G., and H. A. Scheraga. 1965. *Biopolymers* 3: 155.

Némethy, G., I. Z. Steinberg, and H. A. Scheraga. 1963. *Biopolymers* 1: 43.

Pauling, L., and R. B. Corey. 1951. *Proc. Natl. Acad. Sci. U.S.* 37: 729.

Pauling, L., and R. B. Corey. 1953. *Proc. Roy. Soc. (London) Ser. B* 141: 21.

Pauling, L., R. B. Corey, and H. R. Branson. 1951. *Proc. Natl. Acad. Sci. U.S.* 37: 205.

Peller, L. 1959. *J. Phys. Chem.* 63: 1199.

Poland, D. C., and H. A. Scheraga. 1965. *Biopolymers* 3: 275, 283, 305, 315, 335, 357, 369, 379, 401.

Potts, J. T., A. Berger, J. Cooke, and C. B. Anfinsen. 1962. *J. Biol. Chem.* 237: 1851.

Ramachandran, G. N., C. Ramakrishnan, and V. Sasisekharan. 1963. *J. Mol. Biol.* 7: 95.

Riehm, J. P., C. A. Broomfield, and H. A. Scheraga. 1965. *Biochemistry* 4: 760.

Schellman, J. A. 1955. *Compt. Rend. Trav. Lab. Carlsberg, Ser. Chim.* 29: 230.

Scheraga, H. A. 1960. *J. Phys. Chem.* 64: 1917.

Scheraga, H. A. 1962. In *Polyamino Acids, Polypeptides, and Proteins*, ed. M. A. Stahmann. Madison, Wisc.: Univ. of Wisconsin Press. P. 241.

Scheraga, H. A. 1963. In *The Proteins*, Vol. I, ed. H. Neurath. New York: Academic Press, Inc. P. 477.

Schrier, E. E., M. Pottle, and H. A. Scheraga. 1964. *J. Am. Chem. Soc.* 86: 3444.

Scott, R. A., and H. A. Scheraga. 1965. *J. Chem. Phys.* 42: 2209.

Smyth, D. G., W. H. Stein, and S. Moore. 1962. *J. Biol. Chem.* 237: 1845.

Smyth, D. G., W. H. Stein, and S. Moore. 1963. *J. Biol. Chem.* 238: 227.

Spackman, D. H., W. H. Stein, and S. Moore. 1960. *J. Biol. Chem.* 235: 648.

Tanford, C. 1962. *J. Am. Chem. Soc.* 84: 4240.

Wetlaufer, D. B., S. K. Malik, L. Stoller, and R. L. Coffin. 1964. *J. Am. Chem. Soc.* 86: 508.

# The Colors of Bioluminescence: Role of Enzyme and Substrate Structure[1]

**W. D. McElroy and H. H. Seliger**

*Department of Biology*
*The Johns Hopkins University*
*and*
*McCollum-Pratt Institute*
*Baltimore, Maryland*

## Introduction

Biochemical specificity and reactivity of enzymes are strongly influenced by the molecular arrangement ascribed to the native state. Although there is much evidence that proteins can undergo specific and reversible configurational changes, there is little direct evidence that such alterations play a significant role in the catalytic process. However, the influence of temperature and pressure on enzyme-catalyzed reactions leads one to suspect that changes in the secondary and tertiary structure of biocatalysts may be of great importance in determining the rate of catalysis and the reactivity of transients formed in the reaction. Activators or inhibitors that combine at sites other than the "catalytic center" presumably function in this manner.

We shall review the evidence indicating that enzyme structure and configuration are important not only for catalysis but also for determining the resonance energy levels of the excited state that are responsible for light emission. From structural studies on the substrates, luciferin ($LH_2$) and ATP, we can conclude that the nature and strength of binding to the enzyme

[1] The research summarized in this paper was supported in part by the National Science Foundation, the National Institutes of Health, and the Atomic Energy Commission.

of the transient formed in the oxidative reaction are important in determining the color of the light. The inference can be drawn, therefore, that the three-dimensional structure of the enzyme molecule directly influences the allowed electronic transitions of the emitting molecule.

## Chemistry of Light Emission in the Firefly, *Photinus pyralis*

The substrates and enzyme required for light production in extracts from the firefly, *Photinus pyralis*, have now been prepared in a highly purified, crystalline state (McElroy, 1960; McElroy and Seliger, 1961, 1963a). All evidence indicates that these same factors are responsible for light emission in other genera of the Lampyridae and possible other groups in the Coleoptera. The crystallization of firefly $LH_2$ and luciferase (designated as E in reactions) has allowed, for the first time, an extensive quantitative study of the interaction of these substances during the process of light emission. Luciferase, purified by repeated crystallization, is homogeneous as judged by electrophoresis and ultracentrifugation.

The preparation and some of the properties of firefly $LH_2$ have been described by Bitler and McElroy (1957). Recent studies by White *et al.* (1961) have demonstrated the structure of $LH_2$ to be that shown in Fig. 1. This structure was proved by total synthesis. In the last step of the chemical synthesis of luciferin, 2-cyano-6-hydroxybenzthiazole reacts with cysteine. When $D(-)$-cysteine is used, a luciferin, $D(-)$-$LH_2$, is obtained that has all the properties of natural luciferin. When $L(+)$-cysteine is used in the synthesis, the resulting luciferin, $L(+)$-$LH_2$, is inactive for light production, although it is otherwise chemically identical with $D(-)$-$LH_2$. Both $L(+)$-$LH_2$ and $D(-)$-$LH_2$ will react with ATP in the presence of luciferase to liberate pyrophosphate.

*Enzyme-catalyzed light reaction.* When one starts with free $LH_2$ and luciferase, ATP and $Mg^{++}$ are required for light emission. The initial reaction is in reality an adenyl transfer to the carboxyl group of $LH_2$ to form luciferyl-adenylate, $LH_2$—AMP, with the elimination of inorganic pyrophosphate, as indicated in the following reaction:

$$\text{(Reaction 1)} \quad LH_2 + ATP + E \underset{}{\overset{Mg^{++}}{\rightleftharpoons}} E \cdot LH_2\text{—}AMP + PP$$

The release of inorganic pyrophosphate and reversibility of the reaction have been demonstrated in several ways (Rhodes and McElroy, 1958a, b). The over-all light reaction is

$$\text{(Reaction 2)} \quad E \cdot LH_2\text{—}AMP + O_2 \rightarrow \text{light and products}$$

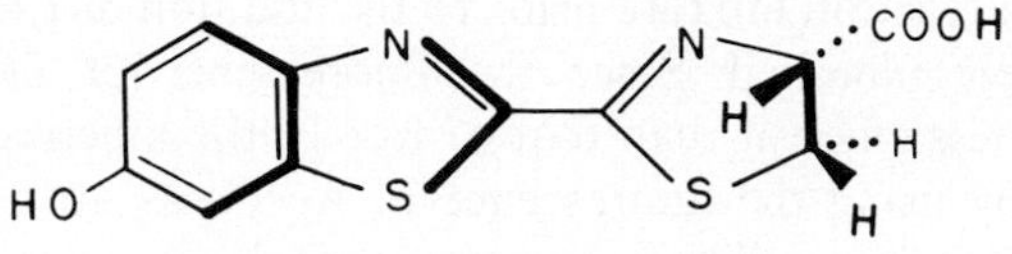

L (+) LUCIFERIN

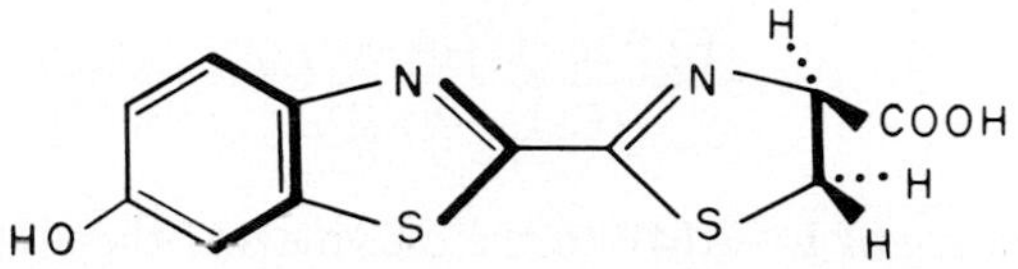

D (−) LUCIFERIN

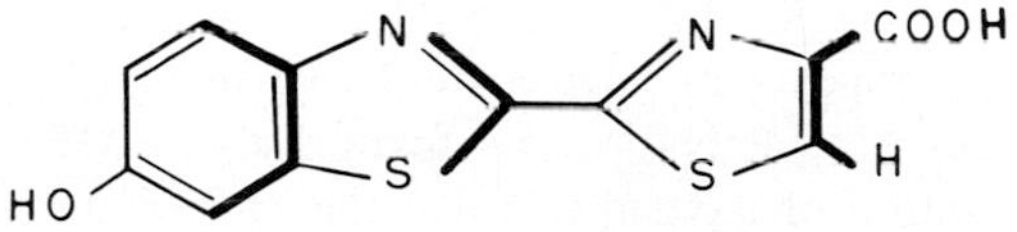

DEHYDROLUCIFERIN

**Fig. 1.** Structure of firefly luciferin and dehydroluciferin.

The product of the light reaction has many of the properties of dehydro-luciferin (L) (see Fig. 1). However, it seems most likely that the latter is not produced from the excited intermediate but rather is an oxidation product that does not lead to light emission.

Unfortunately, we have not yet been able to isolate unambiguously the excited state of the product molecule from which the light quantum is emitted. From the facts obtained so far, we know that the fluorescence yield of the intermediate must be practically 100%. By analogy to the luminol chemiluminescence reaction, it seems most likely that oxygen can add to $E \cdot LH_2$—AMP to form an organic hydroperoxide. The exergonic step could then be described as a dehydration process in which one atom of oxygen remains in the intermediate and the other appears in a water molecule.

It is known that at least one of the oxidation products of $LH_2$ is dehydro-luciferin, which is also activated by ATP and $Mg^{++}$ in the presence of enzyme as indicated in the following reaction:

$$\text{(Reaction 3)} \qquad L + ATP + E \xrightarrow{\;Mg^{++}\;} E \cdot L\text{—}AMP + PP$$

If L is added to a reaction mixture prior to the addition of $LH_2$, light production is completely inhibited. Since the fluorescence of L—AMP on the enzyme is much less efficient than that of free L, the kinetics of the reaction can be studied by using the fluorescence of free L as an assay method. It has been found that the equilibrium constant for the activation step at pH 7.1 is $2.5 \times 10^5$. Furthermore, the dissociation constant, $K$, as defined by the following equation, was determined to be $5 \times 10^{-10}$.

$$K = \frac{\text{(E) free (L—AMP) free}}{\text{(E·L—AMP)}} \tag{1}$$

This tight binding of L—AMP to the enzyme and the ability of inorganic pyrophosphate to react reversibly with the complex accounts for the over-all kinetic behavior of the light-emitting reaction. The product of the light reaction has many of the properties of L—AMP. The inhibition of light by the product can be reversed by pyrophosphate or coenzyme A. The nature of the binding is not clear; however, indirect evidence suggests that the OH group on the benzthiazole ring and the adenylic acid are important factors.

Thus luciferase appears to have a dual role in light emission. The first step involves $LH_2$-ATP activation to form $LH_2$—AMP, and the second involves the utilization of oxygen to form the excited state (Hastings *et al.*, 1953; McElroy *et al.*, 1953). Although we cannot describe completely the organic mechanism involved in this oxidation reaction, certain important facts must be considered in any proposed mechanism. We know, for example, that the total light output is directly proportional to the amounts of ATP and $LH_2$ present; i.e., both substrates are used (Seliger and McElroy, 1959). Furthermore, we know from previous studies that one light quantum is emitted for each $LH_2$ molecule used, for very low concentrations of $LH_2$ at alkaline pH. As the pH is decreased below neutrality, the oxidation of $LH_2$ does not always lead to light emission.

*Emission spectrum.* Figure 2 shows the true emission spectrum of the *P. pyralis* light reaction *in vitro* in glycyl-glycine buffer at pH 7.6. The peak emission for the bioluminescence is 562 m$\mu$, with the band ranging from 500 to 630 m$\mu$. As an absolute minimum, therefore, the energy requirement for the bioluminescence should exceed 57 kcal/mole. Measurements of the spectrum using *P. pyralis* organs give approximately the same emission peak. However, other fireflies show some shifts in their peak emission, and the reasons for this are discussed below.

One might expect that some product would occur in the light-emitting step that would have a fluorescence spectrum similar to the bioluminescence emission spectrum and that could possibly be identified as the light-emitting molecule. Detailed fluorescence studies on $LH_2$, L, and the adenylic deriva-

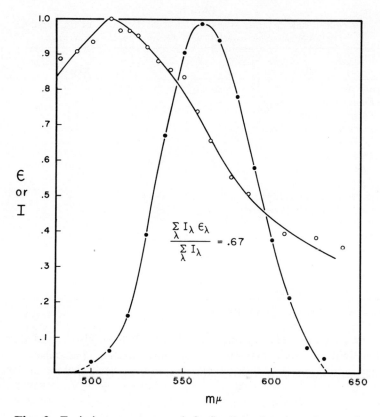

**Fig. 2.** Emission spectrum of firefly light *in vitro*. *P. pyralis* luciferase, *p*H 7.6. ○: spectral sensitivity of photocell; ●: corrected emission spectrum.

tives have been made. We shall not review all the data here. In summary, they clearly indicate that the adenylic derivative of an oxygenated product is the most likely emitter (McElroy and Seliger, 1963b).

*Light reaction of other fireflies.* In Table 1 we present the results of a number of tests on cell-free extracts of various fireflies (McElroy and Harvey, 1951). Crude extracts of the lanterns were made, and, when all the light had disappeared, ATP and *P. pyralis* $LH_2$ were added, either separately or in combination. For most extracts only ATP was necessary to restore light, indicating that both $LH_2$ and luciferase were still present in the extract. In some extracts where the ATP reaction was negative, light could be restored by adding $LH_2$ and ATP. Additional experiments using *Photinus melanotis* and *Diphotus montanus* indicated that the $LH_2$ and ATP disappear at about the same rate in crude extracts. Some glowworm extracts appear to behave

TABLE 1

THE PRODUCTION OF LIGHT BY FIREFLY LANTERN EXTRACTS IN THE PRESENCE
OF ADENOSINE TRIPHOSPHATE AND *Photinus pyralis* LUCIFERIN*

| Firefly | ATP | $LH_2$ | $LH_2 +$ ATP |
|---|:---:|:---:|:---:|
| Jamaican | | | |
|   *Photinus lobatus lobatus* | + | − | + |
|   *Photinus pallens* | + | − | + |
|   *Photinus lobatus morbosus* | + | − | + |
|   *Photinus commissus* | + | − | + |
|   *Photinus melanotis* | − | − | + |
|   *Diphotus montanus* | − | − | + |
|   *Photuris jamaicensis* | − | − | − |
|   Glowworm (unidentified) | − | − | + |
|   Puerto Rican *Pyrophorus* sp. | + | − | + |
| American | | | |
|   *Photinus pyralis*, adult | + | − | + |
|   *Photinus scintillans* | + | − | + |
|   *Photuris pennsylvanica* | + | − | + |
|   Two unidentified species | + | − | + |
|   Glowworm (*P. pyralis*) | − | − | + |

* Symbols: + = light, − = no light.

in this manner also. Harvey and Haneda (1952) have also found that ATP restores light in crude extracts of Japanese fireflies. The negative result obtained with *Photuris jamaicensis* was due to the loss of enzyme in the crude extract. Chromatographic evidence obtained using crude extracts of *Photinus pallens, P. pyralis, Photinus scintillans, Photuris pennsylvanica,* and *Pyrophorus plagiophthalamus* indicates that the luciferins from all these different forms are identical.

## Factors Affecting the Color of Light Emission in *P. pyralis*

*Temperature, pH, and metal ions.* As the pH of the *P. pyralis* extract is lowered, the intensity of the yellow-green bioluminescence decreases, leaving a dull brick-orange glow (Seliger and McElroy, 1960a, b). This variation in bioluminescence emission with pH is shown in Fig. 3. At neutral (and alkaline) pH, there is a single emission band in the yellow-green region. At intermediate pH, a red emission band appears at 616 m$\mu$, and at pH value below 5.5, the yellow-green emission is completely suppressed and only the red band is evident. At acid pH, the number of light quanta emitted per $LH_2$ molecule oxidized is markedly lower than one and indicates a predominantly dark reaction. However, at alkaline pH, although the rate of light emission is reduced to a fraction of the rate at pH 7.6, the quantum yield is essentially unity. The change of yield with $p$H corresponds rather closely in form to the fluorescence yield of $LH_2$ and L at various $p$H's, except that the $p$K has been shifted essentially one $p$H unit toward the acid range for the bioluminescence quantum yield. This may represent the interaction of the enzyme with the benzthiazole OH group or possibly the amino group of AMP, altering in effect the fluorescence or chemiluminescence properties of the bound intermediate that is essential for light emission.

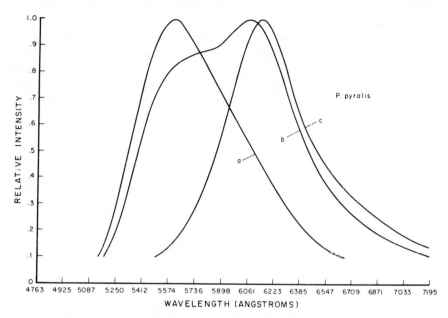

**Fig. 3.** Effect of $p$H on the *in vitro* emission spectrum. *P. pyralis* luciferase. *a*: $p$H 7.6; *b*: $p$H 6.5; *c*: $p$H 5.0.

Recently we have attempted to measure the $p$K of the molecular species emitting red light by observing only the red light as a function of $p$H. Although the data are not conclusive, there is a suggestion that the $p$K is near 6.8. Therefore, a histidine residue might be involved in the binding of the $LH_2$—AMP to the enzyme, which in turn might affect the $p$K of the excited state and consequently the color of the light emitted.

Except for the partial denaturation of the enzyme in acidic buffer, the $p$H effect on the emission spectrum shift is completely reversible. We have been able to observe these same reversible red shifts in emission spectra by increasing the temperature of the reaction, by carrying out the reaction in 0.2 M urea and at normal $p$H values (7.6) in glycyl-glycine buffer, and by adding small concentrations of $Zn^{++}$, $Cd^{++}$, and $Hg^{++}$ as chlorides. The normalized emission spectra of the *in vitro* bioluminescence of purified

*P. pyralis* luciferase for various $Zn^{++}$ concentrations are shown in Fig. 4. The curves do not show relative changes in intensities in going from the yellow-green to the red emission; the efficiency of the light reaction is markedly decreased under conditions where red light is emitted. The maximum red shifts obtained at low *p*H with $Zn^{++}$ and with $Cd^{++}$ are shown in Fig. 5 compared with the normal yellow-green emission. The temperature, urea, and $Hg^{++}$ effects are essentially the same. With $Hg^{++}$, the concentration required for the red shift was 100 times smaller than for either $Zn^{++}$ or $Cd^{++}$ (Seliger and McElroy, 1964).

By using suitable blue-green–transmitting filters and red-transmitting filters, we have been able to establish that there are two *p*H optima and two temperature optima for the bioluminescence emissions, one *p*H optimum and one temperature optimum each for the red and the yellow-green emissions. These are shown in Fig. 6. As would be expected, the red emission has lower *p*H and higher temperature optima.

*Changes in substrate structure.* The preceding facts support the idea that the color of the emitted light depends upon the nature of the binding of the intermediate to the enzyme. It seemed likely, therefore, that a change in

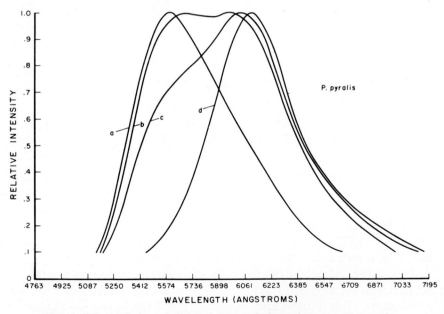

**Fig. 4.** Effect of zinc on the *in vitro* emission spectrum. *P. pyralis* luciferase. *a*: control, *p*H 7.6; *b*: $1.3 \times 10^{-4}$M $ZnCl_2$; *c*: $4 \times 10^{-4}$M $ZnCl_2$; *d*: $2.3 \times 10^{-3}$M $ZnCl_2$. (From Seliger and McElroy, 1964, *Proc. Natl. Acad. Sci. U.S.* 52: 75.)

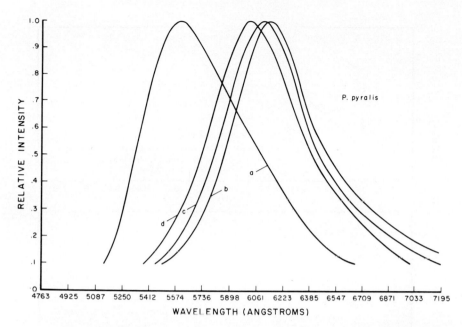

**Fig. 5.** Normalized emission spectra of the *in vitro P. pyralis* bioluminescence showing the maximum red-shifts obtained with acid *p*H, Zn⁺⁺, and Cd⁺⁺. *a*: control, *p*H 7.6; *b*: *p*H 5; *c*: 2.3 × 10⁻³M Zn⁺⁺; *d*: 1.2 × 10⁻²M Cd⁺⁺. (From Seliger and McElroy, 1964, *Proc. Natl. Acad. Sci. U.S.* 52: 75.)

the structure of the substrate molecules (LH₂ or ATP) may alter the binding and in turn affect the color of the light. Unfortunately, the LH₂ cannot be greatly changed and still remain an active light-emitting substrate. It was found that the 6-amino benzthiazole compound is an active substrate, and with this compound a red emission instead of the yellow-green was observed, even at neutral *p*H. This is additional evidence that the 6-hydroxy group in the natural LH₂ is important as a binding site to the enzyme and has an effect on the nature of the emitting intermediate.

Until recently, ATP was thought to be specific for the enzymatic reaction leading to light emission. Deoxy-ATP, UTP, CTP, GTP, ADP, and other pyrophosphate-containing nucleotides were shown to be inactive. Recently, Leonard and associates (personal communication) have prepared an ATP with the ribose attached to the 3 position of the adenine ring (3-iso-ATP). This compound appears to be about 10–15% as effective as normal ATP in the light reaction. The additional interesting observation, however, is that at *p*H 7.5 a significant amount of the light emitted is red when 3-iso-ATP is used. Thus the stereochemistry of the nucleotide attachment to LH₂ and presumably to the enzyme is important in determining the color of the light.

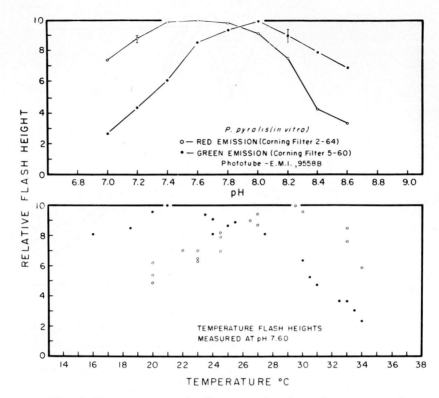

**Fig. 6.** Temperature and *p*H curves for the yellow-green and red *in vitro* bioluminescence of *P. pyralis*. (From Seliger and McElroy, 1964, *Proc. Natl. Acad. Sci. U.S.* 52: 75.)

*Chemiluminescence and color of light.* An investigation of the nonenzymatic chemiluminescence of $LH_2$—AMP and other derivatives in the organic solvent dimethylsulfoxide (DMSO) reveals the presence of two fundamental emission peaks, i.e., two different emitting molecular species (Seliger and McElroy, 1962).

Firefly $LH_2$ was condensed with adenylic acid, metaphosphoric acid, or diazomethane in dry pyridine with dicyclohexylcarbodiimide, according to the method of Khorana. An aliquot was delivered to 2 ml of DMSO in a 10- by 75-mm test tube mounted in front of a 1 P21 phototube. Chemiluminescence was obtained upon addition of a solid pellet of KOH, a droplet of 10 M NaOH, or a drop of tertiary butyl alcohol solution in which a small amount of potassium metal had been dissolved so that tertiary butoxide ions were formed.

Except for the esters of $LH_2$, the observed chemiluminescence was of too low an intensity to estimate color. In the case of $LH_2$—AMP, a drop of

10 M NaOH added to the test tube was surrounded by a yellow-green glow as it sank to the bottom. When the tube was then shaken vigorously, a brilliant red emission over the entire solution volume appeared to the dark-adapted eye. This disappeared in one to two seconds, and the very low intensity steady emission characteristic of the NaOH and DMSO reaction alone remained. This yellow-green light emission from $LH_2$—AMP was seen most clearly upon the initial introduction of the NaOH droplet. Upon successive additions of NaOH, the chemiluminescence emission became more orange until only a red glow was visible. These results are consistent with the appearance of the red flash when either the NaOH or KOH was shaken vigorously in the solution and also with the red flash that was observed when the strongly basic tertiary butoxide ions were added to the solution; they show that the color of the chemiluminescence is strongly dependent on $p$H. This is analogous with the enzymatic reaction that depends upon $p$H for the color of the emission. When the technique for the measurement of transient spectra was used, the red emission spectrum in strongly basic DMSO was obtained. This is shown in Fig. 7. The peak emission at 6255 Å differs from the peak at 6140 Å in the enzymatic reaction. However, this was not unexpected, since with luminol there was also a red shift in chemiluminescence emission from 4300 Å in aqueous solution to 4800 Å in DMSO.

The unique character of the $LH_2$—AMP compound was shown by the fact that the methyl ester of luciferin, $LH_2$—$CH_3$, gave only a yellow-green color; $LH_2$—$PO_4$ gave only a red chemiluminescence under the same experimental conditions that caused $LH_2$—AMP emission to shift from yellow-green to red. Thus, the oxidized product of $LH_2$—AMP can exist in either of two fluorescent-excited molecular species, depending on the $p$H. These results indicate that an essential role of the enzyme in the oxidation of firefly $LH_2$ is to permit, by the binding of the $LH_2$—AMP, the removal of a proton and the subsequent attack by oxygen. On the other hand, in the absence of enzyme, the chemical environment would have to be so basic that $LH_2$—AMP would hydrolyze before oxygen attack could occur. By reacting the $LH_2$—AMP in DMSO, we have inhibited hydrolysis by chemical means even at high $p$H values, effectively accomplishing what the enzyme can do at neutral $p$H. As might be expected, D-$LH_2$—AMP and L-$LH_2$—AMP do not show the stereospecificity in nonenzymatic chemiluminescence that was previously reported for the enzymatic reaction.

## Color of Light in Different Species of Fireflies

It has been known for some time that different species of fireflies emit different colors of bioluminescence, ranging from green through bright yellow. These are valid observations and are not visual artifacts due to selective

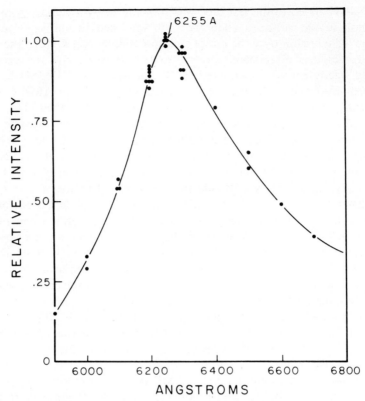

**Fig. 7.** Red chemiluminescence of LH$_2$—AMP. Alkaline dimethylsulfoxide.

cuticle absorption in the light organ. We have recently measured the *in vivo* emission spectra of 20 species of firefly, 16 Jamaican and 4 native American species (Seliger *et al.*, 1964). The large range of *in vivo* spectral variations is summarized in Table 2. Because the spectral curves are symmetric and have reasonably constant half-widths, the peak emissions intermediate between green and yellow are probably not due to mixtures of a green-emitting molecular species and a red-emitting molecular species. The emission is most likely due to a single excited enzyme-substrate complex.

We succeeded in collecting sufficient numbers of *P. pennsylvanica* (U.S.A.), *P. jamaicensis* (Jamaica), and *P. plagiophthalamus* (Jamaica) to extract and partially purify both luciferase and luciferin from each species. The Jamaican elaterid beetle, *P. plagiophthalamus*, has been described by Harvey (1952) as being unique among the fireflies in possessing light organs that emit two different colored lights. A symmetric pair of dorsal organs on the anterior thorax lights up with a constant bright *green* glow when the insect is resting,

TABLE 2

FIREFLY SPECIES AND WAVELENGTH OF MAXIMUM INTENSITY (PEAK WAVE-
LENGTH) ARRANGED IN ORDER OF INCREASING WAVELENGTH

(From Seliger and McElroy, 1964, *Proc. Natl. Acad. Sci. U.S.* 52: 75.)

| Species | Peak wavelength (angstroms) |
| --- | --- |
| *Photuris pennsylvanica* | 5524 |
| *Pyrophorus plagiophthalamus* (dorsal organ) | 5530 |
| *Diphotus* sp. | 5550 |
| *Photuris jamaicensis* ♂. ♀ | 5550 |
| *Photinus pardalus* | 5600 |
| *Photinus pyralis* ♂, ♀ | 5621 |
| *Photinus commissus* | 5640 |
| *Photinus marginellus* | 5646 |
| *Photinus pallens* | 5650 |
| *Photinus xanthophotus* ♀ | 5670 |
| *Photinus leucopyge* | 5690 |
| *Lecontea* sp. | 5700 |
| *Photinus lobatus* | 5700 |
| *Photinus evanescens* | 5700 |
| *Photinus melanurus* | 5700 |
| *Photinus nothus* | 5700 |
| *Photinus* (new species) | 5700 |
| *Photinus morbosus-ceratus* | 5710 |
| *Photinus gracilobus* | 5720 |
| *Photinus scintillans* ♀ | 5748 |
| *Photinus scintillans* ♂ | 5751 |
| *Pyrophorus plagiophthalamus* (ventral organ) | 5820 |

walking, or disturbed in captivity. This light is extinguished when the insect is in flight, and light from a third organ appears. This organ is a large, ventral one, completely shielded in a cleft between the thorax and the first abdominal segment. When the insect is in flight, the elytra are extended, the first abdominal segment is flexed, opening the cleft, and a constant bright yellow light is emitted. In a dark field, a low-flying *Pyrophorus* illuminates the ground below much as do the downward-directed landing lights of an airplane. When the insect alights or is batted down, the elytra close, the yellow light goes off, and the green "parking lights" go on. For this reason and because of the position and shape of the anterior thoracic organs, *P. plagiophthalamus* is also called the "automobile bug."

On the basis of paper chromatography, absorbance and fluorescence spectra, and the pH dependence of the relative fluorescence yield, all of the isolated luciferins, including those from the two different organs of *P. plagiophthalamus*, appear to be identical with *P. pyralis* luciferin. In the *in vitro* light reaction, regardless of the source of luciferin, the spectral distribution of the light emitted by the extracts from each firefly species corresponded with the *in vivo* emission measured previously. The data for *P. pyralis* are shown in Fig. 8. Similar studies have been made using luciferase of *P. plagiophthalamus* dorsal and ventral organs. In each case, the species enzyme alone determined the spectral distribution of the emitted light. The spectra in Fig. 8 are displaced one above the other in order to show the relative distributions more easily. For *P. plagiophthalamus*, slight shifts occur in the peak positions of the *in vivo* emissions relative to the *in vitro* emissions, probably because the color of the light emitted by the particular *in vivo* specimens measured was actually slightly different from the average color of the *in vitro* enzyme extracts obtained from the light organs of approximately 100 insects. In a subsequent collection of a large number of *P. plagiophthalamus*, we

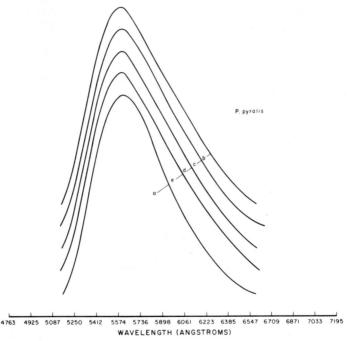

**Fig. 8.** Emission spectra of *P. pyralis*. *a*: *in vivo;* *b*: *in vitro*, *P. pyralis* luciferase + *P. pyralis* LH₂; *c*: *in vitro*, *P. pyralis* luciferase + synthetic LH₂; *d*: *in vitro*, *P. pyralis* luciferase + LH₂ of *P. plagiophthalamus* dorsal light organ; *e*: *in vitro*, *P. pyralis* luciferase + LH₂ of *P. plagiophthalamus* ventral light organ. (From Seliger and McElroy, 1964, *Proc. Natl. Acad. Sci. U.S.* 52: 75.)

distinguished in different insects in this presumably single species three separate colors of *in vivo* emission from the dorsal organs, namely, green, yellow-
green, and lemon yellow, and three separate colors of *in vivo* emission from
the ventral organs, yellow-green, yellow, and orange. Apparently no correlation exists between the emission color of the ventral organ and the emission
color of the dorsal organ. In more than 1000 insects examined, without
exception, both dorsal organs of each insect emitted identical colors of light.

*Effects of pH and metal cations.* The maximum effects of *pH* and metal
cations on the *in vitro* emissions of luciferase of *P. plagiophthalamus* dorsal
organ are shown in Fig. 9. Qualitatively, these spectral shifts are in the same
direction as the *P. pyralis* effects, although the magnitudes of the shifts are
much smaller. In none of our experiments were we able to observe a red-
shift in the emission from the luciferase of the *P. plagiophthalamus* ventral
organ. However, as shown in Fig. 10, *basic solutions,* and, separately, the
addition of metal cations, produced a "blue-shift," opposite to that observed
from both the dorsal organ and from *P. pyralis.*

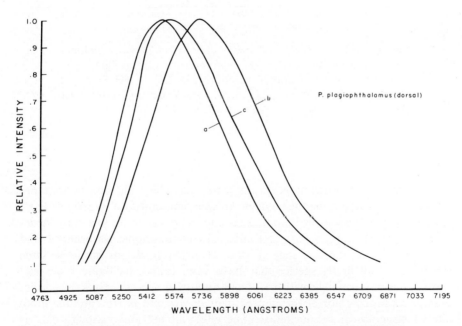

**Fig. 9.** Effects of *pH* and metal cations on *in vitro* bioluminescence of luciferase of *P. plagiophthalamus* dorsal light organ
+ synthetic LH₂. *a*: normal reaction, *pH* 7.6; *b*: *pH* 6.0; *c*:
*pH* 7.6, 5.5 × 10⁻⁴M Zn⁺⁺. (From Seliger and McElroy, 1964,
*Proc. Natl. Acad. Sci. U.S.* 52: 75.)

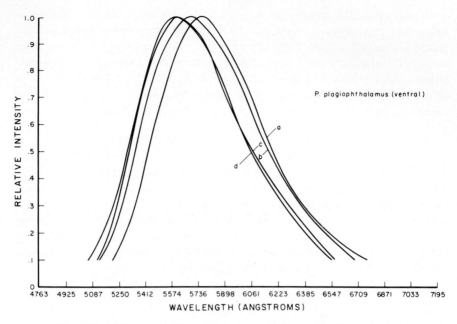

**Fig. 10.** Effects of *p*H and metal cations on *in vitro* bioluminescence of luciferase of *P. plagiophthalamus* ventral light organ + synthetic LH₂. *a*: normal reaction, *p*H 7.6; *b*: *p*H 8; *c*: *p*H 7.6, 5.5 × 10⁻⁴M Zn⁺⁺; *d*: *p*H 7.6, 8 × 10⁻⁵M Cd⁺⁺. (From Seliger and McElroy, 1964, *Proc. Natl. Acad. Sci. U.S.* 52: 75.)

## Discussion

The results obtained thus far indicate that the following factors are important in determining the color of *in vitro* light emission in extracts from several different species of beetles: LH₂ and ATP structure, luciferase structure, *p*H, temperature, metals, and salts. Chromatographic, absorbance, and fluorescence data indicate that all natural firefly luciferins have the same structure. In all firefly species that have been tested, luciferase from any species will produce light with LH₂ from any other species. Thus the species differences in the color of the emitted light *in vivo* and *in vitro* are due to an altered structure of the luciferase. The effect of *p*H and various salts, as well as a change in the structure of the LH₂—AMP, suggest that the strength and nature of the binding of the transient emitter is the important factor that determines the allowed electronic transitions for light emission.

The presence of two different luciferases in the light organs of the same organism, the "automobile bug," indicates the interesting possibility that we are dealing with isozymes. As stated previously, we have noted differences in the color of light emitted from the ventral and dorsal organs. This suggests that genetic as well as developmental differences may be important in the synthesis of specific luciferases. Unfortunately, inadequate material at this time has prevented us from looking more carefully at the physical structure of the luciferases from this organism.

Detailed studies on the nature of the binding and active catalytic sites of the firefly luciferases will be necessary before we can give an adequate explanation of these striking effects of enzyme structure on light emission. Our observations suggest that the fluorescence or changes in fluorescence of small molecules attached to proteins may be extremely valuable for studying small configurational changes that may occur during catalysis or function.

# REFERENCES

Bitler, Barbara, and W. D. McElroy. 1957. *Arch. Biochem. Biophys.* 72: 358.

Harvey, E. N. 1952. *Bioluminescence.* New York: Academic Press, Inc.

Harvey, E. N., and Y. Haneda. 1952. *Arch. Biochem. Biophys.* 35: 470.

Hastings, J. W., W. D. McElroy, and Jane Coulombre. 1953. *J. Cellular Comp. Physiol.* 42: 137.

McElroy, W. D. 1960. *Federation Proc.* 19: 941.

McElroy, W. D., and E. N. Harvey. 1951. *J. Cellular Comp. Physiol.* 37: 83.

McElroy, W. D., and H. H. Seliger. 1961. In *Light and Life*, ed. W. D. McElroy and B. Glass. Baltimore: The Johns Hopkins Press. P. 219.

McElroy, W. D., and H. H. Seliger. 1963a. *Federation Proc.* 21: 1006.

McElroy, W. D., and H. H. Seliger. 1963b. In *Advan. Enzymol.*, ed. F. F. Nord. New York: John Wiley & Sons. P. 119.

McElroy, W. D., J. W. Hastings, Jane Coulombre, and Valerie Sonnenfeld. 1953. *Arch. Biochem. Biophys.* 46:399.

Rhodes, W. C., and W. D. McElroy. 1958a. *Science* 128: 253.

Rhodes, W. C., and W. D. McElroy. 1958b. *J. Biol. Chem.* 233: 1528.

Seliger, H. H., and W. D. McElroy. 1959. *Biochem. Biophys. Res. Commun.* 1: 21.

Seliger, H. H., and W. D. McElroy. 1960a. *Radiation Research*, Suppl. 2: 528.

Seliger, H. H., and W. D. McElroy. 1960b. *Arch. Biochem. Biophys.* 88: 136.

Seliger, H. H., and W. D. McElroy. 1962. *Science* 138: 683.

Seliger, H. H., and W. D. McElroy. 1964. *Proc. Natl. Acad. Sci. U.S.* 52: 75.

Seliger, H. H., J. B. Buck, W. G. Fastie, and W. D. McElroy. 1964. *J. Gen. Physiol.* 48: 95.

White, E., F. McCapra, G. F. Field, and W. D. McElroy. 1961. *J. Am. Chem. Soc.* 83: 2402.

# The Molecular Architecture of Multichain Proteins[1]

### K. E. Van Holde

*Department of Chemistry and Chemical Engineering*
*University of Illinois*
*Urbana, Illinois*

Cell and tissue, shell and bone, leaf and flower, are so many portions of matter, and it is in obedience to the laws of physics that their particles have been moved, moulded, and conformed.

D'Arcy Wentworth Thompson[2]

It would seem a reasonable hypothesis that much of the organization of matter within a cell is dictated genetically, by the prescribed synthesis of certain macromolecules. We must then expect these molecules to be capable of complex and highly specific interactions. Relatively simple examples of such interactions are provided by the so-called multichain proteins, "molecules" which appear to be specific aggregates of a number of polypeptide chains. Such structures have come to be recognized as not at all uncommon, as can be seen from the partial list in Table 1. Two conclusions can be drawn from such a list: the individual polypeptide chains appear to be nearly always of low molecular weight, and proteins that have been reported to have "molecular weights" in excess of 100,000 generally have been shown to consist of several subunits. Synthesis of a large structure from smaller subunits rather than in "one piece" possesses a number of advantages. The efficiency of information storage is high; as an example, the ribonucleic acid (RNA) of

[1] This research was supported in part by a grant (GM-10830-05) from the National Institutes of Health.

[2] *On Growth and Form*, 2nd ed. (Cambridge, England: Cambridge Univ. Press, 1942). P. 10.

TABLE 1

SOME MULTICHAIN PROTEINS*

| Protein | Preparative mol. wt. $\times 10^{-3}$ | Subunit weight† $\times 10^{-3}$ | Polypeptide chain weight $\times 10^{-3}$ |
|---|---|---|---|
| β-Lactoglobulin (bovine) | 36‡ | 18(2) | 18(2) |
| Aldolase (rabbit muscle) | 150 | 50(3) or 25(6) | 50(3) or 25(6) |
| Lactic dehydrogenase (beef heart) | 134 | 72(2) or 34(4) | 34(4) |
| Hemoglobin (mammalian) | 68 | 17(4) | 17(4) |
| Catalase (bovine) | 248 | 42(6) | 42(6) |
| Insulin | 34‡ | 6(6) | 5.733(6) |
| Hemerythrin (*Golfingia gouldii*) | 105 | 14(8) | 14(8) |
| Apoferritin (horse spleen) | 480 | 25(16)? | 25(16)? |
| Hemocyanin (*Loligo pealii*) | 3,750 | 380(10) | 25(160) or 50(80)? |
| Tobacco mosaic virus coat | 37,000 | 17.5(2,100) | 17.5(2,100) |

* Many of the data are from Reithel (1963).
† The values are for the smallest physically identified subunit. The numbers in parentheses give the number of such units in the "preparative" unit.
‡ Capable of forming higher polymers.

tobacco mosaic virus (TMV) need code only for a coat-protein unit of 158 amino acid residues to produce a coat containing in the aggregate over $3 \times 10^5$ residues. The chances of error in reading a short message are much less, and if errors do occur, only a small portion of the product (the defective subunit) need be rejected. In the cell, it is conceivable that damage to a multichain enzyme could be repaired by replacing one subunit, rather than the entire enzyme. With similar advantages, the principle of subunit construction is used at all levels of biological structure. Macromolecular chains are themselves always synthesized from a limited number of kinds of subunits (amino acids, for example), while a complex organism is made up of cells, "subunits" which may be replaced when damaged.

**Structure**

One remarkable feature of the multichain proteins listed in Table 1 is the specificity of their structures. Very few native globular proteins seem to form nonspecific, random aggregates. Horse hemoglobin, for example, invariably contains four and only four polypeptide chains, and X-ray evidence (Perutz *et al.*, 1960) indicates that these chains are arranged in a very specific way. This point may be made more emphatically by considering in detail a group of even more complex multichain proteins. These are the hemocyanins, the copper-containing respiratory pigments found in a wide variety of invertebrate species. We have recently carried out a detailed investigation of the hemocyanin from the squid, *Loligo pealii* (Cohen and Van Holde, 1962, 1963, 1964; Van Holde and DePhillips, 1962; Van Holde and Cohen, 1964a, b). An electron micrograph of the "molecules" of this hemocyanin is shown in Fig. 1; they appear to be right circular cylinders, approximately 330 Å in diameter and 120 Å in length. Very similar structures have been observed for five other molluscan hemocyanins by Van Bruggen and collaborators (1962a, b; 1963). In Fig. 2 is shown the sedimentation diagram of the *Loligo* hemocyanin at the same $pH$ as used for the electron microscope preparations. The homogeneous major component corresponds to the particles observed in Fig. 1. This material has a sedimentation coefficient[3] ($s_{20, w}^0$) of 58.7S and a molecular weight, from light-scattering, of 3,750,000. In slightly alkaline solutions, this component dissociates rapidly into a material with $s_{20} \cong 19S$ and molecular weight (by light-scattering and sedimentation equilibrium) of about 770,000. As the $pH$ is raised, a further dissociation occurs, leading ultimately, at $pH > 10$, to the homogeneous material shown in Fig. 3. This component has an $s_{20, w}^0$ of 11.1S and a molecular weight, as determined by light-scattering and sedimentation equilibrium, of 380,000. Details of the measurements are given by Van Holde and Cohen (1964a). The course of the dissociation with increasing $pH$ is shown in Fig. 4. Light-scattering and sedimentation velocity data indicate that the variation in $s_{20, w}$ between $pH$ 7.5 and $pH$ 10 results from an equilibrium between 11S and 19S components. Small quantities of $Mg^{++}$ in the solutions evidently stabilize the 58S component; similar effects have been seen with other hemocyanins.

From the molecular weight data, a hemocyanin molecule such as shown in Fig. 1 appears to split first into five parts; these five each split into two parts, to yield ten subunits in all. This result correlates well with the observation of Van Bruggen *et al.* (1963) that the structures observed in electron microscopy of the molluscan hemocyanins of high molecular weight appear to show five- or tenfold symmetry. The increases in frictional coefficient and intrinsic viscosity accompanying the dissociation (Van Holde and Cohen, 1964a) are best explained by a lengthwise splitting of the cylinders. Measurements of optical rotatory dispersion in the neighborhood of 233 m$\mu$ indicate that little or no change in helix content accompanies the dissociation.

The dissociation of the 58S component into 19S material and the subsequent splitting to give 11S hemocyanin have been shown to be reversible

---

[3] Throughout this paper, sedimentation coefficients are given in Svedberg units; $1S = 1 \times 10^{-13}$ sec.

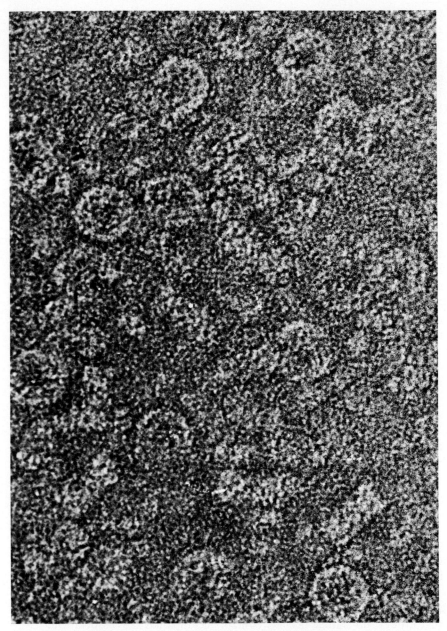

**Fig. 1.** Electron micrograph of *L. pealii* hemocyanin, negative-stained with uranyl acetate at $pH$ 6.6 and sprayed onto a carbon-coated grid. X 500,000.

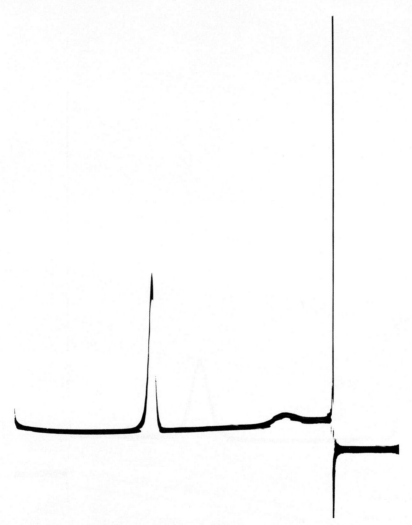

**Fig. 2.** Sedimentation of *L. pealii* hemocyanin 0.1 ionic strength phosphate buffer, *p*H 6.6. Centrifuged 12 min at 42,040 rpm.

(Van Holde and Cohen, 1964b; Van Holde and Harrison, unpublished observation). Thus, the formation of the more complex structures can be imagined as occurring spontaneously in the *in vivo* synthesis of the hemocyanin.

Recently, more complete dissociation of the *Loligo* hemocyanin has been achieved (LaBar, Elfbaum, and Van Holde, unpublished observation). Solutions containing 15% or more of dioxane, at *p*H greater than 10 and at

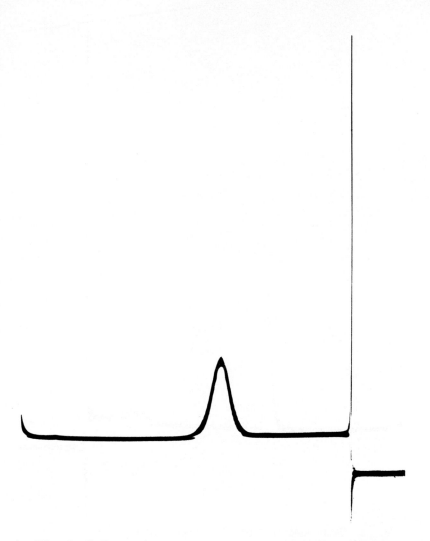

**Fig. 3.** Sedimentation of *L. pealii* hemocyanin in 0.1 ionic strength bicarbonate buffer, *p*H 10.7. Centrifuged 56 min at 42,040 rpm.

temperatures above 30°C, yield more slowly sedimenting components. While a homogeneous preparation has not as yet been obtained, $s_{20, w}$ values of about 5S and 2S have been observed, and the molecular weight as measured by the Archibald technique is well below 100,000.

A sizable body of data concerning the hemocyanins of other molluscan species exists; this is summarized in Table 2. Most exhibit components

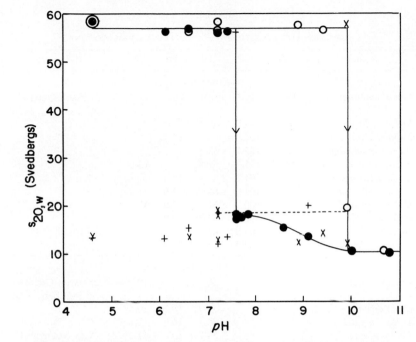

**Fig. 4.** Sedimentation coefficients *vs.* pH for *L. pealii* hemocyanin. ● and +: $s_{20,w}$ values for major and minor components observed when hemolymph was diluted into buffer; ○ and ×: $s_{20,w}$ values for major and minor components observed when hemolymph was diluted into buffer containing 0.01 M $MgCl_2$. Experiments performed at protein concentrations of about 3 mg/ml and rotor speed of ∼ 42,000 rpm.

with sedimentation coefficients in the neighborhoods of 60S and 10S; many also have boundaries with sedimentation coefficients varying between 10S and 20S. In addition, several species possess hemocyanin components with sedimentation coefficients of about 100S. Van Bruggen *et al.* (1962a) have demonstrated by electron microscopy that the 100S component of *Helix pomatia* hemocyanin is an end-to-end dimer of the 60S material. In two instances a 130S component was observed. This may represent a dimerization of the 100S particles. The very long, rod-like aggregates observed in the hemocyanin of *Kelletia kelletia* by Condie and Langer (1964) appear to be further stages in the same polymerization.

The percentage of copper, by weight, of molluscan hemocyanins has consistently been found to be 0.25 ± 0.01 (see Prosser and Brown, 1961). This would correspond to an ultimate subunit weight of about 25,000. Since two copper atoms are required for each oxygen-binding site, a fundamental

TABLE 2

SEDIMENTATION COEFFICIENTS OF MOLLUSCAN HEMOCYANINS

| Source | VI | V | IV | III | II | Reference |
|---|---|---|---|---|---|---|
| | | GASTROPODA | | | | |
| *Limax maximus* | 136.1 | 97.3 | 61.9 | 18.0 | 13.7 | Eriksson-Quensel and Svedberg, 1936 |
| *Littorina littorea* | | 99.7 | 63.3 | 15.0 | | ” |
| *Neptunea antiqua* | | 104.0 | | 14.3 | * | ” |
| *Buccinum undatum* | | 102.1 | 63.8 | | * | ” |
| *Busycon canaliculatum* | 130.4 | 101.7 | 61.1 | | 13.5 | ” |
| *Helix arbustorum* | | 91.2 | 64.1 | 15.0 | 11.1 | ” |
| *Helix nemoralis* | | 101.0 | 65.0 | 16.6 | 11.9 | ” |
| *Helix hortensis* | | 100.0 | 61.9 | 15.9 | 12.1 | ” |
| *Helix pomatia* | | 98.9 | 62.0 | 16.0 | 12.1 | ” |
| *Helix pomatia* | | 103.0† | 65.7† | 19.7† | | Brohult, 1947 |
| *Paludina vivipara* | | 102.5 | 64.5 | 21.8 | | ” |
| | | CEPHALOPODA: DECAPODA | | | | |
| *Rossia owenii* | | | 56.2 | | 10.9 | Eriksson-Quensel and Svedberg, 1936 |
| *Sepia officinalis* | | | 55.9 | 18.7 | 10.6 | ” |
| *Loligo vulgaris* | | | 56.7 | 16.9 | 12.1 | ” |
| *Loligo pealii‡* | | | 58.7† | 19 | 11.1† | Van Holde and Cohen, 1964a |
| *Ommatostrephes sloani pacificus* | | | * | 19.5† | | Omura *et al.*, 1961 |
| | | CEPHALOPODA: OCTOPODA | | | | |
| *Octopus vulgaris* | | | 49.3 | | * | Eriksson-Quensel and Svedberg, 1936 |
| *Eleodone mostacha* | | | 49.1 | | 10.6 | ” |

* Component reported, but S not given.
† Extrapolated to infinite dilution.
‡ A material with $s_{20,w} \cong 5S$ has also been observed; see text.

unit of about 50,000 molecular weight might be postulated. This is in the range observed for the dissociation product of *Loligo* hemocyanin in alkaline dioxane solutions.

On the basis of the uniform copper content, general similarity of sedimentation coefficients, and great similarity of electron micrographs, a general architecture for the molluscan hemocyanins can be tentatively proposed.

Such a scheme is shown in Fig. 5. It must be emphasized that I do not propose that the various hemocyanins are identical. That they are not is shown by the considerable variation in $p$H-stability ranges for the various components in different species and by the absence of certain components from many hemocyanins. Furthermore, the range in $s_{20,w}$ exhibited by a given component can be considerable; for example, the stage IV "component"

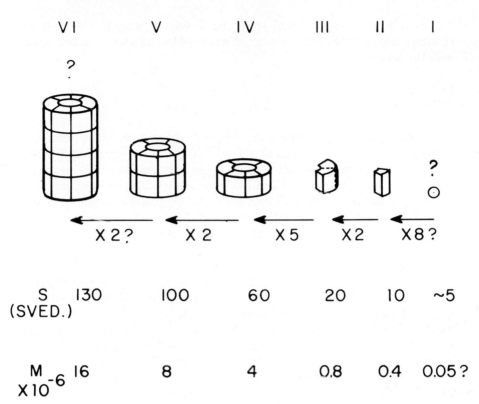

**Fig. 5.** Schematic diagram of proposed hierarchy of structures of molluscan hemocyanins. Stages indicated by roman numerals correspond to those in Table 2, with addition of "Stage I," corresponding to a unit that will hold two copper atoms. Drawings not to scale, and not intended to be representational, except insofar as Stages IV and V resemble structures observed in electron microscopy of several hemocyanins. Sedimentation coefficients and molecular weights are only approximate. See text.

varies in sedimentation coefficient from about 50S in octopods to over 60S in gastropods. Very likely, considerable variation will be found in the amino acid compositions of the individual hemocyanins. Comparison of preliminary results on the *Loligo* hemocyanin (Lloyd and Van Holde, unpublished observation) with data for *H. pomatia* (Claesson, 1956) indicates considerable difference.

The over-all impression is that these complex proteins are built on a more or less uniform hierarchical scheme. The structures of high molecular weight appear to be quite open; holes are visible in the aggregates, and the particle volume deduced from the electron micrographs is considerably greater than the volume of protein inferred from the molecular weight. This kind of structure allows a maximum number of oxygen-binding sites to be in contact with the solvent medium.

## Formation

In attempting to understand the frequent observations of spontaneous formation of specific aggregates of polypeptide chains, we encounter two all-important questions. What interactions cause polypeptide chains to aggregate? What limits their polymerization so as to yield specific structures?

Many kinds of noncovalent intermolecular interactions might be postulated: hydrogen bonds, electrostatic forces, and hydrophobic interactions, to mention a few. While the type of interaction doubtless varies from one protein to another, and while in many proteins all the types may be operative, indirect evidence is emerging that may help to limit the possibilities. The first such evidence comes from the surprising fact that many of these aggregation processes exhibit a *positive* entropy change. This is demonstrated by a shift in the equilibrium toward aggregation as the temperature is raised, and by dissociation as the temperature is lowered. Such behavior is shown, for example, by TMV coat protein (Lauffer, 1962) and by the *L. pealii* hemocyanin (Van Holde and Cohen, 1964b). In the latter, for example, the protein in $Mg^{++}$-free solutions at $pH$ 6 is nearly all in the 19S form at 2°C and nearly all in the 58S form at 25°C. The process is reversible, as is demonstrated by Fig. 6.

Now, in a polymerization process there must be a loss in translational entropy. Steinberg and Scheraga (1963) have shown that even if considerable rotational and vibrational freedom is left to the polymer, the entropy change should be *negative*. To obtain an over-all *positive* entropy change requires some additional randomization of the system. This could result, for example, if water of hydration were released from the subunit when polymerization occurred. According to Némethy and Scheraga (1962), this should occur if hydrophobic bonds are formed in the polymerization. A similar effect would result if charged groups, present upon the surfaces of the subunits, were to be "buried" when polymerization occurred (Lauffer, 1962). Both of these explanations for the entropy change would further predict that the volume of the system should increase upon polymerization. Lauffer observed this effect in the TMV protein polymerization; similarly, Van Holde and Cohen (1964a) found that the partial specific volume of the 58S *Loligo* hemocyanin is 0.740, while that of the 11S component is 0.710. Certain aspects of the *Loligo* hemocyanin polymerization, however, indicate the process to be more complex than a simple hydrophobic bonding. For example, Fig. 4 demonstrates that $Mg^{++}$ will stabilize the 58S structure. The addition of 0.01 M $Mg^{++}$ at $pH$ 8.2

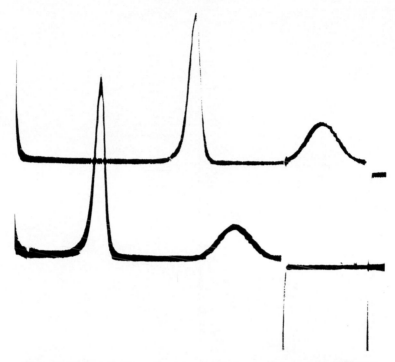

**Fig. 6.** Sedimentation of near-equilibrium mixtures of 19S and 58S *L. pealii* hemocyanins. Solutions had been sedimented for 64 min at 21,740 rpm and 18°C, *p*H 5.8. Solution corresponding to upper schlieren image was entirely dissociated at 2°C, then allowed to reassociate at 18°C for 240 hr. Solution corresponding to lower pattern was dissociated at 2°C, allowed to reassociate nearly completely at 25°C, and finally incubated at 18°C for 202 hr. The near-identity of the two patterns shows that the same equilibrium mixture is obtained regardless of whether 58S or 19S component is the starting material.

will cause the polymerization of dissociated hemocyanin (Van Holde and Cohen, unpublished observation).

Comparison of amino acid compositions supports the idea that hydrophobic bonding plays a major role in many multichain enzymes. In Fig. 7 are listed a number of globular proteins for which good data on amino acid composition are available. Proteins known to exist in solution primarily as single-chain entities are listed on the left; the multichain proteins are listed on the right. The only multichain proteins listed are those that are found as definite aggregates. The vertical scale gives the percentage of a group of "hydrophobic" residues (proline, valine, leucine, isoleucine, and phenyl-

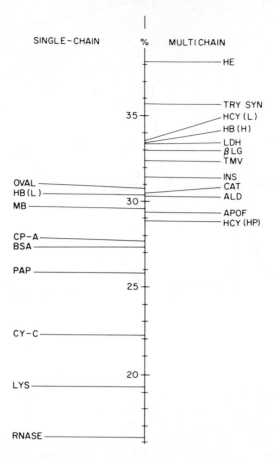

**Fig. 7.** Globular proteins ranked *vs.* percentage of certain hydrophobic residues (proline, valine, leucine, isoleucine, and phenylalanine). Explanations of abbreviations follow, together with sources of composition data. Where the reference is not given, the data are from Tristam and Smith (1963).

ALD: rabbit muscle aldolase; APOF: horse spleen apoferritin; BSA: bovine serum albumin (Spahr and Edsall, 1964); CAT: beef liver catalase; CP-A: carboxypeptidase A; CY-C: horse heart cytochrome *c* (Margoliash et al., 1962); HB(H): human hemoglobin (Hill *et al.,* 1962); HB(L): sea lamprey hemoglobin; HCY(HP): *H. pomatia* hemocyanin (Claesson, 1956); HCY(L): *L. pealii* hemocyanin (Lloyd and Van Holde, unpublished); HE: *Sipunculus nudus* hemerythrin (Holleman and Biserte, 1958); INS: beef insulin; LDH: rat heart lactic dehydrogenase; βLG: bovine β-lactoglobulin (Piez *et al.,* 1961); LYS: hen's egg lysozyme (Canfield, 1963); MB: sperm whale myoglobin (Edmundson and Hirs, 1961); OVAL: hen's egg ovalbumin; PAP: papaya papain; RNASE: beef pancreas ribonuclease (Hirs *et al.,* 1960); TMV: tobacco mosaic virus coat protein (Anderer, 1963); TRY SYN: *Es. coli* tryptophan synthetase.

alanine) contained in each. While some overlap occurs, the distinction between the two categories is clear. Excellent examples are provided by comparison of the hemoglobins and myoglobins. For clarity, not all have been listed, but the hemoglobins are uniformly richer than the myoglobins in the hydrophobic residues. The only exception is the lamprey "hemoglobin," which is, in fact, a single-chain enzyme.

The correlation observed in Fig. 7 can be explained simply. Kendrew (1962) has pointed out that in myoglobin, almost all of the hydrophobic residues are in the interior of the molecule, whereas the surface is composed largely of polar groups. If an enzyme of low molecular weight were to contain too large a fraction of nonpolar groups, not all of these could be covered by the polar cortex. "Patches" of hydrophobic residues would be in contact with the solvent, and these would provide natural sites for association. In a sense, the association process would put these groups back "inside." This concept has been developed in some detail by Fisher (1964), who has proposed quite general relationships between protein composition and structure. The data in Fig. 7 seem to indicate that a small polypeptide chain cannot tolerate more than about 30% of hydrophobic residues; a greater number will lead to association.

Certainly, the conclusion above is a first approximation, and subject to many exceptions. Variation in amino acid sequence, as distinct from composition, must play a role, and the over-all shape of the molecule must be important. An elongated subunit has a larger ratio of surface to volume, and might be expected to polymerize with fewer hydrophobic residues. (However, Fisher (1964) argues that only very hydrophilic proteins will be elongated.) The amino acids selected here do not constitute a unique list. Some of the enzymes listed as "single-chain" proteins may be made to polymerize in unusual circumstances. Lysozyme dimerizes in alkaline solutions (Sophianopoulos and Van Holde, 1961), and ribonuclease can be caused to dimerize by lyophylization from 50% acetic acid (Crestfield et al., 1962).

The behavior of $\beta$-lactoglobulin shows that the situation is not so simple as Fig. 7 might imply (Timasheff and Townend, 1961). This protein contains two types of subunits, designated A and B. The amino acid compositions of the two are almost identical, and both fall in the "high" range. But B-type units will not polymerize alone, whereas A-type will. Furthermore, the entropy change upon polymerization is negative. Clearly, other forces must be involved.

Having considered why subunits polymerize, we must now ask why they produce specific aggregates. Certainly, in such processes as the formation of insulin fibrils, nonspecific aggregation occurs. Other polymerizations may be limited by a second component, as the formation of TMV coat protein appears to be. But most of the subunits cited in Table 1 yield polymers of highly specific size. The *Loligo* hemocyanin is a good example; the process stops at stage IV (see Fig. 1). Furthermore, under many circumstances, this component seems to be highly favored over possible precursors in its synthesis, as well as over higher polymers. The sedimentation diagrams shown in Fig. 6 represent an equilibrium between stage III and stage IV. The synthesis involves the production of a pentamer of the stage III aggregates. Thus, one might expect to observe dimers, trimers, and tetramers as intermediates. Yet there is no evidence for intermediates in Fig. 6; this has proved to be the rule rather than the exception in these experiments.

Perhaps a major determing factor in limiting this protein polymerization is the cyclic nature of the final product. As has already been pointed out, the association process must involve a loss in translational entropy. This must be paid for, by either a negative enthalpy or a positive entropy change in the bond formation. If the compensation is only partial, the formation of dimers, trimers, or tetramers will be relatively unfavorable, but in the addition of the last unit to close the ring an additional bond is formed. A few kilocalories of (negative) free energy thus acquired would make the cyclic structure highly favored over its precursor.

Among the multichain enzymes whose structures are known, the majority are cyclic aggregates. Particles very similar to those of the hemocyanins (but showing hexagonal symmetry) have been observed for the erythrocurins (Levin, 1963), and the hemoglobin structure is clearly not a linear one. Witz et al. (1964) have given evidence for a closed structure for the tetramer of $\beta$-lactoglobulin.

## ACKNOWLEDGMENT

The author wishes to thank several persons who have taken part in the investigations of hemocyanin. A great deal of the research was the work of Dr. L. B. Cohen; others who have participated include Dr. F. LaBar, Mr. S. Elfbaum, Mr. D. Lloyd, Mr. Stephen Harrison, and Dr. H. DePhillips. Mrs. Donna Kubai and Mr. Allen Bell obtained the electron micrograph. The assistance of Mr. R. Hyde and others of the staff of the Marine Biological Laboratory, Woods Hole, Mass., is gratefully acknowledged.

## REFERENCES

Anderer, F. A. 1963. *Advan. Protein Chem.* 18: 1.

Brohult, S. 1947. *J. Phys. and Colloid Chem.* 51: 206.

Canfield, P. E. 1963. *J. Biol. Chem.* 238: 2699.

Claesson, I. M. 1956. *Arkiv Kemi* 10: 1.

Cohen, L. B., and K. E. Van Holde. 1962. *Biol. Bull.* 123: 480.

Cohen, L. B., and K. E. Van Holde. 1963. *Biol. Bull.* 125: 375.

Cohen, L. B., and K. E. Van Holde. 1964. *Biochemistry* 3: 1809.

Condie, R. M., and R. B. Langer. 1964. *Science* 144: 1138.

Crestfield, A. M., W. H. Stein, and S. Moore. 1962. *Arch. Biochem. Biophys.* Suppl. 1: 217.

Edmundson, A. B., and C. H. W. Hirs. 1961. *Nature* 190: 663.

Eriksson-Quensel, I. B., and T. Svedberg. 1936. *Biol. Bull.* 71: 498.

Fisher, H. F. 1964. *Proc. Natl. Acad. Sci. U.S.* 51: 1285.

Hill, R. J., W. Konigsberg, G. Guidotti, and L. C. Craig. 1962. *J. Biol. Chem.* 237: 1549.

Hirs, C. II. W., S. Moore, and W. H. Stein. 1960. *J. Biol. Chem.* 235: 633.

Holleman, J. W., and G. Biserte. 1958. *Bull. Soc. Chim. Biol.* 40: 147.

Kendrew, J. C. 1962. *Brookhaven Symp. Biol.* 15: 216.

Lauffer, M. A. 1962. *Symp. Fundamental Cancer Res., 15th, Houston, 1961.* P. 180.

Levin, O. 1963. *J. Mol. Biol.* 6: 95.

Margoliash, E., J. R. Kimmel, R. L. Hill, and W. R. Schmidt. 1962. *J. Biol. Chem.* 237: 2148.

Némethy, G., and H. A. Scheraga. 1962. *J. Phys. Chem.* 66: 1773.

Omura, T., T. Fujita, F. Yamada, and S. Yamamoto. 1961. *J. Biochem. (Tokyo)* 50: 400.

Perutz, M. F., M. G. Rossman, A. F. Cullis, H. Muirhead, G. Will, and A. C. T. North. 1960. *Nature* 185: 416.

Piez, K. A., E. W. Davie, J. E. Folk, and J. A. Gladner. 1961. *J. Biol. Chem.* 236: 2912.

Prosser, C. L., and F. A. Brown, Jr. 1961. *Comparative Animal Physiology.* Philadelphia: W. B. Saunders Co.

Reithel, F. J. 1963. *Advan. Protein Chem.* 18: 123.

Sophianopoulos, A. J., and K. E. Van Holde. 1961. *J. Biol. Chem.* 236: PC82.

Spahr, P. F., and J. T. Edsall. 1964. *J. Biol. Chem.* 239: 851.

Steinberg, I. Z., and H. A. Scheraga. 1963. *J. Biol. Chem.* 238: 172.

Timasheff, S. N., and R. Townend. 1961. *J. Am. Chem. Soc.* 83: 470.

Tristam, G. R., and R. H. Smith. 1963. *Advan. Protein Chem.* 18: 227.

Van Bruggen, E. F. J., E. H. Wiebenga, and M. Gruber. 1962a. *J. Mol. Biol.* 4: 1.

Van Bruggen, E. F. J., E. H. Wiebenga, and M. Gruber. 1962b. *J. Mol. Biol.* 4: 8.

Van Bruggen, E. . J., V. Schuiten, and E. H. Wiebenga. 1963. *J. Mol. Biol.* 7: 249.

Van Holde, K. E., and L. B. Cohen. 1964a. *Biochemistry* 3: 1803.

Van Holde, K. E., and L. B. Cohen. 1964b. *Brookhaven Symp. Biol.* 17: 184.

Van Holde, K. E., and H. DePhillips. 1962. *Biol. Bull.* 123: 481.

Witz, J., S. N. Timasheff, and V. Luzatti. 1964. *J. Am. Chem. Soc.* 86: 178.

# Molecular Architecture
# and Cell Information

# Molecular Mechanisms of the Immune Response[1]

## Gerald M. Edelman

*Rockefeller University*
*New York City, New York*

Organisms of most vertebrate species react to antigenic substances with several manifestations, collectively known as the immune response. The manifestations of this response include delayed hypersensitivity, immune tolerance, and humoral antibody production. Although their phenomenologic aspects differ, all of these manifestations share one outstanding feature: specificity. Specificity implies that the immune response is elicited only by the particular chemical structure or structures present on the immunizing antigen.

The central problem of immunology is to define the nature of this specificity. A solution to this problem would describe how information is transferred from the three-dimensional structure of the antigen to the immunologically competent cell. It would completely define the path of information transfer to the molecules that mediate the immune response. In the case of tolerance and delayed hypersensitivity, these molecules are not known, and therefore most investigations of these phenomena have been restricted to the behavior of whole cells and tissues. The production of humoral antibodies by plasma cells is the one instance in which both chemical knowledge and cytologic knowledge are comparably developed; this makes feasible a preliminary attempt to discern the molecular mechanism of the immune response.

[1] Supported by Public Health Service Grant No. AM-04256.

99

Recent investigations of the chemical structure of antibodies have led to new notions concerning the bases of this response. Most of the present discussion will be concerned with this knowledge and its implications for theoretical and experimental solutions to the central problem of specificity. A complete answer to the central problem will probably not come exclusively from structural studies of molecules, however, but rather from a correlation of these studies with those of the physiology of antibody-producing cells. For this reason, a brief review of the sequence of events in humoral antibody production is presented before undertaking a detailed description of the structure of antibodies.

## Sequence of Events in Humoral Antibody Production

Extensive studies have been made of the kinetics and heterogeneity of humoral antibody production after administration of antigens (Uhr, 1964). A typical sequence of events is schematized in Fig. 1.

Following the injection of antigen and after a variable latent period, there occurs in the serum an exponential rise of antibody activity that lasts for four to five days. The antibody molecules belong to the $\gamma$M-globulins (sedimentation coefficient = 19S) having molecular weights of about $10^6$ (see Table 1

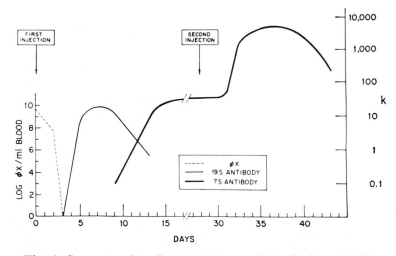

**Fig. 1.** Sequence of antibody response to bacteriophage $\phi$X174 in guinea pig given two intravenous injections of $10^{11}$ plaque-forming units of phage administered one month apart. (From Uhr, 1964, *Science* 145: 456; copyright 1964 by the American Association for the Advancement of Science.)

below). Synthesis continues at a diminishing rate for another four to six days, and then the level of 19S antibodies falls, with a half-life of 24 hr.

About one week after the initial injection, an exponential increase of 7S antibodies of the γG-immunoglobulin class occurs that lasts for about four days. 7S-antibody synthesis may continue thereafter at lower rates for periods of from two years to the entire life of the animal.

One month after the first injection, at the time when the primary 7S response has reached a plateau, a second injection of antigen yields a secondary response of increased 7S-antibody production that occurs in an accelerated manner. Although a secondary response is not seen for 19S-antibody production, a second dose of antigen nine days after the first (when 19S-antibody production has ceased) results in the production of another peak of synthesis of this class of molecules. This suggests that the 19S response depends on continued presence of the antigen at a level higher than that required for 7S-antibody synthesis.

## Cells and Tissues Involved in Humoral
## Antibody Production

The spleen and lymph nodes can be identified as the major sources of cells involved in humoral antibody production, although scattered collections of lymphoid tissue occur in various organs (Stavitsky, 1961). Recent studies (Miller, 1963, 1964; Silverstein, 1964) have suggested that lymphoid organs may be secondary, in the sense that the development of the adult lymphoid system depends upon the thymus. By adult life, however, the thymus plays no major role in the synthesis of antibodies.

There has been considerable controversy concerning the types of cells involved in the immune response (CIBA Found. Study Group, 1963; Gowans and McGregor, 1964). For the purposes of the present discussion, three groups of cells will be considered: the macrophage, the lymphocyte (immunologically competent cell), and the plasma cell.

Whether it is essential in every case for macrophages to process antigen molecules is not known, but the circumstantial evidence for the participation of these cells in the immune response is considerable. Evidence for uptake of antigen by these cells has been found (Garvey and Campbell, 1957; *Mechanisms of Antibody Formation, Proc. Symp.,* 1960; Thorbecke and Benacerraf, 1962), and experiments have been done to demonstrate fragmentation of antigens by macrophages (Campbell and Garvey, 1963). There is no evidence that macrophages are capable of forming antibodies. This capacity belongs to the so-called immunologically competent cells, which can mature into cells which do synthesize antibodies.

Recent studies (CIBA Found. Study Group, 1963; Gowans and McGregor 1964) suggest that the immunologically competent cells are small lymphocytes which may circulate in the blood or reside in the lymph nodes for variable periods of time. The lymphoid cell population is thus in a dynamic state, and cells may wander via the blood from one lymphoid organ to another.

As a result of the antigenic stimulus, some immunologically competent cells may mature into plasma cells. Mature plasma cells contain an extensive endoplasmic reticulum and synthesize $\gamma$-globulin molecules and specific antibodies. In addition to maturation, cellular replication may be involved in the specific immune response (Dutton and Eady, 1964). The recent findings of Jerne and his associates (Jerne et al., 1963) are in accord with this conclusion. By the use of a plaque method, these workers were able to detect antibody formation by single cells of the spleen of mice immunized to red blood cells of sheep. They found that the number of cells producing antibodies rose to a peak four days after injection of the antigen and declined thereafter. Although these experiments do not prove that cellular replication occurs in the immune response, they are consistent with earlier studies (Leduc et al., 1955; Mäkelä and Nossal, 1962; Nossal and Mäkelä, 1962b) that suggest that antibody-forming cells result from division of precursor cells.

Experiments on antibody production by single cells indicate that a single plasma cell can produce antibodies of more than one specificity (Nossal and Mäkelä, 1962a, b; Attardi et al., 1964), although most cells isolated from an animal stimulated with two unrelated antigens produce antibodies to either one or the other antigen.

Whether both 19S and 7S antibodies directed against the same antigen are produced in the same plasma cell has not been decided, although recent studies suggest that they are (Nossal et al., 1964). Antibodies may be found in all classes of $\gamma$-globulins, and molecules in all classes possess structural homologies.

## Properties and Relations of the Classes of Immunoglobulins

Some properties and relationships among the various classes of $\gamma$-immunoglobulins are summarized in Table 1. In terms of concentration in the serum of mammals, $\gamma$G-globulins are predominant, and most structural studies have been performed on antibodies of this class. Molecules of each class have been shown to be multichain structures (Edelman, 1959; Edelman and Poulik, 1961; Franěk, 1961; Edelman, 1964a), and this finding forms the basis for recent proposed nomenclature (Cepellini et al., 1964). Within each class, the molecules consist of two types of polypeptide chains (Edelman and Benacerraf, 1962; Fleischman et al., 1963) that are under control of different

TABLE 1

γ-IMMUNOGLOBULINS *

| Major class | Molecular weight | Heavy chain† | Light chain‡ | Molecular formula |
|---|---|---|---|---|
| γG | $1.6 \times 10^5$ | γ | κ or λ | $\gamma_2\kappa_2$ <br> $\gamma_2\lambda_2$ |
| γA | $1.6 \times 10^5$ <br> (up to $5 \times 10^5$) | α | κ or λ | $\alpha_2\kappa_2$ <br> $\alpha_2\lambda_2$ |
| γM | $10^6$ | μ | κ or λ | $(\mu_2\kappa_2)_n$ <br> $(\mu_2\lambda_2)_n$ |

The number of units in γM-globulins is not completely determined. $n$ may be 5.
* Nomenclature is based on the World Health Organization conference; cf Cepellini et al., 1964.
† ~ molecular weight: 55,000–70,000.
† Not α-proteins; included for purposes of comparison.

genetic loci (Franklin et al., 1962; Harboe et al., 1962). Light chains have molecular weights of 20,000 to 23,000 (Edelman and Gally, 1962; Pain, 1963; Small et al., 1963) and are found in two antigenic types (Mannik and Kunkel, 1962; Fahey and Solomon, 1963). They have been identified with Bence-Jones proteins, immunoglobulins of low molecular weight excreted in disease (Edelman and Gally, 1962). Heavy chains have molecular weights of 55,000 or higher (Pain, 1963; Small et al., 1963), are chemically distinctive in each class (Edelman, 1964a), and bear the carbohydrate moiety (Fleischman et al., 1963). No function has been assigned to the carbohydrate, which appears to be linked covalently as a prosthetic group (Nolan and Smith, 1962).

Heterogeneity is the outstanding chemical feature of the whole molecules of antibodies and their polypeptide chains. This is reflected in their electrophoretic mobilities, content of amino-terminal and carboxy-terminal amino acids, binding constants for antigen, and amino acid composition (Fahey, 1962). A case may be made for the statement that this heterogeneity is a fundamental feature of the immunologic system at the molecular level and that it may largely reflect the capacity of antibodies to bind a variety of chemically unrelated antigens. In addition, the heterogeneity may reflect the number of different biological functions of antibody molecules (Edelman and Benacerraf, 1962) such as complement fixation, fixation to the skin, and placental transfer. These functions will not be discussed further. It should be noted, however, that progress is being made in localizing structures mediating these functions on portions of the antibody molecule other than the antigen-combining site.

From the standpoint of the problem of specificity, the chemical heterogeneity of the portion of the molecule containing the binding site is of most importance. Before discussing the possible nature of the site, however, some structural information on a representative class of γ-globulin molecules, the γG-immunoglobulins, must be reviewed.

### A Model of the 7S γG-Antibody Molecule

Recent studies on the chemical structure of antibodies have suggested a working model (Edelman and Gally, 1964) of the γG-antibody molecule. In Fig. 2 the molecule is shown in an extended form, since no detailed information is available on the over-all flexibility and conformational variability of γ-globulin. The molecule may be capable of taking on several forms, since polarization of fluorescence measurements (Steiner and Edelhoch, 1962; Winkler, 1963), potentiometric titrations (Weltman and Sela, 1964), and viscosity data (Noelken *et al.*, 1965) suggest a certain degree of unfolding or flexibility. Details of folding of the chains within the molecular envelope are

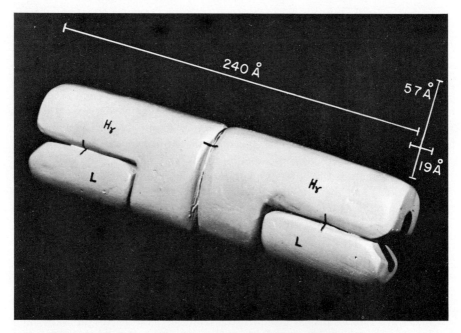

**Fig. 2.** Model of the 7S-antibody molecule. Molecular dimensions taken from Kratky *et al.* (1955). $H\gamma$: heavy polypeptide chain; $L$: light polypeptide chain. Single lines drawn on model represent interchain disulfide bonds.

not known, although it is fairly certain that they contain no $\alpha$-helices (Winkler and Doty, 1961). The dimensions of the molecule as shown in Fig. 2 are based on low-angle X-ray scattering measurements (Kratky *et al.*, 1955) and electron micrographs (Almeida *et al.*, 1963).

One of the main features of the model is that it depicts the multichain structure of the antibody and at the same time assigns roles to both light and heavy chains in forming the active site. The divalent antibody is composed of two light chains and two heavy chains arranged as two light-heavy pairs (Edelman and Gally, 1964). Each chain is linked to its neighbor by a single disulfide bond and by weak interactions. The two half-molecules, each containing a single combining site, are linked through the heavy chains. It is assumed that the heavy chains have identical structures and that there is a twofold rotation axis between them.

The antigen-combining sites have been placed at the ends of the cylinder and may be visualized as small crevices or craters between the light and heavy chains. The dimensions of the sites are based on the measurements of Kabat (1960) in his studies of antidextran antibodies.

The carbohydrate moiety, which is known to be present on the heavy chains (Fleischman *et al.*, 1963), but which so far has not been shown to have a functional role, is not depicted.

This model is consistent with the known steps of degradation of the antibody molecule (Fig. 3). Reduction of interchain disulfide bonds in the absence of urea followed by exposure to urea (Edelman and Poulik, 1961) or acid (Fleischman *et al.*, 1963) solutions leads to dissociation of the chains; neither treatment alone is sufficient. Separated light chains dimerize and may form an interchain disulfide bond (Edelman and Gally, 1962; Gally and Edelman, 1964). Mild reduction followed by treatment with HCl leads to separation of half-molecules (Palmer and Nisonoff, 1964). Hydrolysis with papain (Porter, 1959) cleaves peptide bonds of the heavy chains, and after reduction of the disulfide bond between them, active (S) and inactive (F) fragments are formed.[2] Treatment with pepsin yields fragments closely resembling two S fragments linked by a single disulfide bond (Nisonoff *et al.*, 1961).

The major features of the antibody model have been confirmed by recent experiments which indicate that separated light and heavy chains will reassociate to form 7S molecules with molecular weights of 160,000 (Gally and Edelman, 1964; Olins and Edelman, 1964). Although the chains will reassociate without forming interchain disulfide bonds, it can be shown that these bonds are re-formed if the chains are in the partially reduced state.

A typical experiment showing the reconstitution of human $\gamma$G-globulin molecules from their chains is presented in Fig. 4. Separated light and heavy chains labeled with different iodine isotopes were mixed in propionic acid and

---

[2] In the new terminology (Ceppelini *et al.*, 1964), the S fragment is termed the Fab fragment and the F fragment is termed the Fc fragment.

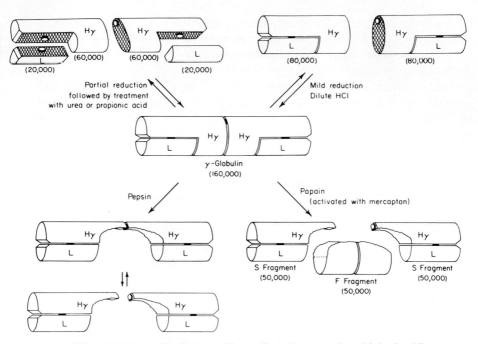

**Fig. 3.** Schematic diagram illustrating the ways in which the 7S-antibody molecule may be degraded. Numbers in parentheses are approximate molecular weights. $H\gamma$: heavy chain; $L$: light chain. Hatched areas indicate regions of noncovalent interchain bonding. Disulfide bonds or half-cystines are indicated in these regions.

dialyzed in neutral aqueous buffers. The mixtures were subjected to ultracentrifugation in sucrose density gradients. A peak of material with a sedimentation coefficient of 7S containing both chains in a molar ratio of 1/1 was found. This 7S material had a molecular weight of 160,000. Separate light and heavy chains, each of which migrated with different velocities, are shown superimposed on the same figure. Light and heavy chains of different antibodies and of immunoglobulins from different individuals of the same species were also shown to form 7S molecules without hindrance.

The interchain disulfide bonds of reconstituted molecules may be reformed by simple reoxidation. Although these have not yet been proven to be the original interchain bonds, it is highly likely that they are in view of findings (Fougereau and Edelman, 1964) on the arrangement of the chains in reconstituted molecules. The gross arrangement of the chains resembled that of native $\gamma$-globulin. This was shown by digesting the molecule with papain and subsequently demonstrating that the S fragments contained the labels of both chains whereas F fragments contained mainly the iodine isotope used to label heavy chains (see Fig. 2).

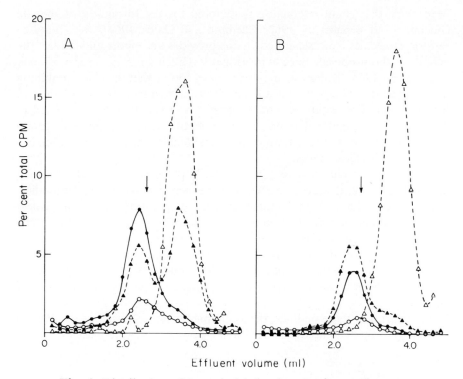

**Fig. 4.** Distribution of isotopic labels after density gradient centrifugation of $H_{I^{125}}L_{I^{131}}$ mixtures. Human H-chain fractions labeled with $I^{125}$, L-chain fractions labeled with $I^{131}$, and the products of their reconstituted mixture in 0.5 N propionic acid, $H_{I^{125}}L_{I^{131}}$, were each analyzed separately by density gradient centrifugation. A. Mass ratio of H to L chains during reconstitution: 3.3/1. B. Mass ratio of H to L chains during reconstitution: 6/1. △—△: labeled L chain centrifuged alone; ○—○: labeled H chain centrifuged alone; — : L-chain label in reconstituted mixture; ●—●: labeled H-chain fraction in mixture. Sedimentation proceeded from right to left. Per cent total cpm, counts per minute, in each fraction expressed as per cent of total counts recovered from cell contents, pellet, and concentrating sac. This total accounts for soluble and insoluble material. ↓ : position of alkaline phosphatase marker.

## Reconstitution of Antibody Activity by Admixture of Light and Heavy Polypeptide Chains

The fact that an active antibody consists of two types of polypeptide chains raises the question of whether either type of chain or both types together control the specificity of the antigen-combining site. A proposal has been made that chain interaction is required for the formation of the site (Edelman and Benacerraf, 1962; Edelman and Gally, 1964); the ability to re-form molecules from separated chains provides an opportunity to test the validity of this proposal. Several investigators (Edelman *et al.*, 1963b; Franěk and Nezlin, 1963; Roholt *et al.*, 1964) have found that specific combining activity was reconstituted after admixture of the relatively inactive light and heavy chains. The results of some experiments of this kind are presented in Table 2, which contains data on guinea-pig antibodies to the haptenic group dinitrophenyl, and in Table 3, which contains similar data on sheep antibodies to f1 and f2 bacteriophages.

The separated chains were mixed in 0.5 N propionic acid and were then dialyzed into neutral aqueous buffer. In the experiments on phage antibodies, the mixture of chains from the same antibody preparation led to the greatest reconstitution of activity. Hybrid mixtures led to lesser degrees of reconstitution in both phage systems, particularly when the heavy chains were derived from the homologous antibody. In experiments on phage antibodies from single animals (Fougereau *et al.*, 1964), hybrid mixtures of homologous light chains and heterologous heavy chains also showed slight enhancement of activity.

In contrast to these findings, the antihapten system showed reconstitution of activity only if homologous light and heavy chains were used (Table 2).

TABLE 2

RECONSTITUTION OF ANTIBODY ACTIVITY BY ADMIXTURE OF LIGHT AND HEAVY CHAINS OF GUINEA-PIG ANTIBODIES TO THE DINITROPHENYL (DNP) HAPTEN

| Sample | Binding of $C^{14}$ DNP cpm* |
|---|---|
| Ab | 900 |
| Ab–P | 790 |
| Ab–RA | 710 |
| Ab–RAP | 480 |
| H(DNP) | 380 |
| L(DNP) | <200 |
| H(DNP) + L(DNP) | 580† |
| H(DNP) + L($\gamma$) | 240 |

*Abbreviations:* Ab, antibody; H(DNP), heavy chain from anti-DNP antibody; L(DNP), light chain from anti-DNP antibody; P, exposed to 0.5 N propionic acid; RA, reduced and alkylated; RAP, reduced and alkylated and exposed to propionic acid for the same length of time as the separated chains; L($\gamma$), light chain from $\gamma$-globulin.

* cpm: counts per minute calculated to be bound per unit absorbancy of protein at 280 m$\mu$ after extrapolation of data from equilibrium dialysis experiments to infinite hapten concentration.

† Maximal value expected if the contributions of heavy and light chains were only additive was 340 cpm. Ratio of absorbancies of heavy to light chains in mixture was 4/1.

TABLE 3

ANTIPHAGE ACTIVITY IN MIXTURES OF POLYPEPTIDE CHAINS OF TWO NON-
CROSS-REACTING ANTIBODIES OBTAINED FROM A SINGLE SHEEP

| Sample | K(per min per unit absorbancy at 280 m$\mu$) | |
|---|---|---|
| | f1  neutralization | f2  neutralization |
| Ab(f1) | 3,700 | 14.0 |
| H(f1) | 51.6 | 0.28 |
| L(f1) | 4.64 | 0.30 |
| Ab(f2) | 12.5 | 500 |
| H(f2) | 1.13 | 11.0 |
| L(f2) | 0.63 | 0.65 |
| H(f1) + L(f1) | 610    (28)* | 0.0 |
| H(f1) + L(f2) | 81    (26) | 0.31 |
| H(f2) + L(f2) | 0.52 | 33.0 (5.8) |
| H(f2) + L(f1) | 9.58 (2.8) | 6.5 (5.6) |

*Abbreviations:* K, first-order rate constant for phage neutralization of protein sample tested; Ab, antibodies; Ab(f1), purified antibodies to f1 bacteriophage; Ab(f2), purified antibodies to f2 bacteriophage; H(f1), heavy chains of antibodies to f1 phage; L(f2), light chains of antibodies to f2 phage; H(f2) + L(f2), polypeptide chains of antibodies to f2 phage mixed in 0.5 N propionic acid and dialyzed into neutral aqueous buffers.    Other designations follow the same conventions.

* Numbers within parentheses are activities of chain mixtures expected if no potentiation occurred, calculated on the basis of the content and activities of both L and H chains.

Similar results have been obtained by Roholt *et al.* (1964), who used rabbit antihapten systems. Another difference between the antiphage and antihapten systems was the degree of reconstitution as compared to the original antibody activity. In the antiphage system, the highest degree of reconstitution was 15%, whereas in the antihapten system it was 60%. Moreover, although the degree of residual activity in heavy chains of the antiphage system may have been caused by contamination with light chains, it appears likely that in the antihapten system, the heavy chains bind the hapten to some extent.

Density gradient centrifugation has revealed that the major part of the reconstituted activity can be ascribed to the formation of reconstituted 7S molecules (Olins and Edelman, 1964). Failure to reconstitute activity is not usually due to failure to reconstitute 7S molecules. Recent experiments have shown that hybrid mixtures of complementary chains from guinea-pig anti-dinitrophenyl antibodies and nonspecific γ-globulin formed 7S molecules, although activity was not reconstituted (Edelman, 1964b).

In additional experiments on chain interaction, light chains and heavy chains of γ-globulins from two different animal species formed 7S molecules (Fougereau *et al.*, 1964; Olins and Edelman, 1964). This fact suggests that the general structural homology of mammalian γ-globulins (Edelman, 1964a) extends to regions of the chains responsible for interchain bonding. Despite the fact that interspecies molecular hybrids could be formed, however, activity was not reconstituted even if the chains were derived from antibodies to the same antigen. For example, sheep and guinea pigs immunized with f1 bacteriophage yielded antibodies the chains of which formed hybrids. In contrast to the findings on intraspecies hybrids, the activity of these interspecies hybrids was not greater than that of the individual chains.

The conclusions derived from experiments on chain interaction have been supported and extended by experiments in which the active sites of antibodies were labeled specifically (Roholt *et al.*, 1963; Metzger *et al.*, 1964). The results of these experiments suggest that both light and heavy chains are labeled and therefore that they both contribute amino acid residues to the antigen-combining site.

Besides providing support for the model of the γG-antibody molecule, the experiments on formation of molecular hybrids suggest several hypothetical mechanisms by which specificity may be achieved. These mechanisms will be discussed after reconsidering certain aspects of the central problem in the light of the foregoing remarks on antibody structure.

## Some Implications of Structural Studies:
## Possible Mechanisms of Specificity and
## Routes of Information Transfer

The central problem remains: how does the immune system recognize and discriminate among the varieties of three-dimensional structures that constitute different antigenic determinants? In analyzing this problem, it might be useful to consider some of the general requirements imposed upon theories of antibody production by current knowledge of antibody synthesis and structure. So far, in major outlines the synthesis of the polypeptide chains of antibodies appears to resemble that of other proteins. Preliminary experiments (Uhr *et al.*, 1964) suggest that antibody synthesis proceeds via DNA-dependent RNA synthesis. Moreover, adequate evidence exists to indicate that light and heavy chains are controlled by independent structural genes as reflected by the presence of allotypic markers (Kelus, 1963) or Gm groups (Franklin *et al.*, 1962; Harboe *et al.*, 1962). It is therefore likely that the sequence of transfer of information is DNA $\rightarrow$ RNA $\rightarrow$ polypeptide chain.

Instructive theories of antibody formation imply that the necessary information to recognize the three-dimensional structure of the antigen is directly transferred by contact from the antigen[3] to the antibody molecule, or to the RNA or DNA involved in its synthesis. Instructive mechanisms avoid the need to store large amounts of information in the antibody-forming

---

[3] The whole antigen molecule may not be required. "Antigen" is being used here in the sense of antigenic determinant.

system. Strictly instructive theories meet a number of embarrassments, however. No simple hypothesis is available to explain how the great variety of antigenic structures can intervene in the DNA or RNA code in a meaningful way. Folding hypotheses in which the antigen is the template for the final conformation of the antibody are difficult to support. Recent experiments suggest that unfolded active fragments of antibodies refold in the absence of antigen and regain their original activity (Buckley *et al.*, 1963). This occurs even if all the disulfide bonds are cleaved (Haber, 1964). The idea of a common precursor (Pauling, 1940) having the same amino acid sequence for all antibody molecules must be abandoned for a variety of reasons. The molecules consist of different types of polypeptide chains, the amino acid compositions of different antibodies are different (Koshland and Englberger, 1963), and antibodies of the same specificities have chains with different allotypic or Gm specificities. It is difficult to see how the antigen, which is presumed to act as a template in an instructive process, can be removed from the antibody molecule after the specific folding is completed. Moreover, recent information (Anfinsen *et al.*, 1961) suggests that the tertiary structure of proteins is largely determined by the primary structure, i.e., the amino acid sequence.

Selective theories imply that the antigen selects among pre-existent or stored sets of information at one or more of the three stages of information transfer. Such theories require recognition of the antigen, either by preformed or pre-existent antibodies, or by cellular receptors other than antibodies. Considering the first possibility, the number of different kinds of preformed antibodies would have to be very large to account for recognition of different antigens. No reasonable estimate of the number of different foreign antigenic determinants is available. Even if one considers, however, that the number of *completely* different haptenic determinants is relatively small because of the presence of similar aromatic rings and similar charge distribution, the number of antigenic determinants on foreign proteins must be very large, since different proteins have aperiodic amino acid sequences and different tertiary structures. It is difficult to see how the necessary information to recognize all antigenic foreign proteins could be inherent in the genome of the antibody-producing animal, unless one assumes that the genes controlling antibody synthesis are highly mutable and that most of the mutations have selective advantage. On the other hand, one might imagine that large numbers of $\gamma$-globulins having different amino acid sequences could be produced by mechanisms other than mutation. A mechanism of this type involving cross-over during somatic cell division has been proposed by Smithies (1963).

If cellular receptors other than preformed $\gamma$-globulins are involved in selective recognition of the antigen, these receptors must constitute a system of recognition at least as refined as the antibody system itself. To explain the diversity and specificity of such a system would be no easier than to explain these properties of the antibodies themselves. In such a system, for example, the three-dimensional message in the antigenic structure must somehow be conveyed from the cellular receptors through the mechanisms of protein synthesis, for which the known coding systems are linear (i.e., one-dimensional).

The purpose of these remarks is to emphasize that, notwithstanding their value, present theories fail to account in detail for the events of antibody synthesis. Other criticisms of the different theories have been made on the basis of failure to account for immunologic tolerance and other aspects of the immune response, but since they are not directly related to the present discussion, they will not be reviewed (see Refs. in Burnet, 1959; Lederberg, 1959; Talmage, 1959; Jerne, 1960; and Szilard, 1960).

Instead, it might be more profitable to consider some ways by which specificity might be acquired in a manner consistent with present facts on antibody structure. Several structural requirements must be met by any theory of antibody formation.

First, a mechanism must be provided to obtain a sufficiently large diversity in structure of the antigen-combining regions among the $\gamma$-globulins. If diversity of the three-dimensional structure results from differences in the amino acid sequences, then the mechanism for diversity must be related to formation of the polypeptide chains on ribosomes. As emphasized above, mutations, germinal or somatic, variations in crossing-over, or some other means of altering particular amino acid sequences must be provided.

Second, a means must be provided for the specific recognition of antigen prior to the events of antibody synthesis. This may be mediated by special cellular receptors rather than by antibodies, but perhaps the simplest way would be via either $\gamma$-globulin molecules themselves or their chains as they are formed in lymphoid cells.

Third, after antigen recognition, a means must be provided to elicit selective synthesis of the proper subsets of light and heavy chains from the enormously diverse population.

These three requirements will be discussed in detail.


## Mechanisms for Diversification of the
## Three-Dimensional Structure of Immunoglobulins

The experiments on the chain structure of antibodies and the antibody model suggest a mechanism by means of which a variety of combining sites directed against different antigens might be built. This mechanism is based on the chain-interaction hypothesis and requires that a sufficiently large number of light and heavy chains of different amino acid sequences be available to interact to form whole molecules. Both the genetic evidence mentioned above and chemical evidence (Edelman et al., 1961; Koshland and Englberger, 1963) suggest that antibodies of different specificities differ in their amino acid sequences. Antibodies of different specificities would be composed of different combinations of light and heavy chains. If antibody-producing cells contain information for the production of $p$ light chains and $q$ heavy chains, then there are $pq$ different ways by which antibody-combining sites might be constructed. In terms of the model of the antibody molecule, this assumes that there is a single most stable conformation of the site for any particular light-heavy pair. If $m$ different conformations were possible, then the number of structurally different sites would be $mpq$. Since there is no evidence to the contrary, it will be assumed here that $m = 1$.

The number of different active sites $pq$ is an upper limit, since several constraints may operate. More than one combination of different light and heavy chains may be capable of forming a site of given specificity; i.e., some combinations of chains may be degenerate with respect to specificity. Several lines of evidence suggest that this is so. Starch-gel electrophoretic experiments on the chains of specifically purified guinea-pig antibodies to haptens showed two to eight sharp bands corresponding to light chains (Edelman et al., 1961). Band patterns of antibodies to the same hapten but from different animals were similar, whereas antibodies of different specificities showed different band patterns. The multiplicity of bands has been shown to be related to the heterogeneity of the antibodies (Edelman et al., 1963a). The great heterogeneity of the binding constants of purified antibodies (Karush, 1962) and the in vitro reconstitution of active hybrid molecules from chains of different antibodies (Edelman et al., 1963b) are also consistent with the notion that degeneracy occurs among native antibodies.

Degeneracy would obviously decrease the number of distinctly different specificities that could be formed by interaction of a given number of light and heavy chains. If there were $10^3$ heavy chains and $10^3$ light chains all having different amino acid sequences, and if on the average any given specificity could be generated by 10 different combinations, then $10^5$ completely different kinds of sites could be formed.

Although the number of possible sites is greatly increased by assuming the chain-interaction hypothesis, still the production of possibly as many as 2,000 or more different chains must be explained. Several mechanisms have been proposed. The most obvious is mutation and selection. Presumably, there would be a selective advantage for those animals that produced the largest number of different polypeptide chains. Alternative mechanisms for producing the large number of variations would include somatic mutation and variation in crossover during the mitosis of immunologically competent cells (Smithies, 1963).

Since, in the model of the antibody molecule, the combining sites are assumed to be at the ends, and since certain relatively fixed regions of the chains are required for interchain bonding, probably only certain restricted regions of heavy and light chains contribute directly to the site. The contributory amino acid residues would not necessarily be in the same linear segment of the amino acid sequence. Moreover, the assumption of fixed-site regions does not prohibitively limit the number of possibilities. If 15 amino acid residues contributed directly to the active site, then genetic variations of the sequences of these amino acids could yield $20^{15}$ different combinations.

In addition to direct interchange of amino acid residues in the site region, amino acid substitution in other regions of the chains (see Fig. 5) could alter the conformation of the active site. For purposes of description, three regions can be distinguished: site regions, modulating regions, and interchain-bonding regions. Changes in the site region would alter specificity directly, whereas changes in the modulating region would alter the conformation of the site indirectly. It is obvious that, within limits, the modulating region and interchain-bonding regions might overlap.

It should be stressed that the mechanism of chain interaction requires that there be no restriction on the pairing or interaction of any light or heavy chains or light-heavy pairs. The reconstitution experiments described above indicate that there is no constraint on hybrid formation. This suggests that the interchain-bonding regions of different molecules may have very similar structures or may not vary greatly in sequence. The light chains composing different Bence-Jones proteins have been found to have many similar tryptic peptides, although they vary in over-all amino acid sequence (Putnam, 1962).

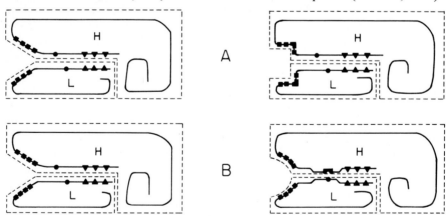

**Fig 5.** Schematic illustration of means by which the conformation of the active site may be influenced. (Only half-molecules are shown; the site is to the left.) A. Differences in conformation of the site resulting from amino acid sequence differences in the site region. B. Differences in conformation of the site resulting from differences in amino sequences not directly involved in the site (modulation). ■ or ◀ : amino acid residues in the site regions; ● or ◣◢ : amino acid residues in the modulating regions; ▼ : amino acid residues in the interchain-bonding region; *L*: light chain; *H*: heavy chain.

It would be of interest to know whether the common peptides and allotypic determinants (Kelus, 1963) are in the interchain-bonding regions.

The assumption of chain interaction working in consort with a genetic mechanism of variation requires that there be complementation between the different cistrons involved in controlling light- and heavy-chain structure. Mutations unfavorably affecting interchain-bonding regions would presumably be selected against, since whole $\gamma$-globulin molecules could not be formed. This might represent a means of stabilizing the products of an otherwise highly mutable system.[4]

## Initial Recognition of Antigen

Given a mechanism for the generation of a large number of different antigen-combining sites, one is still left with the problem of how the antigen is recognized in the primary response and of how, subsequently, the synthesis of the proper subsets of chains is directed. The most conservative selective mechanism would assume that the antigen is first recognized by $\gamma$-globulin molecules (Jerne, 1960) or by their polypeptide chains. Any other mechanism involves the assumption of special cellular receptors (Szilard, 1960) or of sets of macromolecules other than antibodies. In order to transfer the information on the antigen to the synthetic machinery, the set of specific sites would have to be coextensive with the antigen-combining sites of antibodies and would have to correspond to them in an unambiguous manner. It seems unlikely that such a group of sites chemically unrelated to antibodies would have evolved, since its range and degree of specificity would have to equal or exceed those of antibodies themselves.

Although instructive mechanisms avoid the embarrassment of providing for the initial recognition of antigen if they intervene at the level of protein folding, they still fail to account for the fact that only certain subsets of chains appear to be involved in specific antibody response of a given antigen.

## Control of the Specific Synthesis of Chains

It is evident from the research on cellular responses briefly reviewed in earlier paragraphs that an elaborate control mechanism operates in the

---

[4] *Note added in proof.* Recent studies on the amino acid sequence of Bence-Jones proteins (Hilschmann and Craig, 1965) have suggested that light chains have regions of variable sequence nearer the amino end, and a long region of common sequence beginning at the middle of the chain and proceeding to the carboxyl end. A series of point mutations could generate this pattern if amino acid substitution in the "variable" region affected the combining site, but not the gross structure or function of antibodies. On the other hand, mutations involving the "common" region would be selected against if this region were necessary for interchain bonding and functions other than combination with antigen.

immune response. At the molecular level, this system controls the production of the proper subsets of polypeptide chains and stores the information for future use.

This control system has two distinguishable but related manifestations. One is the gross regulation of $\gamma$-globulin synthesis and levels in the organism. The other involves specific assembly of particular antibody molecules. In normal mammals, $\gamma$-globulin levels do not vary greatly, even with immunization. Although both light and heavy chains apparently are synthesized in the same cell (Buffe *et al.*, 1964; Bernier and Cebra, 1964), little is known about the order in which they are synthesized. Recent studies of light chains of normal $\gamma$-globulins and myeloma globulins have a bearing upon this problem. Bence-Jones proteins have been found to be free light chains that are formed *de novo* (Edelman and Gally, 1962). In addition, normal humans have been shown to have light chains both in the circulation and in their urine (Berggård and Edelman, 1963). These chains are possibly generated as a result of either asynchronous synthesis or a failure in linkage or pairing with heavy chains. *In vitro* reconstitution of $\gamma$-globulin proceeds best in the presence of excess light chains (Fougereau and Edelman, 1964); perhaps a similar excess must be present in the antibody-forming cell for efficient synthesis of whole molecules.

Whether specific assembly of antibody molecules from the proper chains depends on the continued presence of the antigen is still not known. One possible control mechanism involves direction by the antigen of both the choice of the proper pairs of chains and the assembly of the chains to form the whole molecule (Edelman and Benacerraf, 1962). This assembly would require only the formation of the most stable ternary complexes among the antigenic determinant and certain light and heavy chains. In cellular terms, this role of the antigen could manifest itself in one of two ways. Each cell may make a large number of different chains in small amounts, and, after exposure to antigen, form stable ternary complexes involving some of these chains. Some mechanism would have to be provided to guarantee that subsequently only those particular chains are synthesized in large amounts by the cell. Alternatively, each cell may be capable of synthesizing only one kind or at most a few variants of each kind of chain. Exposure to the antigen would accelerate chain synthesis in the proper subset of cells. If this process accelerated division and maturation of these cells, the continued presence of antigen would not be necessary. This latter mechanism could account for the secondary response, since the number of cells with the proper chains would be increased by an initial exposure to antigen. It is essentially a selective mechanism.

One possible over-all scheme for specific antibody synthesis is presented in Fig. 6, mainly for heuristic purposes and to emphasize the problems posed at this stage of our knowledge. The diversity of antibodies is assumed to arise from mutation of structural genes, and organisms with the largest population of different $\gamma$-globulins are assumed to have the selective advantage. By chain interaction, the number of active sites is some power greater than the number

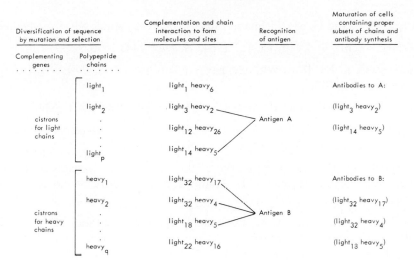

**Fig. 6.** Hypothetical scheme of stages in specific antibody synthesis.

of cistrons controlling chain synthesis. Antigen molecules are assumed to be recognized by "proper" subsets of chains, and, as a result of formation of ternary complexes in the cell, division and maturation are stimulated. The resulting plasma cells synthesize a variety of $\gamma$-globulin molecules that differ in chain types. Notwithstanding this difference, each pair of light and heavy chains forms a site more or less complementary to the antigen. Because this system is degenerate, it has a built-in safety factor. The loss of one or another chain by mutation would not significantly affect the response to a particular antigen.

Obviously, the mechanisms outlined above are highly speculative, and much more knowledge of cell physiology is required to build a sound hypothesis to account for humoral antibody synthesis. The major aim of the foregoing discussion has been to indicate that knowledge of the molecular structure of antibodies provides a point of departure for tracing the path of information over which the message from the antigen is carried. In addition, this knowledge provides necessary boundary conditions for cell physiologists in their attempts to describe the over-all mechanisms of the immune response.

## REFERENCES

Almeida, J., B. Cinader, and A. Howatson. 1963. *J. Exptl. Med.* 118: 327.

Anfinsen, C. B., E. Haber, M. Sela, and F. H. White, Jr. 1961. *Proc. Natl. Acad. Sci. U.S.* 47: 1309.

Attardi, G., M. Cohn, K. Horibata, and E. S. Lennox. 1964. *J. Immunol.* 92: 335.

Berggård, I., and G. M. Edelman. 1963. *Proc. Natl. Acad. Sci. U.S.* 49: 330.

Bernier, G. M., and J. J. Cebra. 1964. *Science* 144: 1590.

Buckley, C. E. III, P. L. Whitney, and C. Tanford. 1963. *Proc. Natl. Acad. Sci. U.S.* 50: 827.

Buffe, D., P. Burtin, and P. Grabar. 1964. *Compt. Rend.* 258: 4629.

Burnet, F. M. 1959. *The Clonal Selection Theory of Acquired Immunity.* Nashville, Tenn.: Vanderbilt University Press.

Campbell, D. H., and J. S. Garvey. 1963. In *Advan. Immunol.*, Vol. III, ed. F. J. Dixon, Jr., and J. H. Humphrey. New York: Academic Press, Inc. P. 261.

Cepellini, R., S. Dray, G. M. Edelman, J. Fahey, F. Franĕk, E. Franklin, H. C. Goodman, P. Grabar, A. E. Gurvich, J. F. Heremans, H. Isliker, F. Karush, E. Press, and Z. Trnka. 1964. *Bull. World Health Organ.* 30: 447.

CIBA Found. Study Group. 1963. *The Immunologically Competent Cell.* Boston: Little, Brown and Company.

Dutton, R. W., and J. D. Eady. 1964. *Immunology* 7: 40.

Edelman, G. M. 1959. *J. Am. Chem. Soc.* 81: 3155.

Edelman, G. M. 1964a. In *Immunopathol., Intern. Symp., 3rd, La Jolla, Calif., 1963*, ed. P. Grabar and P. A. Miescher. Basel, Switz.: Benno Schwabe & Co., Verlag. P. 57.

Edelman, G. M. 1964b. *Molecular and Cellular Basis of Antibody Formation, Proc. Symp., Prague, 1964.* Prague, Czech.: Czech. Acad. Sci. P. 113.

Edelman, G. M., and B. Benacerraf. 1962. *Proc. Natl. Acad. Sci. U.S.* 48: 1035.

Edelman, G. M., and J. A. Gally. 1962. *J. Exptl. Med.* 116: 207.

Edelman, G. M., and J. A. Gally. 1964. *Proc. Natl. Acad. Sci. U.S.* 51: 846.

Edelman, G. M., and M. D. Poulik. 1961. *J. Exptl. Med.* 113: 861.

Edelman, G. M., B. Benacerraf, Z. Ovary, and M. D. Poulik. 1961. *Proc. Natl. Acad. Sci. U.S.* 47: 1751.

Edelman, G. M., B. Benacerraf, and Z. Ovary. 1963a. *J. Exptl. Med.* 118: 229.

Edelman, G. M., D. E. Olins, J. A. Gally, and N. D. Zinder. 1963b. *Proc. Natl. Acad. Sci. U.S.* 50: 753.

Fahey, J. L. 1962. In *Advan. Immunol.*, Vol. 2, ed. W. H. Taliaferro and J. H. Humphrey. New York: Academic Press, Inc. P. 42.

Fahey, J. L., and A. Solomon. 1963. *J. Clin. Invest.* 42: 811.

Fleischman, J. B., R. R. Porter, and E. M. Press. 1963. *Biochem. J.* 88: 220.

Fougereau, M., and G. M. Edelman. 1964. *Biochemistry* 3: 1120.

Fougereau, M., D. E. Olins, and G. M. Edelman. 1964. *J. Exptl. Med.* 120: 349.

Franěk, F. 1961. *Biochem. Biophys. Res. Commun.* 4: 28.

Franěk, F., and R. S. Nezlin. 1963. *Biokhimiya* 28: 193.

Franklin, E. C., H. Fudenberg, M. Meltzer, and D. R. Stanworth. 1962. *Proc. Natl. Acad. Sci. U.S.* 48: 914.

Gally, J. A., and G. M. Edelman. 1964. *J. Exptl. Med.* 119: 817.

Garvey, J. S., and D. H. Campbell. 1957. *J. Exptl. Med.* 105: 361.

Gowans, J. L., and D. D. McGregor. 1964. In *Immunopathol., Intern. Symp., 3rd, La Jolla, Calif., 1963,* ed. P. Grabar and P. A. Miescher. Basel, Switz.: Benno Schwabe & Co., Verlag. P. 89.

Haber, E. 1964. *Proc. Natl. Acad. Sci. U.S.* 52: 1099.

Harboe, M., C. K. Osterland, and H. G. Kunkel. 1962. *Science* 136: 979.

Hilschmann, N., and L. C. Craig. 1965. *Proc. Natl. Acad. Sci. U.S.* 53: 1403.

Jerne, N. K. 1960. *Ann. Rev. Microbiol.* 14: 341.

Jerne, N. K., A. A. Nordin, and C. Henry. 1963. In *Cell Bound Antibodies,* ed. B. Amos and H. Koprowski. Philadelphia: The Wistar Institute Press. P. 109.

Kabat, E. A. 1960. *J. Immunol.* 84: 82.

Karush, F. 1962. In *Advan. Immunol.,* Vol. 2, ed. W. H. Taliaferro and J. H. Humphrey. New York: Academic Press, Inc. P. 1.

Kelus, A. S. 1963. *Biochem. J.* 88: 4P.

Koshland, M. E., and F. M. Englberger. 1963. *Proc. Natl. Acad. Sci. U.S.* 50: 61.

Kratky, O., G. Porod, A. Sekora, and B. Paletta. 1955. *J. Polymer Sci.* 16: 163.

Lederberg, J. 1959. *Science* 129: 1649.

Leduc, E. H., A. H. Coons, and J. M. Connelly. 1955. *J. Exptl. Med.* 102: 61.

Mäkelä, O., and G. J. V. Nossal. 1962. *J. Exptl. Med.* 115: 231.

Mannik, M., and H. G. Kunkel. 1962. *J. Exptl. Med.* 116: 859.

*Mech. Antibody Formation, Proc. Symp., Prague, 1959.* 1960. Prague, Czech.: Czech. Acad. Sci.

Metzger, H., L. Wofsey, and S. J. Singer. 1964. *Proc. Natl. Acad. Sci. U.S.* 51: 612.

Miller, J. F. A. P. 1963. *Brit. Med. Bull.* 19: 214.

Miller, J. F. A. P. 1964. *Science* 144: 1544.

Nisonoff, A., G. Markus, and F. C. Wissler. 1961. *Nature* 189: 293.

Noelken, M. E., C. A. Nelson, C. E. Buckley, III, and Charles Tanford. 1965. *J. Biol. Chem.* 240: 218.

Nolan, C., and E. L. Smith. 1962. *J. Biol. Chem.* 237: 446.

Nossal, G. J. V., and O. Mäkelä. 1962a. *Ann. Rev. Microbiol.* 16: 53.

Nossal, G. J. V., and O. Mäkelä. 1962b. *J. Exptl. Med.* 115: 209.

Nossal, G. J. V., A. Szenberg, G. L. Ada, and C. M. Austin. 1964. *J. Exptl. Med.* 119: 485.

Olins, D. E., and G. M. Edelman. 1964. *J. Exptl. Med.* 119: 789.

Pain, R. H. 1963. *Biochem. J.* 88: 234.

Palmer, J. L., and A. Nisonoff. 1964. *Biochemistry* 3: 863.

Pauling, L. 1940. *J. Am. Chem. Soc.* 62: 2643.

Porter, R. R. 1959. *Biochem. J.* 73: 119.

Putnam, F. W. 1962. *Biochim. Biophys. Acta* 63: 539.

Roholt, O., K. Onoue, and D. Pressman. 1964. *Proc. Natl. Acad. Sci. U.S.* 51: 173.

Roholt, O. A., G. Radzimski, and D. Pressman. 1963. *Science* 141: 726.

Silverstein, A. M. 1964. *Science* 144: 1423.

Small, P. A., J. E. Kehn, and M. E. Lamm. 1963. *Science* 142: 393.

Smithies, O. 1963. *Nature* 199: 1231.

Stavitsky, A. B. 1961. In *Advan. Immunol.*, Vol. 1, ed. W. H. Taliaferro and J. H. Humphrey. New York: Academic Press, Inc. P. 211.

Steiner, R. F., and H. Edelhoch. 1962. *J. Am. Chem. Soc.* 84: 2139.

Szilard, L. 1960. *Proc. Natl. Acad. Sci. U.S.* 46: 293.

Talmage, D. W. 1959. *Science* 129: 1643.

Thorbecke, G. J., and B. Benacerraf. 1962. In *Prog. Allergy*, Vol. VI, ed. P. Kallos and B. H. Waksman. New York: Verlags. Karger. P. 559.

Uhr, J. W. 1964. *Science* 145: 457.

Uhr, J. W., M. Scharf, and S. Tawle. 1964. *Molecular and Cellular Basis of Antibody Formation, Proc. Symp., Prague, 1964.* Prague, Czech.: Czech. Acad. Sci. P. 537.

Weltman, J., and M. Sela. 1964. *Biochim. Biophys. Acta* 93: 553.

Winkler, M. H. 1963. *Abstr. 145th Meeting, Am. Chem. Soc., Division of Biol. Chem., New York, Sept., 1963.* P. 41–C.

Winkler, M. H., and P. Doty. 1961. *Biochim. Biophys. Acta* 54: 448.

# Aspects of Nucleotide Arrangement in Deoxyribonucleic Acids[1]

**Herman S. Shapiro**

*Cell Chemistry Laboratory, Department of Biochemistry*
*College of Physicians and Surgeons*
*Columbia University*
*New York City, New York*

## Introduction

Not many years have elapsed since a compilation of reproducible analyses of the nitrogenous constituents of deoxyribonucleic acids (DNAs) allowed recognition of some regular features among these polymers (Chargaff, 1950, 1955), features that have been incorporated into a feasible physicochemical model for DNA (Watson and Crick, 1953). Investigations into the details of nucleic acid structure center now upon elucidation of their nucleotide sequence or, at least, some general features of nucleotide arrangement. These studies, directed both to RNA and DNA, have assumed some importance due to the impetus of hypotheses and experiments which have attributed a direct as well as an indirect responsibility of nucleotide sequence to the specific disposition of amino acids in proteins.

*Fundamental difficulties within the problem.* Two intrinsic features of DNA make the determination of an exact nucleotide sequence in the polynucleotide chain an inherently difficult task.

The first of these is the complex heterogeneity of DNA from higher cellular

[1] This work has been supported by research grants from the National Institutes of Health, U.S. Public Health Service, and the American Cancer Society.

sources; these DNAs can be fractionated into component subpopulations (Chargaff *et al.*, 1953; Crampton *et al.*, 1954; Chargaff, 1963).

When a DNA-histone complex, either of native or reconstituted association, is serially subjected to NaCl solutions increasing from 0.15 M to 2 M concentration, specific fractions of the nucleohistone dissociate and become solubilized. These fractions, themselves, represent a narrower population range of the original DNA preparation and exhibit a characteristic, gradual shift of composition (Chargaff *et al.*, 1953; Crampton *et al.*, 1954). This fractional dissociation technique solubilizes material of diminishing G, C, and M content[2] and of increasing A and T content with each change to higher ionic strength. In all cases the recognized regularity features of DNA are maintained. The results of a complete fractionation of rye-germ nucleohistone, following the procedures described for wheat-germ nucleohistone (Lipshitz and Chargaff, 1956), are presented in Table 1. The compositional regularities are maintained when M and C are treated together as 6-amino pyrimidine units. The DNAs of small bacteriophages appear not to exhibit such heterogeneity of composition (Sinsheimer, 1959). It is uncertain whether the DNA of low molecular weight reported to be associated with cytochrome $b_2$ (Armstrong *et al.*, 1963) can yet be classified as a single species of DNA.

The second feature that prevents an unequivocal solution of nucleotide arrangement in DNA is the fact that only four or five nucleotide components form an extremely large polymer whose estimated molecular, or rather, particle weight keeps increasing with each new refinement of isolation techniques (Hershey and Burgi, 1960; Cairns, 1963).

An approach to sequence studies is usually facilitated when some unique, identifiable loci can be recognized in a polymer around each of which an orderly arrangement of units can be reconstructed. High specificity of the degrading agent, usually an enzyme, or the low frequency of several uncommon constituents in the polymer help identify such loci. The studies of the amino acid sequence in several small proteins (Anfinsen and Redfield, 1956) and of the nucleotide sequence of specific species of RNA (Ingram and Pierce, 1962; Holley *et al.*, 1965) have been aided by both these conveniences. Analyses of the enzyme digests of the RNA of relatively low molecular weight, the RNA responsible for the transfer of amino acids to the sites of protein syntheses (Hecht *et al.*, 1959), will certainly allow the first direct correlation between a cellularly operational nucleotide sequence and a specific amino acid (Holley *et al.*, 1965).

---

[2] Abbreviations: Py, pyrimidine deoxyribosides; Pu, purine deoxyribosides; C, deoxycytidine; M, deoxy-5-methylcytidine; T, thymidine; A, deoxyadenosine; G, deoxyguanosine; p, esterified phosphoric acid. In order to indicate nucleotides, and oligonucleotides of known sequence, p is placed at the left of the symbol to denote 5′-hydroxyl ester, at the right to denote 3′-hydroxyl ester. Compounds comprising mixtures of structural isomers will be designated by total composition, e.g., $C_2Tp_4$.

## TABLE 1

COMPOSITION OF RYE-GERM DNA FRACTIONS PREPARED BY FRACTIONAL DISSOCIATION OF NUCLEOPROTEIN GEL

(From Shapiro and Chargaff, 1960, *Biochim. Biophys. Acta* 39: 68.)

| Fraction | | | Moles/100 g-atoms P* | | | | | Molar ratios | | | | |
|---|---|---|---|---|---|---|---|---|---|---|---|---|
| No. | NaCl molarity | % of DNA in starting material | A | G | C | M | T | $\dfrac{A+T}{G+C+M}$ | $\dfrac{Pu}{Py}$ | $\dfrac{A}{T}$ | $\dfrac{G}{C+M}$ | $\dfrac{C}{M}$ |
| 1 | 0.60 | 12.9 | 25.9 | 23.9 | 17.0 | 6.8 | 26.3 | 1.09 | 0.99 | 0.98 | 1.00 | 2.50 |
| 2 | 0.65 | 11.2 | 27.4 | 22.9 | 16.2 | 6.4 | 27.1 | 1.20 | 1.01 | 1.01 | 1.01 | 2.53 |
| 3 | 0.70 | 17.8 | 27.5 | 21.6 | 16.6 | 6.1 | 28.2 | 1.26 | 0.96 | 0.98 | 0.95 | 2.72 |
| 4 | 0.75 | 14.4 | 28.1 | 21.8 | 16.6 | 5.8 | 27.8 | 1.26 | 0.99 | 1.01 | 0.97 | 2.86 |
| 5 | 0.80 | 9.2 | 27.9 | 21.2 | 16.8 | 6.1 | 28.0 | 1.27 | 0.96 | 1.00 | 0.93 | 2.75 |
| 6 | 0.90 | 16.2 | 28.9 | 20.7 | 16.5 | 5.4 | 28.6 | 1.35 | 0.98 | 1.01 | 0.95 | 3.06 |
| 7 | 1.7 | 5.3 | 30.3 | 20.0 | 15.8 | 4.7 | 29.2 | 1.47 | 1.01 | 1.04 | 0.98 | 3.36 |

* A, adenine; G, guanine; C, cytosine; M, methylcytosine; T, thymine. The mean proportions of each constituent have been corrected for a 100% recovery.

An invariant content of nearly 1.5 nucleotide percent of 5-methylcytosine (Wyatt, 1951; Chargaff, 1955) in calf-thymus DNA to which we might assign a molecular weight of $10 \times 10^6$ would imply the presence of approximately 450 *unique* M loci in this DNA. These loci and their immediate nucleotide environment are practically indistinguishable by present analytical techniques.

These two considerations of DNA structure, the heterogeneity of DNA and the limited number of components in polymeric association, force any study of nucleotide sequence to have its results interpreted only in statistical terms.

*The implications of random nucleotide distribution.* The basis for subsequent interpretations and discussions arising from studies of nucleotide sequence rests on comparison of experimental results with data derived from theoretical considerations. The expected frequency of specific oligonucleotide sequences in a population of linear polymers, where any nucleotide sequence is possible, may be calculated with the aid of simplified equations of probability theory or by the more sophisticated theory of runs (Mood, 1940). A tabulation of expected frequencies of specific pyrimidine runs (i.e., a series of consecutive, similar events) will, of course, vary with changes of the DNA composition. The expected frequency of pyrimidine runs in which no distinction is made between cytidylic and thymidylic acids will, however, remain constant because of the compositional regularity in a DNA duplex structure in which the purine and pyrimidine contents are equal (Chargaff, 1950, 1955). The formalized equations of Peacocke that have been cited in the literature (Jones *et al.*, 1957) illustrate the mathematics involved. A polynucleotide structure based on a random arrangement of nucleotide units can be derived from simple probability statistics. The compositional regularities in DNA define the frequencies of both purine and pyrimidine moieties to be 0.5. The frequency of each contiguous pyrimidine group defined by length $n$, and flanked by purine nucleotides, is $0.5^{n+2}$, and the number of these runs per total pyrimidine complement in the DNA is $0.5^{n+2}/0.5$, or $0.5^{n+1}$. Finally, the fraction of DNA pyrimidines contributing to each run group of length $n$ is defined by the term $n(0.5)^{n+1}$. The frequencies $F$ of pyrimidine runs having a common length (isostich), increasing from $n = 1$, are 0.25, 0.125, 0.0625, etc. The fractions of pyrimidines contributing to these isostichs are consequently 0.25, 0.25, 0.1875, etc. These values apply equally to the purine arrangement in the DNA. The proportion of individual pyrimidine runs, composed of C and T units, within the restriction of each isostich frequency is obtained from appropriate expansion of the expression $(C + T)^n$, where C and T refer to the molar frequencies of these pyrimidines in the DNA. These calculations reflect a nucleotide arrangement based on a random linear disposition of nucleotides either in a population of DNA polymers or, within the finite size of the polymer, in a single DNA chain.

*The estimation of pyrimidine runs.* The basis of all chemical approaches to the elucidation of nucleotide arrangement in DNA rests upon the easy, specific removal of *either* the purine or pyrimidine moieties without disturbance to the integrity of the remaining nucleotide structure. The studies of nucleotide arrangement that were initially directed to pyrimidine distribution (Shapiro and Chargaff, 1956; Burton and Petersen, 1957; Cohn and Volkin, 1957) relied on this premise.

Investigations into the distribution of pyrimidine nucleotides within the DNA polymer require a preliminary hydrolysis of the purine-deoxyribose bonds. The extreme acid lability of the purine $N^9$-deoxyribose $C_{1'}$ glycoside bond makes the course easy (Levene and Bass, 1931). Apurinic acid (APA), the generic name designated to the products prepared by mild acid treatment of DNA, are nondialyzable and contain a pyrimidine and phosphorus complement unchanged from that of the parent polymers (Tamm *et al.*, 1952a). Each APA preparation is as unique in its pyrimidine sequences as the DNA from which it originated. The structure, furthermore, is modified by the presence of reactive aldehydo groups at former purine nucleotide loci (Tamm *et al.*, 1952b). The properties of APA and some of its derivatives have been described (Tamm and Chargaff, 1953).

Pyrimidine nucleoside 3',5'-diphosphates (p-Py-p) had been early recognized to be among the products of moderate acid degradation of DNA (Levene and Jacobs, 1912), a process during which DNA, not then recognized to be a complex polymer, naturally passed through a transitory state of depurinization. As a result of renewed interest in these breakdown products (Dekker *et al.*, 1953), an elimination reaction involving the phosphate ester that is $\beta$ to the reactive aldehyde was cited as the mechanism responsible for the process after initial removal of the purines. The course of a series of $\beta$-elimination reactions that would lead to the release of p-Py-p, as we later postulated (Shapiro and Chargaff, 1957a), is depicted in Fig. 1. After liberation of purines, the first eliminations occur at the broken lines *A* and *B*, leading to formation of a double bond between the second and third carbon atoms of the deoxyribose. A second elimination occurring $\beta$ to this double bond, at position $C_{5'}$ would release the pyrimidine nucleoside 3',5'-diphosphate. A release of longer pyrimidine runs through a similar series of reactions should also take place. Elimination reactions are known to proceed easily in alkaline media as well (Linstead *et al.*, 1953), and identification of an $\alpha$—$\beta$ unsaturated pentose phosphate among the products of alkaline digestion of apurinic acid has clarified several aspects of the elimination mechanism involved during the breakdown of the polymer (Bayley *et al.*, 1961).

Our choice of conditions for the elimination reaction was based upon the decomposition kinetics of model compounds (Shapiro and Chargaff, 1957a) and upon the rate of release of pyrimidine nucleoside diphosphates from

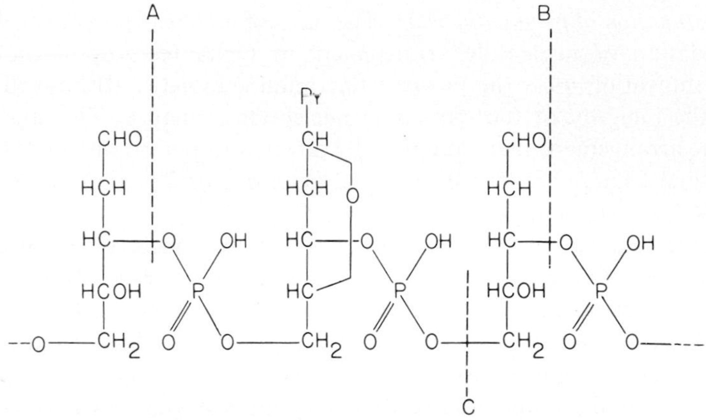

**Fig. 1.** Schematic structure of a trinucleotide segment in DNA illustrating the liberation of pyrimidine runs during acid decomposition. See text.

DNA (Shapiro and Chargaff, 1957b). Two-per-cent solutions of DNA digested in sealed tubes with 0.1 M $H_2SO_4$, 100°C, 35 min were the standard conditions employed. The components of the digest were originally separated chromatographically using Dowex-2 anion-exchange resin columns and estimated by UV spectrophotometry. Subsequent introduction of DEAE-cellulose chromatographic techniques (Spencer and Chargaff, 1961) and direct two-dimensional filter paper chromatographic procedures (Shapiro and Chargaff, 1963) have facilitated these studies. In addition to deoxycytidine and thymidine diphosphate, pCp and pTp, a series of compounds of higher order has been isolated, all of which maintained the general structure $Py_n p_{n+1}$ (Cohn and Volkin, 1957; Shapiro and Chargaff, 1957b). These runs reflect their origin from areas in the DNA where they were flanked by purine nucleotides. Quantitative estimations of the frequency of several pyrimidine runs were sufficient to formulate early conclusions on the nonrandom arrangement of nucleotides in DNA which could not hitherto have been recognized (Shapiro and Chargaff, 1957c).

## Some Features of Pyrimidine Distribution

Initial investigations on the nucleotide arrangement in DNA were conducted on material from calf thymus; human spleen; and two species of sea urchin, *Arbacia lixula* and *Paracentrotus lividus* (Shapiro and Chargaff, 1957b). In each case considerably less than the expected 25% of the pyrimidine complement of the DNA was encountered among the solitary pyrimidine runs. Approximately 30% of the total pyrimidines were estimated as isostichs of length 1 and 2 rather than the expected figure of 50% based on randomness. Moreover, the molar ratio of the individual runs of length 1, pCp/pTp, differed from the molar ratio of these nitrogenous constituents in the DNA, C/T. This identity would have been expected in a linear polymer featuring a random disposition of nucleotides.

*The disposition of 5-methylcytidylic acid.* The relative frequencies of C and its methylated derivative, M, among the several fractions of rye-germ DNA is not constant (Table 1). This immediately dismisses the concept of a random replacement of cytosine by 5-methyl cytosine in the pattern of nucleotide sequence. The frequency of specific pyrimidine runs in these fractions was estimated through preliminary ion-exchange chromatographic fractionation of the acid digests followed by secondary paper chromatographic separation of the components (Shapiro and Chargaff, 1960). These results and subsequent extended studies (Spencer and Chargaff, 1963a) brought into focus some features of the special placement of M in the polymer. The preferential disposition of M adjacent to purine nucleotides, most likely guanylic acid (Sinsheimer, 1954), was clearly established. There was in all fractions, furthermore, a better correlation of the relative frequency of the two *5-methyl* pyrimidines, thymine and methylcytosine, in runs of length 1 than there was of the relative frequency of the two *6-amino* pyrimidines, cytosine and methylcytosine. These and other correlations confirmed the nonrandom nature of the nucleotide arrangement among the fractions of rye-germ DNA and particularly the nonrandom replacement of C by the methylated derivative, M.

Extension of these studies to the longer pyrimidine runs was made possible by DEAE-cellulose chromatographic procedures (Spencer and Chargaff, 1961) developed for oligonucleotide separation (Tener *et al.*, 1958). A representative DEAE-cellulose fractionation by gradient concentration elution is reproduced in Fig. 2, which shows a distinct separation of the component isostich groups. The recovery of pyrimidines is quantitative. Identification and estimation of individual components relied upon a two-dimensional paper chromatographic separation of the components of each isostich. These techniques confirmed the nonrandom replacement of C by M within the longer pyrimidine runs of the DNA structure of wheat- and rye-germ DNA.

The question of the mechanism by which a disproportionate introduction of a structurally similar nucleotide is effected is not entirely clear. Certainly a nearest-nucleotide-neighbor influence involving a purine nucleotide is a pertinent factor. Whether this influence is exerted prior to the polymerization stage of the precursors — the alignment stage — or at a postpolymerization stage, during which enzymic methylation of a protopolymer containing no methylcytosine occurs, is yet to be clarified. A group of methylating enzymes that exist in microorganisms has been described (Gold *et al.*, 1963), but no definite evidence exists for a specificity of methylation in DNA which would

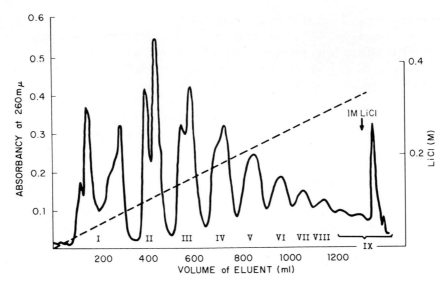

**Fig. 2.** Chromatographic fractionation of an acid hydrolysate of wheat-germ DNA into isostich groups, $n = 1$ to 9 (Fractions I to IX). DEAE-cellulose (1.0 g, 325 mesh, 15 cm by 1 cm column) was used to adsorb a neutralized acid hydrolysate of 20 mg DNA (1 ml 0.1 M $H_2SO_4$, 100°C, 35 min). Components were eluted with an increasing linear concentration gradient of LiCl to 0.32 M in 0.01 M lithium acetate, *p*H 5, using a nine-chamber mixing device. Total volume of eluent was 1,350 ml. After gradient elution, column was washed with 200 ml 1.0 M LiCl. Absorbancy was recorded by a continuous-flow UV monitor. (From Spencer and Chargaff, 1963, *Biochim. Biophys. Acta* 68: 9.)

fit the present data. In this respect, the specificity of these enzymes is not as unequivocal in action as the several enzymes responsible for the glucosylation of hydroxymethylcytosine (HMC) in phage DNA (Josse and Kornberg, 1962). Nucleotide arrangement studies in phage $T_4$ DNA do clearly indicate that a strong nearest-nucleotide-neighbor effect governing glucosylation of specific HMC does exist (Lunt *et al.*, 1964).

*General patterns of nucleotide arrangement.* Hitherto, most discussions and interpretations of the nucleotide arrangement in DNA have been satisfied by the demonstration of some degree of displacement between experimentally observed frequencies of runs and those calculated from a random distribution of nucleotides. The degree of this nonrandomness varies with the cellular origin of the DNA (Shapiro and Chargaff, 1957c). At present, more attention is directed toward the derivation of empirical correlations among the experimental data with the aim of eliciting some features of nucleotide arrangement common to all DNAs. These studies are thus concerned with structural orderliness in the DNA polymer, an orderliness which may be expected to be preserved among DNAs within the accepted scheme of uniformity of genetically controlled cellular functions. Some results of these investigations will be discussed presently.

*Diversity of nucleotide composition.* The wide range of DNA composition from diverse cellular sources permits classification of DNAs into distinct groups (Chargaff, 1955): the AT-type, in which adenine and thymine predominate and the dissymmetry ratio, $(A+T)/(G+C)$, exceeds 1; the GC-type, in which guanine and cytosine abound, and the dissymmetry ratio is below 1; and the equimolar type, with a dissymmetry ratio near 1. Among the tissue sources that are available for the preparation of nucleic acids, bacteria offer material from which DNAs of a wide range of composition are readily isolated. Analyses compiled in several reviews (Chargaff, 1955; Lee *et al.*, 1956; Belozersky and Spirin, 1960; Brawerman and Shapiro, 1962) indicate a range extending from the extreme AT-type exhibited by *Clostridium perfringens* (var. Fred), $(A+T)/(G+C) = 2.70$, to the extreme GC-type found in *Micrococcus lysodeikticus*, $(A+T)/(G+C) = 0.39$. The oft-studied DNAs of the Enterobacteriaceae, *Escherichia coli* and *Salmonella typhimurium*, are midpoints in this value range, exhibiting an equimolar complement of nucleotides. These variations of composition do, however, arrange themselves in an orderly manner, so that organisms showing close species relationship have similar DNA compositions. These observations have already given cause for a taxonomic re-evaluation of one microorganism (Lee *et al.*, 1956).

Does the exhibition of such a range of DNA compositions in bacteria and the implied similar, but not necessarily identical, range of an RNA fraction directly responsible for protein synthesis obscure some features of nucleotide arrangement common to the DNAs of all these organisms? On the contrary, it is expected that a study of DNA preparations of wide compositional differences should make similarities of structure more readily discernible, if they exist. For this reason, the pyrimidine nucleotide runs in the DNAs from *Rhodopseudomonas spheroides*, *E. coli*, *S. typhimurium*, *Salmonella typhosa*, *Bacillus subtilis*, and *Bacillus cereus* were determined (Shapiro, *et al.*, 1965). The DNA of coliphage $T_3$, which has a composition similar to the host *E. coli* DNA, was included in this study to determine how profound is the similarity of structures between these viral and host nucleic acids. The compositions of these DNA preparations are compiled in Table 2. Unless specific efforts have been made to eliminate polysaccharides, preparations of bacterial DNA usually have non-nucleic acid phosphorus associated with them, which probably originates from cell-wall structures. All analytical results, however, are eventually expressed on the basis of DNA phosphorus.

## TABLE 2

### COMPOSITION OF DEOXYRIBONUCLEIC ACIDS UNDER SURVEY

(From Shapiro et al., 1965, *Nature* 205: 1068.)

| Prep. No. | Source | Moles per 100 g-atoms of DNA phosphorus* | | | | Molar ratios | | |
|---|---|---|---|---|---|---|---|---|
| | | A | G | C | T | (A+T)/(G+C) | (A+G)/(C+T) | (A+C)/(G+T) |
| 1 | *B. cereus* MB-19 | 31.2 | 18.8 | 18.2 | 31.8 | 1.70 | 1.00 | 0.98 |
| 2 | Coliphage T$_3$ | 24.9 | 24.5 | 25.6 | 25.1 | 1.00 | 0.97 | 1.02 |
| 3 | *E. coli* B | 24.5 | 24.7 | 25.9 | 24.9 | 0.98 | 0.97 | 1.02 |
| 4 | *E. coli* 15 t⁻arg⁻ | 24.8 | 25.3 | 25.4 | 24.5 | 0.97 | 1.00 | 1.01 |
| 5 | *S. typhimurium* LT-7 | 24.7 | 24.6 | 26.7 | 24.1 | 0.95 | 0.97 | 1.06 |
| 6 | *S. typhosa* 643 | 24.0 | 26.0 | 25.7 | 24.3 | 0.93 | 1.00 | 0.99 |
| 7 | *Ser. marcescens* | 20.4 | 29.4 | 29.6 | 20.6 | 0.69 | 0.99 | 1.00 |
| 8 | *Rh. spheroides*, strain 2.4.1 | 16.1 | 33.9 | 33.8 | 16.2 | 0.48 | 1.00 | 1.00 |
| 9 | *Rh. spheroides*, strain CCI | 16.1 | 33.1 | 35.3 | 15.3 | 0.46 | 0.97 | 1.06 |

* See footnote, Table 1.

*Common features of nucleotide arrangement in bacterial DNA.* A proper evaluation of data from these studies requires the employment of standardized conditions of hydrolysis and techniques of analysis. The several procedures which have been devised for the separation of pyrimidine runs from DNA digests are each less than perfect because of intermediate manipulations or treatment of the hydrolysate (Shapiro and Chargaff, 1964). The techniques presently in use in this laboratory rely on two procedures: 1) DEAE-cellulose fractionation of the pyrimidine isostichs (Spencer and Chargaff, 1961), exemplified in Fig. 2; and 2) direct examination of the DNA digest by paper chromatography (Shapiro and Chargaff, 1963). A schematic identification pattern of a typical two-dimensional paper chromatographic separation of pyrimidine runs is reproduced in Fig. 3. The chromatographic pattern reveals a series of components, whose identities have been ascertained by independent means, aligned in a specific orientation. The arrangement is orderly with respect to both length of run and regular changes in composition. Consequently, the area in which a suspected component should be found is precisely predictable. This serves as a guide in recognizing infrequently encountered runs. Quantitative estimations of the pyrimidine runs are based on molar extinction data which have been previously tabulated (Spencer and Chargaff, 1963b).

The molar frequency of pyrimidine isostichs in a DNA constructed on the plan of random distribution of nucleotides is an exponential relationship with respect to isostich length, $n$. The number of isostichs per total pyrimidine complement, $0.5^{n+1}$, makes this clear. An easier recognition of this mathematical relationship is possible when the logarithms of the frequencies are employed. The consequent straight line, defined by

$$\log F = -0.301\, n + \log 50 \tag{1}$$

is included in Fig. 4 as the broken line. The experimental estimation of isostichs made either by the summation of runs from two-dimensional chromatograms or from phosphorus data derived from DEAE-cellulose fractionation also shows an exponential correlation to isostich length. The line $A$, Fig. 4, formulated from analyses of bacterial DNA preparations 1, 3, 5, and 9 and of $T_3$ coliphage DNA, 2, Table 2, employing the former procedure, is

$$\log F = -0.282\, n + \log 28.8 \tag{2}$$

while line $B$, Fig. 4, based on analyses of DNA preparations 4, 6, 7, and 8, Table 2, employing the latter technique, is

$$\log F = -0.282\, n + \log 42.5 \tag{3}$$

These two lines, though not coincident, because of differences in technique, have an identical slope, $-0.282$. This value is not significantly different from the slope, $-0.301$, derived from the equation based on randomness.

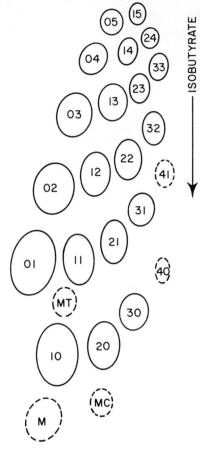

**Fig. 3.** Schematic representation of separation of pyrimidine oligonucleotides, $Py_np_{n+1}$, by two-dimensional chromatography. Composition of each run indicated by a cipher and digit or by two digits, with number of C units followed by number of T units; e.g., 10 is $Cp_2$, 01 is $Tp_2$, 13 is $CT_3p_5$, 32 is $C_3T_2p_6$, etc. Areas containing 5-methylcytidylic acid are marked separately. Zones indicated by broken lines are positions where the runs $MCp_3$, $MTp_3$, $C_4p_5$, and $C_4Tp_6$ have been encountered with hydrolysates of calf-thymus DNA. Isopropanol-ammonia development for 70 hr was followed by 24-hr development in the buffered ammonium isobutyrate solvent. Whatman 1 filter sheets, 46 cm × 50 cm. (From Shapiro and Chargaff, 1963, *Biochim. Biophys. Acta* 76: 1.)

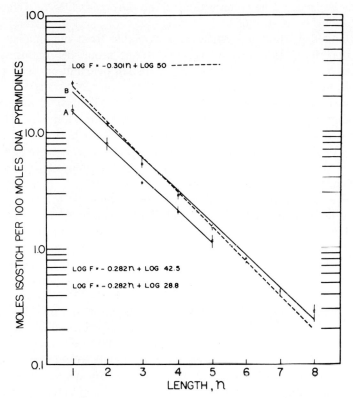

**Fig. 4.** *A*: frequencies of pyrimidine isostichs of length 1 to 5 in DNA of *B. cereus, E. coli, S. typhimurium, Rh. spheroides,* and coliphage T₃ (preps. 1, 3, 5, 9, and 2 in Table 2). Direct two-dimensional paper chromatography. *B*: frequencies of pyrimidine isostichs of length 1 to 8 in DNA of *E. coli, S. typhosa, Ser. marcescens,* and *Rh. spheroides* (preps. 4, 6, 7, and 8 in Table 2). DEAE-cellulose fractionation. Solid lines represent the best fit calculated from experimental values, whose spread and arithmetic mean are also shown. Broken line indicates the frequencies expected from a random distribution of nucleotides. Equations refer to the lines in the same order as they appear.

The striking agreement of isostich distribution among the several preparations of DNAs of different compositions suggests that a common frequency of pyrimidine and presumably purine isostichs can be allocated to microbial DNAs. Into this fixed structural feature, which reflects the fixed complement of Py in DNA, the more complex frequency and arrangement of specific pyrimidine oligonucleotide runs is distributed. This distribution will obviously depend on the composition of the particular DNA. Refer to the term $(C + T)^n$ on page 126.

The limited pyrimidine isostich data available from mammalian DNAs suggest that the DNAs of each large taxonomic group of organisms might be characterized by a distinct pyrimidine isostich distribution. The slope of the equation relating logarithm of isostich frequencies to their lengths in calf-thymus and human-spleen DNAs is $- 0.238$ (Shapiro *et al.*, 1965), a value significantly different from the term based on randomness. This relationship confirms an early observation that there is a bias toward a lower frequency of shorter runs and higher frequency of longer runs than expected by randomness of nucleotide arrangement, with the point of intersection at $n = 4$ (Spencer and Chargaff, 1963a).

The equations that have been derived are of some use to extrapolate the frequency of isostichs that cannot be adequately estimated by present techniques. Before this can be done, it is necessary to instill some confidence that there is no deviation of these linear relationships. Using Eq. (3), the longest pyrimidine isostich that can be accommodated in a DNA containing 5,500 pyrimidine nucleotides is of length 12. Analyses for pyrimidine and purine isostichs in isotopically labeled bacteriophage $\phi$X174 DNA afford data for the limit length of isostich in a DNA of defined length and one closely allied to a bacterial source: 5,500 nucleotides in the single-strand species and an assumed complementary structure composed of 11,000 nucleotides. A pyrimidine isostich of length 11 is the limit run in the single-strand form, while one tract of 14 purines has been estimated (Sedat and Sinsheimer, 1964). In the complementary duplex, therefore, the existence of a pyrimidine isostich of length 14 would be anticipated. Within the limits of the experimental difficulties attendant upon the estimation of purine isostichs, the agreement of the experimentally determined limit with that value predicted from extrapolation of Eq. (3) (Fig. 4, *B*) is good.

If the protostructure of DNA originated through random condensation of nucleotide precursors from a milieu of uncertain composition, then the complementary DNA diad structure, whenever it may have developed, would exhibit the pyrimidine isostich frequency defined by Eq. (1). The over-all change from this initial structure to the polynucleotide structure of the bacterial DNAs encountered in the present studies is not very extensive. This does not imply any specific placement of bacteria in the scale of cellular evolution. Some of the nucleotide transitions that may have accumulated during the course of the polymer replication are of the type $Pu1 \rightleftarrows Pu2$ and $Py1 \rightleftarrows Py2$, where each change would define the change in the complementary polynucleotide strand. These alterations would produce neither a change in the frequency of pyrimidine or purine isostichs nor a change in the polynucleotide framework, the spacing of isostichs, in organisms that may arise as a consequence. This nucleotide framework would, moreover, remain fixed whether the transitions were random or biased within the polymer. Alternatively, a lengthy series of random transitions of the type Pu $\rightleftarrows$ Py would allow variation of nucleotide sequence, so that, while the frequency of isostichs is maintained, the polymer framework may shift. Although the disposition of isostichs escapes recognition because of the analytical procedures, it is unlikely that the isostich framework in diverse bacterial DNAs is an invariant feature of their structure. Consequently, these Pu $\rightleftarrows$ Py transitions would appear to account for any structural variations among bacterial DNAs.

These interpretations may be extended to DNAs of a taxonomically higher group of organisms. In contrast to the structure of bacterial DNAs, the pyrimidine isostich frequency observed in mammalian DNAs differs significantly from the random nucleotide sequence, and is reflected in the change in slope from $- 0.301$ to $- 0.238$ in the derived equations. This change may be appreciated as a cumulative effect of *nonrandom* Pu $\rightleftarrows$ Py transitions within the polymer.

*Specific features of nucleotide arrangement in bacterial DNA.* We have seen that within the limits of the analytical techniques employed in these studies, the frequency of pyrimidine isostichs in bacterial DNAs is not significantly distinguishable from a polynucleotide structure constructed on the basis of randomness. However, the relative proportion of specific pyrimidine runs within these confines is independent of the profile of isostich frequency. The appropriate expansion of the term $(C + T)^n$, employing the C and T content in the DNA preparations from *Serrata marcescens*, *E. coli*, *S. typhosa*, and *Rh. spheroides*, allows calculation of the expected frequency of single, double, and triple C and T runs. These expected values and those values experimentally determined are included in Table 3. While the isostich frequency in bacterial DNAs may maintain the features of a random disposition of purines and pyrimidines, the finer details of arrangement concerning the individual pyrimidine is obviously nonrandom. Interpretation of these and other unpublished results indicates that among the nucleotide transitions cited previously, a particular bias for C $\rightleftarrows$ T transitions within Py runs longer than length 2 could account for the distortions observed.

Of further correlations that may be derived from the analyses of the bacterial DNAs, two may be mentioned at this time. These are the frequencies of the homopolymeric runs of cytidylic acid, $C_1$, $C_2$, $C_3$, etc., and of thymidylic acid, $T_1$, $T_2$, $T_3$, etc., compared to the compositions of the DNA preparations. Interest in these specific correlations was prompted by the observation that the longer runs of thymidylic acid up to $T_5$ were easily detected, while the detection of cytidylic acid runs longer than $C_3$ was difficult (Shapiro and Chargaff, 1963; Spencer and Chargaff, 1963a). We have observed a positive linear correlation between the composition of the DNA preparation and the contribution of pyrimidines to the respective homo-

## TABLE 3

RELATIVE FREQUENCIES OF PYRIMIDINE RUNS IN BACTERIAL DNA SPECIMENS*

| $n$ | Molar ratio† | E. coli 15 t⁻arg⁻ | | S. typhosa 643 | | Ser. marcescens | | Rh. spheroides, strain 2.4.1 | |
|---|---|---|---|---|---|---|---|---|---|
| | | Found | Random | Found | Random | Found | Random | Found | Random |
| 1 | C/T | 1.13 | 1.04 | 1.12 | 1.06 | 1.80 | 1.44 | 2.18 | 2.09 |
| 2 | $C_2/T_2$ | 1.43 | 1.08 | 1.40 | 1.12 | 3.01 | 2.07 | 4.71 | 4.36 |
| 3 | $C_3/T_3$ | 0.82 | 1.14 | 0.74 | 1.18 | 1.40 | 2.95 | 5.70 | 9.06 |

* Data from Shapiro et al., 1965.
† The ratios of the molar proportions of homologous runs of cytidylic acid and thymidylic acid found experimentally are compared with those expected from a random distribution in the DNA.

polymeric runs, $C_n$ and $T_n$ (Shapiro *et al.*, 1965). The arrangement of these series of lines clarifies the difficulty in observing the longer C runs. By extrapolation, these lines can permit an estimation of the frequency of runs that are experimentally difficult to estimate. Runs of C longer than $C_4$ have been observed when 0.5 g to 1.0 g of DNA is subjected to acid digestion (Petersen and Burton, 1964), but routine estimation of infrequent runs would be rather more amenable to analysis by the use of standard techniques applied to isotopically labeled DNA (Hall and Sinsheimer, 1963). There is, consequently, no abrupt cut-off for the frequency of C runs in DNA. These, and other correlations that, however, differ from the relations expected from a random disposition of constituents, add confidence to the concept of some general orderliness of nucleotide arrangement among DNAs of diverse compositions.

*Some conclusions.* We may conclude that the pyrimidine nucleotide isostich distribution in DNAs is constant. Variations that do exist reflect differences among widely separated taxonomic groups. Within this pattern, the disposition of individual sequences composed of T and C, though nonrandom, will follow an orderly pattern influenced by the composition of the DNA. A more inclusive generalization of the features of nucleotide arrangement awaits compilation of further data from a larger selection of cell sources.

### Purine Nucleotide Arrangement

The elimination mechanism that manifests itself during the acid digestion of DNA by the liberation of pyrimidine runs requires preliminary removal of the constituent purines. Similarly, a release of purine runs from DNA in studies of purine nucleotide arrangement requires a procedure that specifically removes the pyrimidine moieties and yet avoids the acidic conditions conducive to easy scission of the purine glycoside linkages. These requirements are satisfied by the reaction of anhydrous hydrazine on DNA (Takemura, 1959), a procedure that has been modified to obtain an apyrimidinic acid comparable in structure to apurinic acid (Chargaff *et al.*, 1963). The immediate product of the hydrazinolysis of DNA is a hydrazone derivative that reacts anomalously with the diphenylamine deoxypentose reagent. Similar observations were made with the hydrazone derivatives formed from cytidylic and thymidylic acids (Temperli *et al.*, 1964). Only after treatment with benzaldehyde does normal color development for deoxypentose become evident. The course of the hydrazinolytic reaction was investigated through the identification of products formed with pyrimidine nucleotides as model substrates. Deoxycytidylic acid yields stoichiometric quantities of urea, 3(5)aminopyrazole, and the hydrazone of 2-deoxyribosephosphate. The products of thymidylic acid decomposition are urea, 4-methyl,5-pyrazalone, and the hydrazone of 2-deoxyribosephosphate. These hydrazones could be quantitatively converted to 2-deoxyribosephosphate and benzalazine in the presence of benzaldehyde. The course of the reaction is depicted in Fig. 5. Treatment of the hydrazinolysis product of DNA with benzaldehyde effects the conversion of the hydrazone derivatives at former purine nucleotide loci into reactive aldehydo groups.

*Some comparisons of purine and pyrimidine arrangements.* Studies directed to elucidation of the purine nucleotide arrangement in DNA have immediate applicability. Together with available data on pyrimidine nucleotide arrangement, an experimental test of the complementarity and antiparallel nature of the nucleotide sequence within a DNA duplex structure becomes possible.

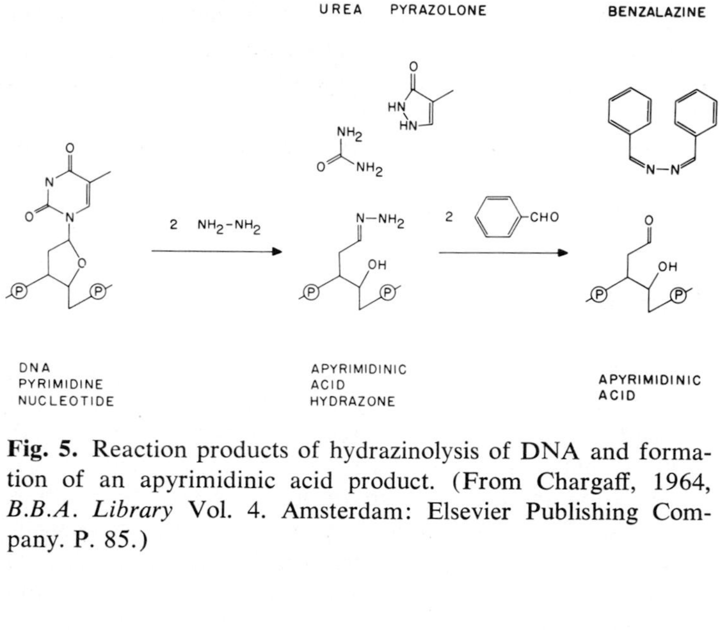

**Fig. 5.** Reaction products of hydrazinolysis of DNA and formation of an apyrimidinic acid product. (From Chargaff, 1964, *B.B.A. Library* Vol. 4. Amsterdam: Elsevier Publishing Company. P. 85.)

The DNA polymer, under current physicochemical concepts of a double-strand helix, may be considered as a continuous sequence at A–T and G–C nucleotide pairs. Such a structure strictly defines the relation and identity of purine and pyrimidine runs in the total DNA molecule. Two of the implied regularities are: 1) the frequency of purine isostichs is equal to the frequency of pyrimidine isostichs; 2) the frequency of a specific purine oligonucleotide on strand 1 is equal to the frequency of the complementary pyrimidine sequence on strand 2. An antiparallel association of polynucleotide strands, the 3′–5′ internucleoside linkages running in opposite directions, means that while pApAp should equal pTpTp, pApGp should equal pCpTp, but not pTpCp. This general problem is presently under investigation. Previous nearest-nucleotide-neighbor analyses applied to isotopically labeled products of polymerizing enzymes allude to such an antiparallel, complementary structure for DNA (Josse *et al.*, 1961). The present approach applied to native DNA is a more rigorous test.

The experimental details for the preparation of apyrimidinic acid are published (Chargaff *et al.*, 1963). The composition of an apyrimidinic acid of calf-thymus DNA is compared to compositions of an apurinic acid and a total DNA preparation (Table 4). The liberation of purine runs from apyrimidinic acid is accomplished under alkaline conditions, conditions that are conducive to the $\beta$-elimination reaction (Linstead *et al.*, 1953) and that have been shown to be equally applicable to the liberation of pyrimidine runs from apurinic acid (Shapiro and Chargaff, 1964). Apyrimidinic acid, 2% solution in 0.3 N KOH, was digested 35 min at 100°C in a boiling-water bath. Purine nucleotide isostichs were obtained by subsequent DEAE-cellulose fractionation similar to the gradient concentration elution procedure employed for the separation of pyrimidine runs (Spencer and Chargaff, 1961). The distribution of organic phosphate and UV optical density among the several fractions of purine isostichs follows the corresponding distributions among pyrimidine isostichs (Chargaff *et al.*, 1965). From this comparison, we may conclude that a general complementarity of nucleotide base-pairing holds for the calf-thymus DNA, material known to have a physical configuration of a well-ordered double helix by X-ray diffraction analysis (Watson and Crick, 1953; Wilkins *et al.*, 1953).

Preliminary studies on calf-thymus DNA (Spencer *et al.*, 1964) have indicated that for a given value of *n* the frequencies of adenylic acid and thymidylic acid runs are equivalent. Examination of the dinucleotide units CT and AG extends such correlations from a consideration of the complementarity features in DNA into a test of the antiparallel nature of the diad. The relative frequency of the sequence isomers pCpTp and pTpCp may be deter-

TABLE 4

COMPOSITION OF APURINIC AND APYRIMIDINIC ACID DERIVATIVES OF
CALF-THYMUS DNA

| Preparation | Moles of component per 100 g-atoms P* | | | | Molar ratios | | |
|---|---|---|---|---|---|---|---|
| | A | G | C | T | (A + T)/(G + C) | A/G | T/C |
| Calf-thymus DNA† | 28.7 | 21.5 | 21.2 | 28.6 | 1.34 | 1.33 | 1.35 |
| Apurinic acid‡ | — | — | 21.5 | 28.5 | — | — | 1.33 |
| Apyrimidinic acid† | 28.1 | 21.9 | — | — | — | 1.28 | — |

* See footnote, Table 1.
† From Chargaff *et al.*, 1965.
‡ From Chargaff, 1955.

mined enzymatically by employing the independent action of prostate phosphatase followed by snake-venom diesterase. Chromatographic separation and estimation of the ratio of the two nucleosides or the two nucleotides in the hydrolysate reflect the original ratio of isomers. The value of pCpTp/pTpCp is 0.79 (Chargaff *et al.*, 1965). A direct evaluation of the purine dinucleotide isomers can be made because pApGp and pGpAp or their dephosphorylated dinucleotides are readily separable by paper chromatography in the buffered ammonium isobutyrate solvent system. Spectrophotometric analysis of the components shows a ratio of pApGp/pGpAp of 0.75. These limited analyses do, therefore, indicate a total antiparallel character of the calf-thymus DNA duplex. Further analyses of the frequency of longer isomeric pyrimidine and purine runs are currently in progress.

**Concluding Remarks**

The elucidation of an explicit nucleotide sequence for a nucleic acid exhibiting what is generally termed a highly polymeric structure is an unfeasible task. Certain features of the nucleotide arrangement of DNAs, however, may be elicited by the techniques presently available. When data from a greater variety of DNA preparations become available, further generalizations and peculiarities of the nucleotide arrangement may become obvious. The plan of structure that has so far emerged is one that follows an orderly pattern, albeit not the one expected from a random linear array of constituent mononucleotides.

## ACKNOWLEDGMENT

Thankful acknowledgment is made to Prof. E. Chargaff for the frequent discussions during the course of investigations on the nucleotide arrangement in DNA and to Drs. Rivka Rudner and Hans Türler for discussions that were helpful during the preparation of this manuscript.

## REFERENCES

Anfinsen, C. B., and R. R. Redfield. 1956. In *Advan. Protein Chem.*, Vol. XI. New York: Academic Press, Inc. P. 1.

Armstrong, J. M., J. H. Coates, and R. K. Morton. 1963. *Biochem. J.* 88: 266.

Bayley, C. R., K. W. Brammer, and A. S. Jones. 1961. *J. Chem. Soc.* 1961: 1903.

Belozersky, A. N., and A. S. Spirin. 1960. In *The Nucleic Acids*, Vol. III, ed. E. Chargaff and J. N. Davidson. New York: Academic Press, Inc. P. 147.

Brawerman, G., and H. S. Shapiro. 1962. In *Comp. Biochem.*, Vol. IV B, ed. M. Florkin and H. S. Mason. New York: Academic Press, Inc. P. 107.

Burton, K., and G. B. Petersen. 1957. *Biochim. Biophys. Acta* 26: 667.

Cairns, J. 1963. *J. Mol. Biol.* 6: 208.

Chargaff, E. 1950. *Experientia* 6: 201.

Chargaff, E. 1955. In *The Nucleic Acids*, Vol. I, ed. E. Chargaff and J. N. Davidson. New York: Academic Press, Inc. P. 307.

Chargaff, E. 1963. *Essays on Nucleic Acids*. Amsterdam: Elsevier Publishing Company.

Chargaff, E. 1964. *B.B.A. Library*, Vol. 4. Amsterdam: Elsevier Publishing Company. P. 85.

Chargaff, E., J. Buchowicz, H. Türler, and H. S. Shapiro. 1965. *Nature* 206: 145.

Chargaff, E., C. F. Crampton, and R. Lipshitz. 1953. *Nature* 172: 289.

Chargaff, E., P. Rüst, A. Temperli, S. Morisawa, and A. Danon. 1963. *Biochim. Biophys. Acta* 76: 149.

Cohn, W. E., and E. Volkin. 1957. *Biochim. Biophys. Acta* 24: 359.

Crampton, C. F., R. Lipshitz, and E. Chargaff. 1954. *J. Biol. Chem.* 211: 125.

Dekker, C. A., A. M. Michelson, and A. R. Todd. 1953. *J. Chem. Soc.* 1953: 947.

Gold, M., J. Hurwitz, and M. Anders. 1963. *Proc. Natl. Acad. Sci. U.S.* 50: 164.

Hall, J. B., and R. L. Sinsheimer. 1963. *J. Mol. Biol.* 6: 115.

Hecht, L. I., M. L. Stephenson, and P. C. Zamecnik. 1959. *Proc. Natl. Acad. Sci. U.S.* 45: 505.

Hershey, A. D., and E. Burgi. 1960. *J. Mol. Biol.* 2: 143.

Holley, R. W., J. Apgar, G. A. Everett, J. T. Madison, M. Marquisee, S. H. Merrill, J. R. Penswick, and A. Zamir. 1965. *Science* 147: 1462.

Ingram, V. M., and J. G. Pierce. 1962. *Biochemistry* 1: 580.

Jones, A. S., M. Stacey, and B. E. Watson. 1957. *J. Chem. Soc.* 1957: 2454.

Josse, J., and A. Kornberg. 1962. *J. Biol. Chem.* 237: 1968.

Josse, J., A. D. Kaiser, and A. Kornberg. 1961. *J. Biol. Chem.* 236: 864.

Lee, K. Y., R. Wahl, and E. Barbu. 1956. *Ann. Inst. Pasteur* 91: 212.

Levene, P. A., and L. W. Bass. 1931. *Nucleic Acids.* New York: The Chemical Catalog Co.

Levene, P. A., and W. A. Jacobs. 1912. *J. Biol. Chem.* 12: 411.

Linstead, R. P., L. N. Owen, and R. F. Webb. 1953. *J. Chem. Soc.* 1953: 1211.

Lipshitz, R., and E. Chargaff. 1956. *Biochim. Biophys. Acta* 19: 256.

Lunt, M. R., J. C. Siebke, and K. Burton. 1964. *Biochem. J.* 92: 27.

Mood, A. M. 1940. *Ann. Math. Statist.* 11: 367.

Petersen, G. B., and K. Burton. 1964. *Biochem. J.* 92: 666.

Sedat, J., and R. L. Sinsheimer. 1964. *J. Mol. Biol.* 9: 489.

Shapiro, H. S., and E. Chargaff. 1956. *Federation Proc.* 15: 352.

Shapiro, H. S., and E. Chargaff. 1957a. *Biochim. Biophys. Acta* 26: 596.

Shapiro, H. S., and E. Chargaff. 1957b. *Biochim. Biophys. Acta* 26: 608.

Shapiro, H. S., and E. Chargaff. 1957c. *Biochim. Biophys. Acta* 23: 451.

Shapiro, H. S., and E. Chargaff. 1960. *Biochim. Biophys. Acta* 39: 68.

Shapiro, H. S., and E. Chargaff. 1963. *Biochim. Biophys. Acta* 76: 1.

Shapiro, H. S., and E. Chargaff. 1964. *Biochim. Biophys. Acta* 91: 262.

Shapiro, H. S., R. Rudner, K. Miura, and E. Chargaff. 1965. *Nature* 205: 1068.

Sinsheimer, R. L. 1954. *J. Biol. Chem.* 208: 445.

Sinsheimer, R. L. 1959. *J. Mol. Biol.* 1: 43.

Spencer, J. H., and E. Chargaff. 1961. *Biochim. Biophys. Acta* 51: 209.

Spencer, J. H., and E. Chargaff. 1963a. *Biochim. Biophys. Acta* 68: 9.

Spencer, J. H., and E. Chargaff. 1963b. *Biochim. Biophys. Acta* 68: 18.

Spencer, J. H., R. E. Cape, and T. Jaworska. 1964. *Abstr. Intern. Congr. Biochem., 6th, New York, 1964.* I: 87

Takemura, S. 1959. *Bull. Chem. Soc. Japan* 32: 920.

Tamm, C., and E. Chargaff. 1953. *J. Biol. Chem.* 203: 689.

Tamm, C., M. E. Hodes, and E. Chargaff. 1952a. *J. Biol. Chem.* 195: 49.

Tamm, C., H. S. Shapiro, and E. Chargaff. 1952b. *J. Biol. Chem.* 199: 313.

Temperli, A., H. Türler, P. Rüst, A. Danon, and E. Chargaff. 1964. *Biochim. Biophys. Acta* 91: 462.

Tener, G. M., H. G. Khorana, R. Markham, and E. H. Pol. 1958. *J. Am. Chem. Soc.* 80: 6223.

Watson, J. D., and F. H. C. Crick. 1953. *Nature* 171: 964.

Wilkins, M. H. F., A. R. Stokes, and H. R. Wilson. 1953. *Nature* 171: 738.

Wyatt, G. R. 1951. *Biochem. J.* 48: 584.

# Molecular Architecture of s-RNA

## G. L. Cantoni

*Laboratory of General and Comparative Biochemistry*
*National Institute of Mental Health*
*U. S. Department of Health, Education, and Welfare*
*Public Health Service*
*National Institutes of Health*
*Bethesda, Maryland*

## Molecular Biology

S-RNA molecules are perhaps unique among nucleic acids in that they perform a variety of functions. There is a great temptation to try to assign these diverse functions of s-RNA to specific areas of the molecule and to establish if and/or how the nucleotide sequences involved in these diverse functions might overlap.

The principal function of s-RNA is the transfer of activated amino acids from the cell cytoplasm to the growing peptide chains in the ribosomes. At least two steps can be recognized in the over-all process. These two steps have different requirements and take place in different cellular locations: the first step, amino acid activation, takes place in the soluble portion of the cell; the second step, transfer of the activated amino acid to the growing polypeptide chain, occurs in the ribosomes. The first step is described in Reactions (1a) and (1b):

(Reaction 1a)   $$\text{Amino acid} + \text{ATP} + \text{Enzyme} \underset{\xrightarrow{\hspace{0.8cm}}}{\xleftarrow{\hspace{0.8cm}} \text{Mg}^{++}}$$
$$\text{Aminoacyl} \sim \text{AMP—Enzyme} + \text{PP}_i$$

(Reaction 1b)   $$\text{Aminoacyl} \sim \text{AMP—Enzyme} + \text{s-RNA} \rightleftarrows$$
$$\text{Aminoacyl} \sim \text{s-RNA} + \text{AMP} + \text{Enzyme}$$

147

The mechanism of this step has become reasonably well understood, thanks to the work of Berg and Ofengand (1958), Hoagland *et al.* (1958), and others (reviewed by Berg, 1961; Brown, 1963).

It can be surmised from this formulation that the specificity in Step 1 depends on protein–nucleic acid interaction, namely, on the interaction between amino acid specific s-RNA and the corresponding amino acid–AMP synthetase complex.

Step 2 is a complex series of reactions involving ribosomes; aminoacyl-s-RNAs; m-RNA; GTP; and at least two soluble protein fractions with multiple requirements, such as, $Mg^{++}$, $K^+$, SH compounds. (In the earlier studies, ATP or an ATP-generating system appeared to be a requirement also; it is not entirely clear whether, in fact, ATP is needed for the polymerization reaction.) A minimum description of the growth of a polypeptide chain involves the following reactions:

(Reaction 2a)[1]

$$NH_2 \text{ peptidyl}_1 \sim \text{s-RNA}_1$$

$$\vdots$$

$$\text{Aminoacyl}_2 \sim \text{s-RNA}_2 + 50S \text{ ribosome} \cdots \text{m-RNA} \cdots 30S \text{ ribosome}$$

$$+ GTP \xrightarrow[\text{Enzyme 1—SH}]{Mg^{++}, K^+, —SH}$$

$$NH_2 \text{ peptidyl} \sim \text{s-RNA}_1$$

$$\vdots$$

$$50S \text{ ribosome} \cdots \text{s-RNA}_2 \cdots \text{m-RNA} \cdots 30S \text{ ribo-}$$
$$\wr \qquad\qquad\qquad\qquad \text{some} + (GDP + P_i)$$
$$\text{aminoacyl}_2$$

(Reaction 2b)

$$NH_2 \text{ peptidyl}_1 \sim \text{s-RNA}_1$$

$$\vdots$$

$$50S \text{ ribosome} \cdots \text{s-RNA}_2 \cdots \text{m-RNA} \cdots 30S \text{ ribo-}$$
$$\wr \qquad\qquad\qquad\qquad\qquad \text{(ATP)?}$$
$$\text{aminoacyl}_2 \qquad \text{some} \xrightarrow{\text{Enzyme 2}}$$

$$NH_2 \text{ peptidyl}_1 \text{ aminoacyl}_2 \sim \text{s-RNA}_2$$

$$\vdots$$

$$70S \text{ ribosome} + \text{s-RNA}_1$$

[1] The reactions should not be interpreted to imply any exact mode as to the linkages among 50S ribosome, 30S ribosome, s-RNA, and m-RNA.

(Reaction 2b′)

$$
\left\{
\begin{array}{l}
\text{NH}_2 \text{ peptidyl} \sim \text{s-RNA} \\
\qquad \vdots \\
\qquad 50\text{S ribosome} \cdots 30\text{S ribosome} + \text{s-RNA} \rightarrow \\[4pt]
\quad \text{NH}_2 \text{ peptidyl} \sim \text{s-RNA} \\
\qquad\qquad \vdots \\
\qquad\qquad 50\text{S ribosome} \cdots 30\text{S ribosome} \\
\qquad\qquad \vdots \\
\qquad\qquad \text{s-RNA}
\end{array}
\right.
$$

Uncharged s-RNA can be bound to the 50S moiety of a 70S ribosome (Cannon *et al.*, 1963) (see also Kaji, 1963, 1964, who describes a specific, m-RNA–dependent binding of uncharged s-RNA). Perhaps this observation suggests that Reaction (2b′) is a partial reversal of Reaction (2b) and that this interaction and the sites involved are not primarily related to the m-RNA translation function. The terminal —CpCpA sequence of s-RNA however is required for this type binding (see also below). On the other hand, a *specific* binding site for aminoacyl-s-RNA is suggested by Reaction (2a), which is dependent on m-RNA (Kaji and Kaji, 1963, 1964; Nakamoto *et al.*, 1963; Bernfield and Nirenberg, 1965, and GTP (Arlinghaus *et al.*, 1964). The peptide-chain growth through repetition of Reactions (2a) and (2b) must be accompanied in some unknown manner with movement of m-RNA on the 30S particle. It is not known if the polypeptidyl-s-RNA binds to a different site (Gilbert, 1963) from that which binds aminoacyl-s-RNA. In other words, we cannot choose at the present time between 1) the shuttling back and forth of the growing peptide chain between two equivalent sites in 50S particle; and 2) a process involving the specific binding of aminoacyl-s-RNA at site 1, reaction with peptidyl-s-RNA bound at site 2, and movement of the s-RNA chain carrying the elongated, growing peptide chain to site 2, freeing site 1 to accept a new aminoacyl-s-RNA. This second possibility appears more attractive from a mechanistic point of view. The description of only two sites is only schematic; it is indeed possible that there are more than two sites for binding of s-RNA to ribosomes, although present evidence suggests that only two s-RNAs are bound at any one time (Warner and Rich, 1964).

In Reaction (2b), which attempts to represent the peptide-elongation reaction, puromycin (Traut and Munro, 1964) or an oligonucleotide fragment $\cdots(\text{Xp}_n)\text{CpCpA-aminoacyl}$, where X cannot be guanosine and $n = 0, 1, 2, 3$, etc. (Takanami, 1964), can substitute for aminoacyl-s-RNA. In this case, however, the incomplete polypeptide is released in solution as polypeptidyl-puromycin or polypeptidyl-aminoacyl-ApCpCp($\text{X}_n$)$\cdots$ (see also Allen and Zamecnik, 1962; Nathans, 1964; Takanami, 1964; Traut and Munro, 1964). These observations indicate that, in addition to the $\cdots$CpCpA amino acid terminus, another portion of the s-RNA chain interacts with the ribosomal 50S moiety and contributes to the stability of the s-RNA peptide-ribosomal complex. It is noteworthy that the $\cdots$pCpA bond in this complex is protected from ribonuclease attack.

There is conflicting evidence on the requirement for GTP in the binding of s-RNA to the ribosomal site (compare Nakamoto *et al.*, 1963, and Arling-haus *et al.*, 1964). Two enzyme fractions are required for Step 2, perhaps one to catalyze the binding of s-RNA and ribosome, and the other to link the aminoacyl residues in the peptide chain. Recent evidence seems to suggest that only the first of these enzymes requires sulphydryl groups for activity (Traut and Munro, 1964; also Arlinghaus *et al.*, 1964).

In the simplest formulation, the key event in the translation of the linear triplet code in m-RNA into the polypeptide sequence in proteins, namely, the interaction between s-RNA and m-RNA, would be through complementary base-pairing of the Watson–Crick type. Indeed, the hypothesis that information translation occurs through complementary base-pairing may be part of the "central dogma," as Crick calls it. It may be well to point out, however, that a restrictive interpretation of this hypothesis is no longer permissible in view of the recent findings of Davies *et al.* (1964) and Gorini and Kataja (1964a, b). A specific informational role for the microsomal protein and/or RNA in this interaction is strongly implied by the discovery of a modulating effect of streptomycin on the specificity of coding by synthetic polyribonucleotides. Indeed, an "extreme" and perhaps "heretical" hypothesis has been proposed as a possible alternative by Spirin (1964). In this formulation, there would be no direct interaction between m-RNA and s-RNA; rather, the coding triplet in m-RNA would interact with a multi-functional ribosomal protein and, by "an allosteric" effect, cause it to develop a specific affinity for the corresponding s-RNA amino acid.

Personally, however, I find the hypothesis of direct interaction between m-RNA and s-RNA more attractive, and there is some evidence in favor of it and no evidence clearly incompatible with it.

While the main functions of s-RNA are described in Reactions (1a) and (1b), and (2a) and (2b), involvement of s-RNA in amino acid transfer of a special kind is suggested by the finding of Coronado *et al.* (1964) that the hydroxylation of proline and lysine prior to incorporation in peptide bond takes place while these amino acids are linked to s-RNA. Here, then, the Reaction (1a) and (1b) would be followed by (1c):

$$\text{(Reaction 1c)} \qquad \text{Prolyl} \sim \text{s-RNA} \xrightarrow{\text{O}_2} \text{Hydroxylprolyl} \sim \text{s-RNA}$$

prior to utilization of the hydroxylprolyl-s-RNA in Step 2.

In addition to these functions, which are intimately linked to the carrier role of s-RNA in cellular metabolism, a more complex function of s-RNA as a regulator or modulator of protein synthesis is suggested by some experiments. There is no general agreement that s-RNA indeed plays such a role, and even less is known as to how it may fulfill it.

In the broadest terms, it appears, on the basis of fragmentary experimental evidence, that s-RNA, but not aminoacyl-s-RNA, exhibits an inhibitory and control role on the synthesis of m-RNA by DNA-dependent RNA polymerase (Stent and Brenner, 1961; Gros et al., 1963; Zillig et al., 1964). In this way, depletion of amino acids, destined to stop protein synthesis, would also interrupt the translation of genetic information in DNA. It is not easy to see, however, how lack of a single amino acid would lead to this result, unless uncharged s-RNA is very active as an inhibitor of RNA polymerase. S-RNA also has been implicated in attempts to explain the phenomenon of polarity, or the order of genes in an operon, on a molecular basis (Ames and Hartman, 1963; Ames and Martin, 1964). There is, however, as yet no direct experimental evidence to support these stimulating hypotheses on regulator functions of s-RNA.

**Structure**

Current concepts on the conformation of s-RNA imply a highly asymmetric structure, perhaps consisting of a single chain folded back on itself, with the halves forming a double helix with each other. Direct evidence for a structure of this kind, such as would be provided by X-ray diffraction patterns, is not available.[2] However, a great deal of indirect evidence based on a variety of physicochemical, chemical, and enzymological approaches has led to the formulation of a structure of this type.

The evidence is as follows:

1. Ultracentrifugation studies and hydrodynamic shape. The molecular weight of average s-RNA derived from a variety of sources, such as *Escherichia coli*, yeast, mammalian liver, *Neurospora*, and others, is relatively uniform; values centering around 25,000 ± 1,000, or 70 nucleotides, have been reported by several investigators (Tissieres, 1959; Brown and Zubay, 1960; Osawa, 1960; Luborsky and Cantoni, 1962). That no important differences in molecular weight exist among several amino acid specific s-RNAs is also well established (Klee and Cantoni, 1960; Ofengand et al., 1961).

Ultracentrifugal analysis of average rabbit-liver s-RNA at low concentration, however, revealed a 12% sedimentation heterogeneity which may be due to small differences in the chain length or hydrodynamic shape (Luborsky

[2] Earlier conclusions based on X-ray diffraction patterns by Spencer and coworkers (1962) are no longer valid, since it has been shown that the material that they studied is not s RNA, but possibly a degradation product thereof (Spencer, 1963).

and Cantoni, 1962). With this reservation, then, the earlier conclusions of Klee and Cantoni (1960) and of Ofengand et al. (1961) that chain length is not a significant parameter in the determination of biological specificity are valid.

The sedimentation behavior of s-RNA indicates that this molecule is highly asymmetric and that the secondary structure of s-RNA is different from that of RNA of high molecular weight and is relatively more similar to the structure of DNA (Luborsky and Cantoni, 1962).

2. Ultraviolet hypochromicity. On heating in dilute salt, s-RNA exhibits marked hyperchromicity. It is to be assumed that hyperchromicity on heating is due to helix → coil transition (Doty et al., 1959). The following observations may then be made.

(a) The melting temperature is higher than that observed for other RNAs of comparable chain length, and the transition is not as broad, although it is much broader than it is for DNA.

(b) The broadness of transition observed in average s-RNA cannot be ascribed to the fact that average s-RNA consists of a complex mixture of different molecular species, since the melting curves of highly purified serine, alanine, and tyrosine s-RNAs are still considerably broader than those of DNA (of comparable chain length?). Fresco (1963) and Fresco et al. (1963) have reported that purified tyrosine, valine, and alanine s-RNAs exhibit biphasic melting curves. Fresco and his collaborators (1963) interpret this expression of noncooperative melting as an indication that helical regions in s-RNA are interrupted by nonhelical segments of undetermined length. The melting curve of purified serine s-RNA (Felsenfeld and Cantoni, 1964) does not exhibit a break in its profile, or, if a break exists, it is much less evident than in the purified s-RNAs studied by Fresco (1963).[3] A more detailed interpretation of the melting curve in terms of specific nucleotide sequence for serine s-RNA has been attempted by Felsenfeld and Cantoni (1964), using the multiwavelength-denaturation analysis technique developed by Felsenfeld and Sandeen (1962), and the results of this analysis agree quite closely with a tentative base-sequence model proposed on the basis of chemical analysis of partial oligonucleotide sequences (Cantoni et al., 1963).

(c) Mg++ has a dramatic effect on both the melting temperature and the sharpness of transition (Giacomoni and Spiegelman, 1962; Nishimura and Novelli, 1963). Mg++ also affects the helix → coil transition of DNA (Dove and Davidson, 1962) and of other ribonucleic acids (Boedtker, 1960). The effect on s-RNA, however, is more pronounced. With DNA, Mg++ and other divalent cations have a large effect on the melting temperature and a relatively small effect on the broadness of the helix → coil transition. With TMV RNA (Boedtker, 1960), the Mg++ affects both the temperature and the broadness

---

[3] It is of interest that s-RNA partially digested by snake-venom phosphodiesterase exhibits biphasic melting curves (Jacobson et al., 1964).

of the helix → coil transition, but in the presence of $Na^+$, and at high $Na^+$-to-$Mg^{++}$ ratios, the temperature of the helix → coil transition is determined by the $Na^+$ rather than by the $Mg^{++}$ concentration. With s-RNA, on the other hand, the $Mg^{++}$ determines the melting profile even in the presence of 500-fold excess of $Na^+$. The sharpness of the helix → coil transition in the presence of $Na^+$ and of very low concentrations of $Mg^{++}$ indicates that the s-RNA structure is capable of a degree of cooperative melting comparable to that seen in a perfectly base-paired structure. The effect of $Mg^{++}$ must thus be an expression of an important and characteristic feature of s-RNA structure. This is clearly revealed by examination of the melting curves of s-RNA that has been subjected to chemical modifications designed to affect base-pairing capacity of the Watson–Crick type. Formaldehyde treatment or methylation (Duval, Ebel, and Cantoni, unpublished observation) produces only a quantitative change in the melting curve profile *in the absence* of $Mg^{++}$; namely, there is a *decrease* in the magnitude of the hyperchromic effect, and melting is less cooperative, as shown by broadening of the transition phase. The important *qualitative* difference is that $Mg^{++}$ has essentially no effect under these conditions, which must indicate that the chemical modifications have markedly altered the structure of s-RNA. The hyperchromicity that develops in methylated or formaldehyde-treated s-RNA on heating could thus be caused by base-base interaction of a single-stranded type as is seen in poly-A or poly-C (Fasman *et al.*, 1964). Such a structure could be stabilized both by hydrogen bonds between complementary base pairs and by nonspecific base-base hydrophobic interaction.

(d) The hyperchromicity developed on heating is perfectly reversible on cooling, and reversibility is not time-dependent. In this respect, s-RNA is quite unlike native DNA (Geiduschek, 1961) and DNA enzymatically synthesized on native DNA template (Schildkraut *et al.*, 1964); the easy reversibility suggests that the bases involved are in close proximity to each other and do not require reorientation to re-form a hypochromic structure. It should be pointed out, however, that although it is certainly true that ultraviolet (UV) hyperchromicity is a manifestation of helix → coil transition, UV hypochromicity does not necessarily represent a Watson–Crick base-paired type of structure.

3. Fasman *et al.* (1964) recently performed a careful analysis of the optical rotatory dispersion (ORD) of s-RNA. The conclusion reached by these authors is that s-RNA exists in a highly ordered (probably helical) secondary structure. The relative contributions of hydrophobic forces and hydrogen bonds for the maintenance of the helical structure have been estimated, and the conclusion of these authors is that hydrophobic forces contribute most importantly to the stabilization of secondary structure. It should be pointed out, however, that, in these experiments, the specific effect of $Mg^{++}$ was

not investigated. It is fair to say, moreover, that the assignment of stabilization forces between hydrophobic and hydrogen bond is fraught with experimental and theoretical difficulties.

4. Rate of tritium-hydrogen exchange has been used by the Englanders (1965) to probe the structure of s-RNA. It is assumed that only the hydrogens involved in hydrogen bonds exchange slowly enough to be measured. These authors detected a variety of rates of deuterium exchange in average s-RNA and have shown that the rate depends on the stability of the corresponding helical segments. There are *ca.* 87 hydrogens available for the usual type of hydrogen-bonding in a 70-nucleotide s-RNA chain of average composition; of these, 77 are used in hydrogen-bonding. This indicates that about six bases plus the odd bases and the terminal $\cdots$CpCpA on the average are not involved in the usual type of hydrogen-bonding and must, therefore, be arranged in one or more than one single-stranded loop. In addition, there is a group of hydrogens exhibiting very slow exchange behavior, which must reflect some very stable structure, which might be common to most molecules. Quantitatively, this group of hydrogens corresponds to about seven base pairs per molecule and thus qualitatively and quantitatively agrees with the structural base-sequence model proposed by Cantoni *et al.* (1963) and analyzed further by Felsenfeld and Cantoni (1964). This agreement is, however, based on the interpretations of the experimental results, which interpretations in turn depend on a variety of working hypotheses. It can, therefore, only be considered suggestive until more data can be marshalled for and/or against the interpretations and the model.

5. Other data from physicochemical studies, such as circular dichroism (Mommaerts *et al.*, 1964), nuclear magnetic resonance (McTague *et al.*, 1964), and rate of reaction with formaldehyde (Penniston and Doty, 1963a, b; Kisselev and Frolova, 1964; Marciello and Zubay, 1964), all imply a highly asymmetric structure, and some of these data seem to favor a single chain folded back on itself like a hairpin, with the two halves forming a double helix.

Assuming for the present that this interpretation of the physicochemical data is valid, areas of uncertainty concerning at least two features of this s-RNA structure remain unresolved. One is the existence and location of imperfection in the base-paired limb. The other is the fine structure of the region involved in the turn. A minimum of three nucleotides is required for the turn. Since all estimations agree that base-pairing is not as complete as would be required if only a three-nucleotide sequence were responsible for the turn (Felsenfeld and Sandeen, 1962; McCully and Cantoni, 1962; Armstrong *et al.*, 1964; Marciello and Zubay, 1964), two possibilities present themselves: 1) the region that is not base-paired linking the two base-paired limbs is longer than three nucleotides; and 2) there are areas that are not base-paired breaking up the continuity of the helical region, in addition to the three nucleotides required for the turn. Various combinations of these basic alternatives are shown in Fig. 1.

At the present state, a choice between these alternatives is difficult, for, to paraphrase Shakespeare, "equalities are so weighed that curiosity in neither can make choice of either's virtue."

## Chemistry

It was realized quite early in the history of s-RNA that it differed both in chemical composition and in biochemical characteristics from other ribonucleic acids. From a chemical point of view, s-RNA has several distinct characteristics and one unique feature. In average s-RNA, that is, in a population of different amino acid specific s-RNA chains, A + U and G + C are present in equivalent amounts (Singer and Cantoni, 1960; Brown, 1963), a finding that suggested several years ago that an important fraction of the bases might be base-paired in the Watson–Crick type. In addition to the four major components, there is a variety of methylated purines and pyrimi-

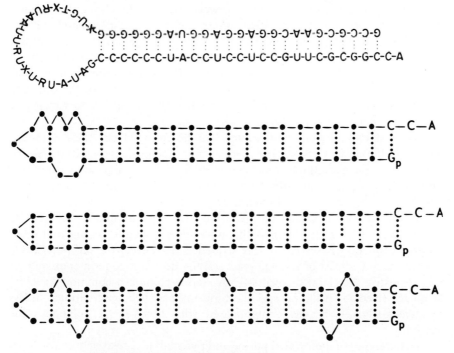

**Fig. 1.** Possible models for s-RNA.

dines. The compositions of s-RNA preparations obtained from a wide variety
of biological sources by different extraction procedures are strikingly similar
(Brown *et al.*, 1962; Cantoni, 1962). The finding that molecular weight is not
a significant parameter in the determination of biological specificity suggested
that the specificities of s-RNAs are attributable to differences in base sequence
and/or composition.

From a multitude of investigations from several different laboratories on
s-RNAs of different biological origins and different amino acid specificities,
certain additional features of the s-RNAs have emerged. All chains have
similar terminal sequences. At the 3'-OH terminus, the common sequence is
$\cdots$CpCpA (Hecht *et al.*, 1959; Berg *et al.*, 1961). The aminoacyl residue is
bound in ester linkage to the 2'- or 3'-OH (Zachau *et al.*, 1958; Feldman and
Zachau, 1964; Wolfenden *et al.*, 1964).

At the 5'-phosphate terminus, 5'-pGp is found in 80–90% of the chains
(Singer and Cantoni, 1960; Zillig *et al.*, 1960). A small fraction of chains end
with 5'-pAp and 5'-pUp (Ralph *et al.*, 1963; Bell *et al.*, 1964), but it is not
known whether these chains are still biologically active and whether they represent specific molecules. It should be pointed out that, in the few cases where
purified amino acid specific s-RNAs have been analyzed, pGp has been found
to be the only nucleotide present at the 5'-phosphate terminus; removal of
5'-pGp may lead to loss of activity. However, loss of the 5'-monoester phosphate (Harkness and Hilmoe, 1962) or its chemical modification (RajBhandary *et al.*, 1964) does not lead to modification of the amino acid acceptor
function. The code for s-RNA amino acid recognition is universal (von Ehrenstein and Lipmann, 1961). Once bound to s-RNA, the amino acid as such
cannot be recognized by the protein-synthetizing machinery of the cell, and
its position in the peptide chain is determined by the s-RNA to which it is
attached (Chapeville *et al.*, 1962).

At least two obvious conclusions can be drawn from these findings:
1) neither the $\cdots$CpC*p*A nor the pGp terminal sequence is part of the amino
acid recognition site; 2) the amino acid polymerase, the enzyme that links the
activated amino acid in s-RNA in a peptide chain, is neither amino acid
specific nor sensitive to the biological origin of s-RNA.

It has been claimed that all s-RNA chains have a common GTCΨUG
sequence (Holley *et al.*, 1964). If this were true, it would suggest that some
common function is served by this sequence. However, the tetranucleotide
fraction of a $T_1$ digest of average yeast s-RNA does not contain enough T or
ΨU to justify the claim that all s-RNA chains contain a common TCΨUG
sequence (Neelon, Ishikura, and Cantoni, unpublished observations) unless
average s-RNA is heavily contaminated with non-s-RNA polynucleotide
material.

The presence of methylated purine and pyrimidine is relatively characteristic for s-RNA (Dunn, 1959; Cantoni *et al.*, 1962). It is true that these com-

ponents have been found also in other RNAs (microsomal) (Starr and Fefferman, 1964) and in DNA (Wyatt, 1950; Dunn and Smith, 1955), but they are found in higher amounts in s-RNAs and are completely absent in viral RNAs. The function of the methylated bases has received much attention, but is yet to be clarified. The following facts have been established.

1. The pattern of methylation is different in s-RNAs derived from different biological sources. This can be shown by both chemical analysis (Dunn *et al.*, 1960; Zamecnik, 1962; Peterkofsky *et al.*, 1964; Holley *et al.*, 1963; Cantoni *et al.*, 1965) and enzymatic analysis (Hurwitz *et al.*, 1964). Enzymatically, s-RNA from *E. coli* can be over-methylated, using s-RNA methylase partially purified from other organisms (Hurwitz *et al.*, 1964). It is interesting that the patterns of methylation for s-RNAs specific for the same amino acid, but derived from two different species, are different: thus, it has been shown in this laboratory that serine s-RNA from yeast contains one residue of 2-dimethyl-guanylic acid per chain, whereas serine s-RNA from *E. coli* does not contain dimethylguanylic acid residues (Nathenson *et al.*, 1965).

2. The methylated bases are clustered close together (McCully and Cantoni, 1962; Staehelin, 1964).

3. They are not located in the first one-third of the molecule (Nihei and Cantoni, 1962; Hurwitz *et al.*, 1964).

4. The absence of methylated bases does not affect acceptor activity when s-RNA is assayed with homologous enzymes (Littauer *et al.*, 1963; Starr, 1963) though they may influence specificity toward heterologous enzymes (Peterkofsky, 1964).

5. In the *E. coli* methionine auxotroph mutant of Fleissner and Borek (1962), the m-RNA–dependent amino acid transfer step is somewhat less effective in methyl-poor s-RNA than in fully methylated s-RNA systems. A more critical test of the possible role of the methylated bases in the regulation of transfer specificity has not been done and is difficult, if not impossible, to do at the present state of our technology.

6. The degree of methylation of s-RNA may alter the sensitivity of s-RNA toward endonucleases, as the methylated bases may be more resistant to some of the specific (McCully and Cantoni, 1962) and nonspecific endonucleases (Littauer, 1964) than are the corresponding nonmethylated bases in s-RNA.

A variety of hypotheses on the role of methylation in s-RNA has been based upon the above facts. For instance, it has been suggested that 1) methylated bases modulate the coding properties of s-RNA, 2) they determine the specificity of interaction with activating enzymes, 3) they insure single-strandedness in the coding triplet region, and 4) they impart resistance to enzymatic attack in bases not base-paired and thus potentially are less suscept-ible to attack. These hypotheses are not mutually exclusive, and only further experimentation will reveal whether they are, in fact, valid.

The unique feature in s-RNA chemistry is the presence of two or three pseudouridylic acid residues per chain. Pesudouridylic acid is a riboside of a unique structure, since the ribose chain is attached to the $C_5$ instead of the $N_1$ position of uridine. Chemically, this imparts several distinct features to the molecule (Tomasz and Chambers, 1964a, b), in addition to providing unique structural properties. How these features are related to biological function is not known; one suggestion is that pseudouridine functions as a punctuation mark, and this will be discussed below.

Over-all nucleotide composition and partial base sequences are different in the various amino acid specific s-RNAs (Cantoni et al., 1963; Holley et al., 1963; Armstrong et al., 1964). With regard to degenerate species of s-RNA, it has been shown that these differ with regard not only to the coding se-quences, but also to those areas of the molecule (which may or may not include the coding triplets) that are involved in the interaction with the acti-vating enzymes. Berg et al. (1962) and Herbert et al. (1964) have shown that at least two nucleotide sequences are immediately adjacent to the terminal-CpCpA triplet in leucine and valine s-RNAs. A reasonable interpretation of this finding is that these sequences correspond to two degenerate species of leucine and valine s-RNA, respectively. The experiments of Bennett et al. (1963) reveal the interesting fact that degenerate species of leucine and serine E. coli s-RNA behave differently when tested as substrates with activating enzymes derived from E. coli and yeast. On the other hand, since highly purified activating enzymes can recognize all the corresponding degenerate species of homologous s-RNAs, there must be large areas of the molecule that are identical or at least quite similar. A quantitative evaluation of the areas of similarity that are necessary and the degree of difference that is per-missible is not yet possible, but may be forthcoming soon.

The simplest hypothesis concerning the amino acid donor site is that it consists of a nucleotide triplet complementary in composition to the codon on m-RNA. There is as yet no firm evidence that such a triplet in fact exists in s-RNA, although most of the available evidence is compatible with this hypothesis and none is clearly incompatible with it. In purified s-RNAs, various workers have detected triplets with base compositions complementary to those of the codons. Such is the case for serine s-RNA, PypApGpApΨUp; alanine, GpGpC; valine, GpApApCp.[4] Miura (1964) found that ApApApΨU occurs in average s-RNA in about one out of 20 chains; Zamecnik (1962)

---

[4] It would be of great interest to know if the sequence GpApApCpΨUp is present in valine s-RNA. This cannot be decided from published data (Armstrong et al., 1964). On the other hand, it is clearly possible, since in valine s-RNA, two pseudouridines per chain are in PypΨU sequences.

reported preliminary results of Berquist on the presence of ApApAp sequences in phenylalanine s-RNA of undetermined purity. More significant
would be the identification of the ApApAp triplet in pure phenylalanine
s-RNA, or at least the demonstration of enrichment of this triplet parallel to
enrichment in phenylalanine acceptor activity, during phenylalanine s-RNA
purification.

The suggestion that pseudouridine might function as a punctuation mark
has been advanced by Miura (1964) on the basis of the finding of ApApApΨUp
in average s-RNA and by Cantoni et al. (1963) on the basis of the finding of
the sequence PypApGpApAp in purified serine s-RNA. It may thus be noted
that speculation on the possible function of pseudouridine as a punctuation
mark for the coding triplet has developed along parallel lines in various
laboratories. Pseudouridine is an attractive candidate as a punctuation mark
because of its ability to form hydrogen bonds with guanosine and cytidine
as well as with adenosine.

Even if we should provisionally accept the hypothesis that AAAΨU and
AGAΨU are the coding triplets in phenylalanine s-RNA and serine s-RNA,
respectively, the location of the punctuation mark is specified only if we
assume that base-pairing interaction is of the classical Watson–Crick type,
that is, antiparallel. However, some other type of specific base-pairing interaction might be possible, considering that the sequences involved are short.
It is therefore not clear whether the hypothetical pseudouridine punctuation
mark would signify the beginning or the end of the coding triplet, since the
hypothetical coding sequences in phenylalanine and serine s-RNA are symmetrical. This is shown below.

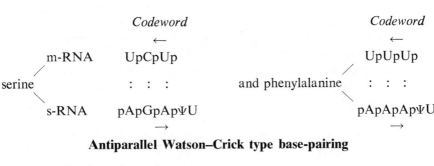

**Antiparallel Watson–Crick type base-pairing**

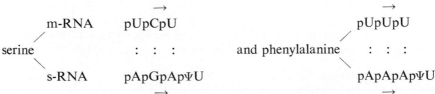

**Parallel, but specific, type of base-pairing**

It is by no means certain that the nucleotide sequences involved in the interaction with the activating enzyme are completely different from those responsible for interaction with m-RNA; there is, however, some evidence that suggests that different molecular arrangements are responsible for these two functions of s-RNA. This may be deduced from the experiment quoted above of Bennett *et al.* (1963) on the specificity of heterologous activating enzymes for only one of the two degenerate species of leucine s-RNA.[5]

More direct evidence was developed by Yu and Zamecnik (1963), who concluded from a study of the effect of bromination on the amino acid accepting activities of s-RNA that the nucleotide sequence responsible for recognition of the phenylalanine-activating enzyme contains at least one bromine-sensitive residue, probably a pyrimidine. Thus, it must differ from the pApApAp sequence that is suggested as a codeword in s-RNA by the discovery (Nirenberg and Matthaei, 1961) that poly-U codes for phenylalanine. Similar conclusions were reached by Weil *et al.* (1964) on the basis of bromination and methylation of s-RNA. These authors have found a decrease in the lysine-acceptor capabilities of s-RNA after chemical methylation. Since chemical methylation cannot modify the pUpUpU sequence, which in s-RNA would correspond to the codeword for lysine in m-RNA (Gardner *et al.*, 1962), Weil and coworkers concluded that the nucleotide sequence sensitive to methylation is different from the "coding" triplet.

## Conclusions

From the combined evidence reviewed above, the following emerge.

1. The amino acid is attached to the 2'- or 3'-OH.

2. The terminal adenosine is necessary not only for amino acid attachment but also for interaction with the activating enzyme.

3. Structural alterations in the 5'-phosphate end of the chain are without effect on the acceptor activity, though their effect on amino acid donor function remains untested.

4. The evidence is only circumstantial that the interaction with m-RNA involves a triplet with composition complementary to the amino acid codewords. The presumptive evidence is strong that the ribosomes exercise an important or perhaps decisive modulating influence on the reading of the code in m-RNA.

5. The sequence of nucleotides involved in the interaction with activating enzymes is different from that required for translation of the m-RNA code.

---

[5] Probably more than two species of degenerate leucine s-RNA exist corresponding to the five codewords for leucine, (UUU), (UUC), (UUG), (UUA), and (UCC). In the experiments of Bennett *et al.* (1963), the relationships among the activating enzymes and two of the five possible degenerate species was explored.

One may tentatively conclude that these two nucleotide sequences are not overlapping.

6. The methylated bases are clustered in relatively close proximity.

7. The function of the methylated bases is still obscure, in spite of suggestive experiments that they are somehow related to specific interactions with the activating enzymes.

8. Most of the bases are base-paired in helical configuration. It cannot be unequivocally decided whether there is only one base-paired region or more than one and what degree of imperfection exists in the base-paired region.

9. Differences in base sequence among degenerate species of s-RNA extend beyond the coding areas.

10. The pattern of methylation is both species-specific and amino acid specific.

Much remains to be discovered about the structure of s-RNA and the relationship of the structure to the biological functions performed by this extraordinary biological object.

## REFERENCES

Allen, D. W., and P. C. Zamecnik. 1962. *Biochim. Biophys. Acta* 55: 865.

Ames, B. N., and P. E. Hartman. 1963. *Cold Spring Harbor Symp. Quant. Biol.* 28: 349.

Ames, B. N., and R. G. Martin. 1964. *Ann. Rev. Biochem.* 33: 235.

Arlinghaus, R., J. Shaeffer, and R. Schweet. 1964. *Proc. Natl. Acad. Sci. U.S.* 51: 1291.

Armstrong, A., H. Hagopian, V. M. Ingram, I. Sjöquist, and J. Sjöquist. 1964. *Biochemistry* 3: 1194.

Bell, D., R. V. Tomilison, and G. M. Tener. 1964. *Biochemistry* 3: 317.

Bennett, T. P., J. Goldstein, and F. Lipmann. 1963. *Proc. Natl. Acad. Sci. U.S.* 49: 850.

Berg, P. 1961. *Ann. Rev. Biochem.* 30: 293.

Berg, P., and E. J. Ofengand. 1958. *Proc. Natl. Acad. Sci. U.S.* 44: 78.

Berg, P., F. H. Bergmann, E. J. Ofengand, and M. Dieckmann. 1961. *J. Biol. Chem.* 236: 1726.

Berg, P., U. Lagerkvist, and M. Dieckmann. 1962. *J. Mol. Biol.* 5: 159.

Bernfield, M. R., and M. W. Nirenberg. 1965. *Science* 147: 479.

Boedtker, H. 1960. *J. Mol. Biol.* 2: 171.

Brown, G. L. 1963. In *Progress in Nucleic Acid Research*, ed. J. N. Davidson and W. E. Cohn. New York: Academic Press, Inc. P. 259.

Brown, G. L., and G. Zubay. 1960. *J. Mol. Biol.* 2: 287.

Brown, G. L., Z. Kosinski, and C. Carr. 1962. In *Acides Ribonucleiques et Polyphosphates*. Editions Du Centre National de la Recherche Scientifique, Paris. P. 183.

Cannon, M., R. Krug, and W. Gilbert. 1963. *J. Mol. Biol.* 7: 360.

Cantoni, G. L. 1962. In *Acides Ribonucleiques et Polyphosphates*. Editions Du Centre National de la Recherche Scientifique, Paris. P. 201.

Cantoni, G. L., H. V. Gelboin, S. W. Luborsky, H. H. Richards, and M. F. Singer. 1962. *Biochim. Biophys. Acta* 61: 354.

Cantoni, G. L., H. Ishikura, H. H. Richards, and K. Tanaka. 1963. *Cold Spring Harbor Symp. Quant. Biol.* 28: 123.

Cantoni, G. L., H. Ishikura, H. H. Richards, and K. Tanaka. 1965. *Nucleic Acids, Structure, Biosynthesis and Function*. Symposium organized by the Regional Research Laboratory, Hyderabad, 1964. New Delhi: Council of Scientific and Industrial Research. P. 257.

Chapeville, F., F. Lipmann, G. von Ehrenstein, B. Weisblum, W. J. Ray, Jr., and S. Benzer. 1962. *Proc. Natl. Acad. Sci. U.S.* 48: 1086.

Coronado, A., E. Mardones, J. Celis, and J. E. Allende. 1964. *Abstr. Intern. Cong. Biochem., 6th, New York, 1964*. P. 49.

Davies, J., W. Gilbert, and L. Gorini. 1964. *Proc. Natl. Acad. Sci. U.S.* 51: 883.

Doty, P., H. Boedtker, J. R. Fresco, R. Haselkorn, and M. Litt. 1959. *Proc. Natl. Acad. Sci. U.S.* 45: 482.

Dove, W. F., and N. Davidson. 1962. *J. Mol. Biol.* 5: 467.

Dunn, D. B. 1959. *Biochim. Biophys. Acta* 34: 286.

Dunn, D. B., and J. D. Smith. 1955. *Nature* 175: 336.

Dunn, D. B., J. D. Smith, and P. F. Spahr. 1960. *J. Mol. Biol.* 2: 113.

Englander, S. W., and J. J. Englander. 1965. *Proc. Natl. Acad. Sci. U.S.* 53: 370.

Fasman, G. D., C. Lindblow, and L. Grossman. 1964. *Biochemistry* 3: 1015.

Feldman, H., and H. G. Zachau. 1964. *Biochem. Biophys. Res. Commun.* 15: 13.

Felsenfeld, G., and G. L. Cantoni. 1964. *Proc. Natl. Acad. Sci. U.S.* 51: 818.

Felsenfeld, G., and G. Sandeen. 1962. *J. Mol. Biol.* 5: 587.

Fleissner, E., and E. Borek. 1962. *Proc. Natl. Acad. Sci. U.S.* 48: 1199.

Fresco, J. R. 1963. In *Informational Macromolecules*, ed. H. J. Vogel, V. Bryson, and J. O. Lampen. New York: Academic Press, Inc. P. 121.

Fresco, J. R., L. C. Klotz, and E. G. Richards. 1963. *Cold Spring Harbor Symp. Quant. Biol.* 28: 83.

Gardner, R. S., A. J. Wahba, C. Basilio, R. S. Miller, P. Lengyel, and J. F. Speyer. 1962. *Proc. Natl. Acad. Sci. U.S.* 48: 2087.

Geiduschek, E. P. 1961. *Proc. Natl. Acad. Sci. U.S.* 47: 950.

Giacomoni, D., and S. Spiegelman. 1962. *Science* 138: 1328.

Gilbert, W. 1963. *J. Mol. Biol.* 6: 389.

Gorini, L., and E. Kataja. 1964a. *Proc. Natl. Acad. Sci. U.S.* 51: 487.

Gorini, L., and E. Kataja. 1964b. *Proc. Natl. Acad. Sci. U.S.* 51: 995.

Gros, F., J. M. Dubert, A. Tissieres, S. Bourgeois, M. Michelson, R. Soffer, and L. Legault. 1963. *Cold Spring Harbor Symp. Quant. Biol.* 28: 299.

Harkness, D. R., and R. J. Hilmoe. 1962. *Biochem. Biophys. Res. Commun.* 9: 393.

Hecht, L. I., M. L. Stephenson, and P. C. Zamecnik. 1959. *Proc. Natl. Acad. Sci. U.S.* 45: 505.

Herbert, E., C. J. Smith, and C. W. Wilson. 1964. *J. Mol. Biol.* 9: 376.

Hoagland, M. B., M. L. Stephenson, J. F. Scott, L. I. Hecht, and P. C. Zamecnik. 1958. *J. Biol. Chem.* 231: 241.

Holley, R. W., J. Apgar, G. A. Everett, J. T. Madison, S. H. Merrill, and A. Zamir. 1963. *Cold Spring Harbor Symp. Quant. Biol.* 28: 117.

Holley, R. W., G. A. Everett, J. T. Madison, M. Marquisee, and A. Zamir. 1964. *Abstr. Intern. Congr. Biochem., 6th, New York, 1964.* P. 9.

Hurwitz, J., M. Gold, and M. Anders. 1964. *J. Biol. Chem.* 239: 3474.

Jacobson, K. B., S. Nishimura, W. E. Barnett, R. J. Mans, P. Cammarano, and G. D. Novelli. 1964. *Biochim. Biophys. Acta* 91: 305.

Kaji, A., and H. Kaji. 1963. *Biochem. Biophys. Res. Commun.* 13: 186.

Kaji, A., and H. Kaji. 1964. *Abstr. Federation Proc.* 23: 478.

Kisselev, L., and L. Frolova. 1964. *Abstr. Intern. Congr. Biochem., 6th, New York, 1964.* P. 65.

Klee, W. A., and G. L. Cantoni. 1960. *Proc. Natl. Acad. Sci. U.S.* 46: 322.

Littauer, U. Z. 1964. *Abstr. Intern. Congr. Biochem., 6th, New York, 1964.* P. 11.

Littauer, U. Z., K. Muench, P. Berg, W. Gilbert, and P. F. Spahr. 1963. *Cold Spring Harbor Symp. Quant. Biol.* 28: 157.

Luborsky, S. W., and G. L. Cantoni. 1962. *Biochim. Biophys. Acta* 61: 481.

Marciello, R., and G. Zubay. 1964. *Biochem. Biophys. Res. Commun.* 14: 272.

McCully, K. S., and G. L. Cantoni. 1962. *J. Biol. Chem.* 237: 3760.

McTague, J. P., V. Ross, and J. H. Gibbs. 1964. *Biopolymers* 2: 163.

Miura, K. 1964. *J. Mol. Biol.* 8: 371.

Mommaerts, W. F. H. M., J. Brahms, J. H. Weil, and J. Ebel. 1964. *Compt. Rend.* 258: 2687.

Nakamoto, T., T. W. Conway, J. E. Allende, G. J. Spyrides, and F. Lipmann. 1963. *Cold Spring Harbor Symp. Quant. Biol.* 28: 227.

Nathans, D. 1964. *Proc. Natl. Acad. Sci. U.S.* 51: 585.

Nathenson, S. G., F. C. Dohan, Jr., H. H. Richards, and G. L. Cantoni. 1965. *Biochemistry* 4: 2412.

Nihei, T., and G. L. Cantoni. 1962. *Biochim. Biophys. Acta* 61: 463.

Nirenberg, M. W., and J. H. Matthaei. 1961. *Proc. Natl. Acad. Sci. U.S.* 47: 1588.

Nishimura, S., and G. D. Novelli. 1963. *Biochem. Biophys. Res. Commun.* 11: 161.

Ofengand, E. J., M. Dieckmann, and P. Berg. 1961. *J. Biol. Chem.* 236: 1741.

Osawa, S. 1960. *Biochim. Biophys. Acta* 43: 110.

Penniston, J. T., and P. Doty. 1963a. *Biopolymers* 1: 145.

Penniston, J. T., and P. Doty. 1963b. *Biopolymers* 1: 209.

Peterkofsky, A. 1964. *Proc. Natl. Acad. Sci. U.S.* 52: 1233.

Peterkofsky, A., C. Jesensky, A. Bank, and A. H. Mehler. 1964. *J. Biol. Chem.* 239: 2918.

RajBhandary, V. L., R. J. Young, and H. G. Khorana. 1964. *J. Biol. Chem.* 239: 3875.

Ralph, R. K., R. J. Young, and H. G. Khorana. 1963. *J. Am. Chem. Soc.* 85: 2002.

Schildkraut, C. L., C. C. Richardson, and A. Kornberg. 1964. *J. Mol. Biol.* 9: 24.

Singer, M. F., and G. L. Cantoni. 1960. *Biochim. Biophys. Acta* 39: 182.

Spencer, M. 1963. *Cold Spring Harbor Symp. Quant. Biol.* 28: 77.

Spencer, M., W. Fuller, M. H. F. Wilkins, and G. L. Brown. 1962. *Nature* 194: 1014.

Spirin, A. S. 1964. Paper presented at the Gordon Research Conference on Nucleic Acids, New Hampton, New Hampshire.

Staehelin, M. 1964. *J. Mol. Biol.* 8: 470.

Starr, J. L. 1963. *Biochem. Biophys. Res. Commun.* 10: 428.

Starr, J. L., and R. Fefferman. 1964. *J. Biol. Chem.* 239: 3457.

Stent, G., and S. Brenner. 1961. *Proc. Natl. Acad. Sci. U.S.* 47: 2005.

Takanami, M. 1964. *Proc. Natl. Acad. Sci. U.S.* 52: 1271.

Tissieres, A. 1959. *J. Mol. Biol.* 1: 365.

Tomasz, M., and R. W. Chambers. 1964a. *J. Am. Chem. Soc.* 86: 4216.

Tomasz, M., and R. W. Chambers. 1964b. *Abstr. Intern. Congr. Biochem., 6th, New York, 1964.* P. 90.

Traut, R. R., and R. E. Munro. 1964. *J. Mol. Biol.* 10: 63.

von Ehrenstein, G., and F. Lipmann. 1961. *Proc. Natl. Acad. Sci. U.S.* 47: 941.

Warner, J., and A. Rich. 1964. *Proc. Natl. Acad. Sci. U.S.* 51: 1134.

Weil, J. H., N. Befort, B. Rether, and J. P. Ebel. 1964. *Biochem. Biophys. Res. Commun.* 15: 447.

Wolfenden, R., D. H. Rammler, and F. Lipmann. 1964. *Biochemistry* 3: 329.

Wyatt, G. R. 1950. *Nature* 166: 237.

Yu, C. T., and P. C. Zamecnik. 1963. *Biochim. Biophys. Acta* 76: 209.

Zachau, H. G., G. Acs, and F. Lipmann. 1958. *Proc. Natl. Acad. Sci. U.S.* 44: 885.

Zamecnik, P. C. 1959. *Harvey Lectures Ser. 54:* 256.

Zamecnik, P. C. 1962. *Biochem. J.* 85: 257.

Zillig, W., D. Schactschabel, and W. Z. Krone. 1960. *Z. Physiol. Chem.* 318: 100.

Zillig, W., P. Traub, and P. Palm. 1964. *Abstr. Intern. Congr. Biochem., 6th, New York, 1964.* P. 34.

*Molecular Architecture*

*and Biological Structures*

# Architecture of the α-class of Fibrous Proteins[1]

**Carolyn Cohen**

*Children's Cancer Research Foundation*
*and*
*Harvard Medical School*
*Boston, Massachusetts*

## Introduction

The role of the α-class of fibrous proteins in the living organism is not merely structural. These large molecules are concerned with such vital processes as contractil ty and blood coagulation. In this paper, a point of view will be developed regarding the structure of these proteins in relation to the activities they carry out. It will be shown that the design of the α-helical coiled coil, which is the polypeptide chain conformation characteristic of these proteins, leads to rod-shaped molecules having a high degree of stability. The molecular structure of different members of this class of proteins can be envisaged as consisting of both coiled-coil and globular domains, in varying arrangements and proportions, so that the α-class comprises a series of molecules having diverse properties but built on a common plan.

The assembly and functioning of two members of this group of proteins, myosin and fibrinogen, will be described. Muscle contraction and blood coagulation may be thought of as presenting analogous structural problems. When muscle contracts, do the myosin filaments shorten? And when blood clots, do the fibrinogen molecules change length? In each case evidence indi-

[1] This work was supported in part by a grant from the National Institutes of Health U. S. P. H. S. AM–02633.

cates that an intermolecular change, rather than an intramolecular folding, is the basis of the process. This concept is consistent with models where the coiled-coil regions define a fixed length for the molecules. Specific problems in the architecture of the myosin and fibrin filaments related to their functioning will also be indicated.

## The α-Helical Coiled Coil

Astbury's great contribution to protein crystallography was the classification of the fibrous proteins. On the basis of the wide-angle X-ray diffraction diagram, he distinguished three structures: the α and the β of the k–m–e–f class, and the collagen class (Astbury, 1947). He realized that these divisions represent three basic polypeptide chain designs — and that proteins with otherwise diverse properties might have a fundamentally similar architecture. Thus he demonstrated that α-keratin, myosin, epidermin, and fibrinogen all give the same X-ray fingerprint and must therefore have regions of similar backbone structure. He recognized also that the simplicity of design in the fibrous proteins is relevant to the structure of the more complicated globular proteins. Not only could the α to β transformation be achieved in the k–m–e–f system by stretching, but a shortened or "supercontracted" form could be obtained by denaturation; in this state, the fibrous proteins resembled denatured globular proteins in yielding a disoriented β or so-called cross-β X-ray diagram (Astbury, 1945). Although he did not achieve the solution of the exact nature of the polypeptide "folds" in these fibrous proteins, he clearly set the problem and was supremely aware of its significance.

The correct solutions were made possible in the past decade by three converging lines of investigation: the development of helical diffraction theory, the synthesis of polypeptides of high molecular weight, and the accumulation of information on the stereochemistry of amino acids and peptides. In the case of the collagen structure, helical diffraction theory showed, in 1953, that the diagram could be interpreted formally in terms of a helix with ten asymmetric units in three turns (Cohen and Bear, 1953; Cowan et al., 1953). It was not until 1955 that X-ray studies of polyproline and polyglycine and model-building showed that the correct structure was a three-chain coiled coil (Cowan et al., 1955; Ramachandran and Kartha, 1955; Rich and Crick, 1955; Bear, 1956). The "pleated sheet" structure proposed by Pauling and Corey (1953a) for the β class was related to the extended polypeptide grid suggested earlier by Astbury and others, but gave a better fit with the X-ray diagram and stereochemical requirements. The solution to the α-diagram has had a longer and perhaps more novel history. Astbury knew that the α structure was some kind of "fold," since the chains could be extended to about twice their length in going to the β form. Various types of polypeptide helices had been examined, the most systematic effort probably being the study by Bragg, Kendrew, and Perutz in 1950 (Bragg *et. al.*, 1950). The essential factor that was missing in their analysis, however, was the requirement that the peptide group be planar. Pauling and Corey incorporated this feature in their model-building, and in 1951 the α-helix was discovered (Pauling *et al.*, 1951).

The α-helix could be shown straightaway to account well for X-ray diagrams from synthetic polypeptides. It is interesting to note, however, that in their 1951 paper Pauling and coworkers relied heavily on equatorial data which are, in fact, the least critical of tests for a helical structure. In 1952, Cochran, Crick, and Vand were able to analyze the diagrams from synthetic α-polypeptides more rigorously by the newly developed helical diffraction theory (Cochran *et al.*, 1952). The meridional and near-meridional intensity distribution, in particular, could be readily examined, and excellent agreement was found between the X-ray diagram from poly-γ-methyl-L-glutamate and that diagram predicted from the α-helix.

Furthermore, shortly after the α-helix was described, Perutz (1951) pointed out that a strong meridional reflection at 1.5 Å was expected from the rise-per-residue repeat of the structure. He demonstrated this diffraction not only in synthetic α-polypeptides, but also in keratin and muscle. Thus by 1952 it seemed clear that the α-helix could account well for synthetic polypeptide diagrams and was closely related to the fibrous protein α diagram. An important difference between the two X-ray patterns remained unexplained; the synthetic polypeptides have a layer line at 5.4 Å with off-meridional reflections, whereas the α-proteins give a strong meridional reflection at 5.1 Å.

The answer to this problem was arrived at independently by Crick and by Pauling and Corey in 1953 (Crick, 1953; Pauling and Corey, 1953b). They proposed that the axis of the α-helix itself forms a helix so that the structure consists of coiled coils. Their arguments were derived from significantly different premises. Pauling and Corey envisaged repeating sequences of residues throwing the helix axis into a supercoil. The basis of the helical distortion resides in the chemical composition of the single chain. Depending on the size of the repeat, various cables could be constructed. In contrast, Crick based his proposal on the interaction of α-helices. He pointed out that to interlock side chains between two helices (so-called knobs-into-holes packing), there must be an integral number of residues in two turns. The α-helix has a near but not exact repeat in two turns; i.e., there are 3.6 rather than 3.5 residues per turn. To achieve a fit, the axes must be inclined at a small angle. The helices can then be made to twist around one another, forming a coiled coil. This kind of structure accounted well for the main features of the X-ray diagram: the 1.49-Å meridional reflection caused by the rise per residue in the α-helix, and the 5.1-Å meridional reflection caused by layers of side chains occurring at this repeat along the axis of the structure.

Moreover, this structure predicted a new near-equatorial reflection whose spacing was related to the large pitch of the supercoil. Some indications of this reflection could be found in diagrams from porcupine quill, but the diffuseness and lack of orientation of dried proteins obscured this part of the diagram. The ideal system in which to look for this diffraction would be a concentrated, highly oriented gel of α-protein. In fact, this constitutes a description of some specialized molluscan muscles.

Certain molluscs have so-called catch muscles that maintain tension over long periods of time. These muscles contain large amounts (up to 50%) of a highly α-helical protein, paramyosin. A specimen particularly suitable for these X-ray studies, because of its ease of dissection, size, and high degree of orientation, is the Anterior Byssal Retractor Muscle (ABRM) of *Mytilus edulis.*

X-ray diagrams recently obtained from the ABRM clearly show the near-equatorial reflection predicted for the coiled coil (Cohen and Holmes, 1963). Furthermore, a strong 5.1-Å meridional reflection is present. These features cannot be accounted for by a simple tilting of α-helices, and furnish strong evidence for the validity of the coiled-coil hypothesis.

Although whole muscle contains myosin as well as paramyosin, one can interpret the diagram on the assumption of a single diffracting system. The model that best accounts for the position and intensity distribution of the near-equatorial layer line is a two-chain poly-L-alanine coiled coil. Scattering from side chains is effectively wiped out by the electron density of water. The pitch of the major helix is about 180 Å, and in this distance the minor helix (or α-helix) makes 36 turns. Further refinements of the structure, including whether the chains run parallel or antiparallel, possible specific bonding patterns, and some notion of the nature of the side-chain distribution, remain to be elucidated by more detailed study of the higher-order reflections.

This significance of the coiled-coil structure is that it provides stability for highly charged polypeptide chains in an aqueous environment. The important point about the coiled coil is not the twisting of each helix axis to form another helix, but the systematic pattern of side-chain interactions which are thereby permitted. Studies of single-chain synthetic polypeptides indicate that the α-helix in these systems is in effect marginally stable in aqueous solution. It seems probable that, as predicted by Crick (1953), a sequence of residues occurs along the α-helices, permitting hydrophobic bonding between chains. Thus a sequence might be postulated where nonpolar residues occur on "inward-pointing" portions and polar residues occur on the outside. The charged side chains would provide solubility and mediate intermolecular interactions.

The generality of the concept of stabilization by interchain bonding in proteins is evident. In contrast to polyproline, which is a single-chain helix, collagen is a three-chain coiled coil. The β structure forms systematically bonded sheets, and feather keratin may in fact be a supercoiled "pleated sheet." The globular proteins, exemplified by our present picture of myoglobin, have a complex pattern of side-chain interactions, which stabilizes both the α-helix and the conformational departures from this structure. Thus the polypeptide "folds" Astbury was seeking have turned out in fact to entail a high level of organization even in the simplest fibrous protein system.

## Molecular Structure of the α-Proteins

Having described the nature of the structure giving rise to the α X-ray diagram, we may now examine those proteins having this common structural feature in terms of two questions. How much of each protein is in the coiled-coil conformation? What is the over-all molecular structure? That is, where is the coiled coil located in the molecule?

That there are large differences in the molecular structure of members of the α-class is obvious from the great diversity these proteins display in amino acid composition and in mechanical, solubility, and functional properties. Thus, despite similarities in their wide-angle X-ray diagrams, these proteins have been shown by Bear (1944, 1945) to have marked differences at small angles (where the large-scale features of structures may be seen). Although formal models can be constructed that account satisfactorily for the small-angle X-ray data, the unambiguous interpretation of these diagrams in terms of the molecular structure is by no means straightforward.

To deduce a model for the molecular structure of a fibrous protein, more information in general is required than that obtained from optical or X-ray studies of the solid state. It is difficult to estimate the size of the ordered regions giving rise to the X-ray diagram, although some rough indications may be obtained on the basis of diffuse *vs.* crystalline scattering. Fibrin gives a "poorer" α diagram than does keratin or myosin, but one cannot get useful quantitative information from such an observation. However, while the insolubility of keratin has been a serious hindrance in the analysis of its molecular structure, several α-proteins are known that are readily soluble in aqueous solution. The muscle proteins are noteworthy in making up a majority of this list (see Table 1). These proteins may thus be characterized in solution by physicochemical and optical methods. Electron microscopy may also be carried out on the dispersed state, as well as on ordered aggregates.

One can obtain an estimate of the α-helix content of the soluble α-proteins by use of the Moffitt equation describing the optical rotatory dispersion of an α-helix (Moffitt and Yang, 1956; Cohen and Szent-Györgyi, 1957). In Table 1 are listed all the presently known soluble α-proteins with estimated helix contents based on a value of $b_0 = 660$ for a fully helical molecule. Wide variation occurs in the amount of α-helix in the α-proteins, ranging from a

TABLE 1

MOLECULAR STRUCTURE OF α-PROTEINS

| Proteins | Helix content (by rotatory dispersion) % | Mol. wt. | Model | Molecular length* (angstroms) |
|---|---|---|---|---|
| Tropomyosin | >90 | 53,000[1] | | 400 |
| Light meromyosin Fr. 1 | >90 | 135,000[2] | | 800 |
| Paramyosin | >90 | 200,000[3] | | 1400 |
| Myosin | 65 | 530,000[2] | | 1500 |
| Heavy meromyosin | 50 | 350,000[2] | | 500 |
| Fibrinogen | 30 | 340,000[4] | | 460 |
| Epidermin | ~40 | 640,000[5] | | |
| Flagellins | ~40 | 20,000–40,000[6,7] | | 30–40 |
| Myoglobin† | 70 | 17,000[8] | | 30 |
| Bovine serum albumin† | 45 | 68,000[9] | | 50 |

* Estimates from hydrodynamic, light-scattering, and electron microscopic data.
† Not α-proteins; included for purposes of comparison.

(1) Bailey, 1948
(2) Holtzer et al., 1962
(3) Lowey et al., 1963
(4) Shulman, 1953

(5) Matoltsy, 1964
(6) Erlander et al., 1960
(7) Ada et al., 1963
(8) Edmundson and Hirs, 1961
(9) Phelps and Putnam, 1960

completely or almost completely helical state to a helix content of about 30%. Thus, although fibrinogen is a fibrous protein, i.e., is asymmetric in shape, its helix content is less than that of "orthodox" globular proteins such as myoglobin and bovine serum albumin.

A generalization does emerge, however, if one examines available hydrodynamic and light-scattering data for these fibrous proteins. Assuming a formal elliptical shape for the model, it appears that, for a given molecular length, as the helix content decreases, the axial ratio decreases also. In terms of a realistic molecular model, therefore, the completely helical proteins may be pictured as simple rods, and a good account can be made of their solution properties. But how the less helical molecules are constructed is not so obvious.

One kind of model is based on the notion that these large fibrous α-proteins are made up of two distinct domains — one α-helical coiled coil and the other globular in structure (Cohen, 1961). The coiled-coil domain gives rise to the α diagram and to the "fibrous" character of the molecule, i.e., its asymmetry. The polypeptide chains in globular regions need not be in the random coil or nonhelical form, but may have α-helices arranged as in any globular protein. Such a picture was first predicted for myosin and heavy meromyosin on the basis of X-ray diffraction, optical, and hydrodynamic properties (Cohen, 1961; Lowey and Cohen, 1962) and has recently been confirmed by electron microscopy of individual myosin molecules (Rice, 1961a, b; Huxley, 1963; Zobel and Carlson, 1963; Rice, 1964). Fibrinogen has been shown by electron microscopy to consist of globular units connected by a thin rod (Hall and Slayter, 1959). It seems plausible to identify the connection between globular units as the coiled-coil part of the structure.

Our information on epidermin is more limited, but a recent report on a soluble pre-keratin fraction indicates a high molecular weight for the molecule (640,000) (Matoltsy, 1964), and preliminary measurements give a helix content of about 40% (Cohen and Matoltsy, unpublished). Hydrodynamic data and electron microscopy will show whether the molecule resembles myosin or fibrinogen.

The smallest $\alpha$-helical molecule thus far reported is "flagellin," the protein obtained from flagella by acid disintegration (Weibull, 1948). Astbury and coworkers have shown that flagella isolated from a variety of bacteria give an $\alpha$ diagram (Astbury and Weibull, 1949; Astbury et al., 1955). Electron micrographs of negatively stained flagella reveal a beaded surface structure. Both a hollow core (Kerridge et al., 1962) and an apparently impenetrable center (Lowy and Hanson, 1964) have been described. In a recent paper, an analogy was made between the packing of flagellin subunits and actin monomers (Lowy and Hanson, 1964). Thus, if the flagellum were a two-component system like actomyosin, a core might give rise to the $\alpha$ diagram and the globular units would be on the surface. If, on the other hand, the flagellum were a one-component system, then the $\alpha$ diagram must be derived from the globular-appearing subunits. In at least one organism, Proteus vulgaris, almost all the protein in the flagella can be obtained as a monodisperse subunit of low molecular weight (20,000–40,000) (Weibull, 1948; Erlander et al., 1960). The helix content is of the order of 40% (Yaguchi et al., 1964). If this flagellin subunit does make up the entire flagellum, one could picture the molecule as some kind of tadpole-shaped structure with a globular head and a short coiled-coil tail (which might be very difficult to visualize in the electron microscope). These units would aggregate to give the beaded structure of the flagellum. The reconstitution of flagella-like filaments from the flagellin subunits has, in fact, recently been reported (Ada et al., 1963; Abram and Koffler, 1964). If the flagellin subunits were truly ovoid in shape, then the region giving rise to the $\alpha$ diagram would not be a separate domain but, rather, $\alpha$-helical coiled-coil sections within the molecule oriented along the axis of the flagellum. In this extreme case of a small molecule, the formalism of a distinct globular and coiled-coil domain may break down.

At present, myosin is the best-characterized molecule among the $\alpha$-proteins that are not completely helical. We can only speculate on the molecular structure of fibrinogen — and guess rather more freely about epidermin and flagellin. But the concept of basic similarities in the plan of the fibrous $\alpha$-proteins may provide electron microscopists with some indication of the kind of molecule that may eventually be visualized. Included in Table 1 are schematic models for the proteins of the $\alpha$-class.

A further point seems noteworthy: What is the relation between amino acid composition of these proteins and their helix contents? The most instructive picture is obtained in the case of the muscle proteins (see Table 1), where few, if any, disulfide bonds are present. Here there seems to be a remarkable correlation between the absence of proline and high $\alpha$-helix content (Szent-Györgyi and Cohen, 1957). Thus, light meromyosin (LMM), tropomyosin, and paramyosin have no proline and are $> 90\%$ helical. One should note, however, that other amino acids that do not favor $\alpha$-helix formation, such as serine, threonine, and valine (Blout et al., 1960), are also present in relatively low amounts in these highly helical proteins. The other approach to the question of amino acid composition and shape of a protein is not the presence of amino acids that are specifically favorable or unfavorable to $\alpha$-helix formation, but the total composition of the protein in terms of percentage of nonpolar vs. polar residues (Waugh, 1954). The highly helical $\alpha$-proteins contain relatively few formers of hydrophobic bonds but carry a uniquely high charge. The most stable form for this molecule would then be an extended rod that gives the largest surface area for the polar groups. Thus, although flagellin from P. vulgaris has no proline, it does have a high content of serine and threonine and a high proportion of nonpolar residues (Weibull, 1951; Kobayashi et al., 1959); these features may determine the globular shape of the molecule.

In summary, the molecular structure of the $\alpha$-class of proteins shows great diversity; the $\alpha$-helical coiled-coil portion of the molecule may constitute almost all of the molecule or a relatively small portion. The role of the coiled coil in the assembly and functioning of these proteins will now be discussed for myosin and fibrinogen.

## Myosin Filaments

In his Croonian lecture of 20 years ago on the "Structure of Biological Fibres and the Problem of Muscle," Astbury presented evidence that "no deep-seated change is observed in the diffraction pattern of muscle" upon contraction (Astbury, 1947). This observation was puzzling, since the prevailing concept was that muscle consists of a set of myofilaments that shorten during contraction and that these filaments contain myosin (or actomyosin) which folds reversibly. The feature of elasticity characteristic of the k–m–e–f class of proteins (contrasted with the inextensibility of collagen) was assumed to be related directly to the contractility of muscle. Astbury was forced to conclude that the wide-angle X-ray results on muscle indicated that the part of the myosin molecule that folds during contraction does not contribute to the diffraction pattern. As we shall show, our present evidence indicates that this conclusion is probably correct — but that it arises from a different concept of the structural basis for contraction.

Striated muscle consists of two sets of filaments, one containing myosin and the other actin. In the past decade, a new picture of the structure of muscle and a new theory of muscle contraction have been conceived, due largely to the work of H. E. Huxley. The shortening of muscle is postulated as arising from the relative motion of the two sets of filaments, without changes in the structure or organization of the filaments in the shortened state (Huxley and Hanson, 1954; Huxley and Niedergerke, 1954; Hanson and Huxley, 1955). In cross-striated muscles, the filaments form regular and separate arrays that give the muscle a banded appearance in the light microscope. The length of the so-called anisotropic (A) band is precisely the length of the myosin filaments. The isotropic (I) band varies in length with extent of shortening or stretch, the actin-containing filaments in the I band interdigitating with the array of the myosin-containing filaments in the A band. The problem of the contraction of muscle is thus focused on the way the myosin-containing filament is built so that it may interact with the actin filaments and generate motion.

The morphology of the filaments in vertebrate striated muscle has been studied intensively in recent years by electron microscopy and X-ray diffraction, and the following picture has emerged (see, for example, Huxley, 1957, 1960, 1963). The filaments containing myosin are 1.50 $\mu$ long and are spindle-shaped, tapering at the ends. The exact diameter of the filaments is not yet established and depends on the methods used in fixation. Thus, in PTA-stained, osmium-fixed material, a diameter of about 100 Å to 120 Å has been found. More recently, fixation with glutaraldehyde has yielded larger diameters (Huxley, 1965). The surface of the filament is "rough," and so-called bridges project along its length (and close to the end), except for a narrow "bare" zone about 0.15–0.2 $\mu$ long at the center. The bridges appear to be arranged in a helical pattern having a sixfold screw with pitch of about 400 Å (by electron microscopy) (Huxley, 1957). Information on the bridge structure is difficult to obtain, but the length of the bridge may be estimated from knowledge of the filament lattice. The myosin filaments exist in a hexagonal array with a center-to-center distance of 450 Å in living rest-length rabbit psoas muscle (Huxley, 1953). The actin filaments occupy trigonal positions in the lattice in the zone of overlap, so that one actin is "shared" by three myosins. The center-to-center distance of the myosin and actin filaments is 260 Å. Thus, the length of the bridge between the filaments is of the order of 150 Å, based on diameters of 140 Å for myosin and 80 Å for actin (Hanson and Lowy, 1963). These bridges are the site of enzymatic activity and interaction with actin (Huxley, 1957, 1960). In effect, they may be thought of as "hooks" which pull the actin into the myosin lattice.

To analyze the architecture of the myosin filament, information is needed on the molecular structure of the myosin monomer and its mode of aggregation. The most recent values for the molecular weight of myosin range from 500,000 to 600,000 (Kielley and Harrington, 1960; Holtzer *et al.*, 1961; Lowey and Cohen, 1962; Mueller, 1964), with a figure of 530,000 ± 30,000 probably being the best present estimate. The exact length of the molecule is not established, since interpretation of light-scattering radius of gyration and various hydrodynamic properties requires a knowledge of mass distribution. The direct visualization of the myosin molecule by electron microscopy has given good agreement on the general picture of a long, thin rod (the LMM molecule plus part of the heavy-meromyosin (HMM) molecule) with a globular unit (the bridge) at one end (Huxley, 1963; Rice, 1963; Zobel and Carlson, 1963) (see Fig. 1 A). A broad distribution of molecular lengths with mean about 1,500 Å, and differences in the size of the bridge, have been reported.

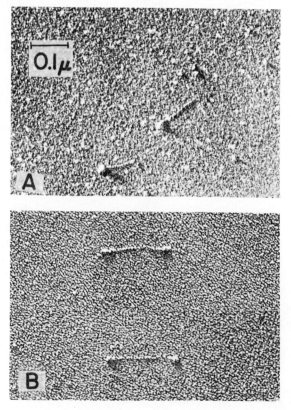

**Fig. 1.** Electron micrographs of myosin molecules. Carbon replica on mica with platinum shadowing. A: monomers; B: dimers. (Courtesy, R. V. Rice.)

A reasonable estimate of length for the monomer from all available data would be 1,500 Å ± 300 Å.

One of the most significant recent discoveries has been the recognition that myosin tends to form aggregates *in vitro* that resemble the native muscle filaments. If the ionic strength of a solution of myosin is lowered, the protein precipitates in the form of tactoidal structures (Jakus and Hall, 1947; Huxley, 1963). When negatively stained and examined in the electron microscope, the aggregates appear to have a rough surface at either end and a bare zone at the center (Huxley, 1963). In the early stages of aggregation, the filaments are short and have few irregular projections at either end, but the central bare zone is about the same size as in the larger aggregates. There is a range of sizes in the synthetic aggregates, but many are similar to native filaments. Aspects of these structures can be readily accounted for, as Huxley has pointed out, by building the filament from an initial antiparallel dimer of myosin molecules with globular portions pointing in opposite directions (see Fig. 1 B). This filament would then grow by the addition of more molecules in some kind of overlapping arrangement to account for the tapering at the ends (see Fig. 2).

While this picture goes a long way in explaining some of the features of the construction of the myosin filament, the exact morphology is by no means clear. What is required is that myosin form an ordered aggregate of a defined size with functional groups (enzymatic and actin-binding sites) in a regular array at the surface. Thus the construction of the myosin filament differs from that of other fibrous systems, such as collagen or fibrin, for example, where the exact sizes of the aggregates are not critical in their functioning and where the role of the protein is structural. This unusual assembly problem is due to the unique position of myosin among proteins: it is the only naturally occurring fibrous molecule with enzymatic activity. And it appears that this functional division is reflected in the form of the molecule and its aggregates, the rod-like α-helical portion of myosin being oriented along the filament and the globular bridge containing the "active site" projecting on the outside.

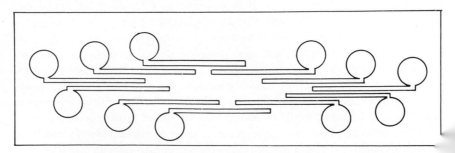

**Fig. 2.** Diagrammatic illustration of myosin aggregate (adapted from H. E. Huxley, 1963).

How might a filament of this size be built so that the enzymatic sites are on the surface in a regular helical array? The symmetry of the structure indicates a sixfold screw axis operating on a molecule or group of molecules. It appears that the structure unit may in fact be a single molecule. In a direction parallel to the symmetry axis, the myosin molecules must be related to one another so that there is a bridge every 400 Å. Since the length of the molecule is several times greater than this period, in addition to overlapping, the molecules must be "tilted" slightly to allow the bridges to be in a row at the surface. Tilt angles of the order of 3° are sufficient to expose any "buried bridges" when the molecules aggregate to form the filament. In projection, the filament has a sixfold rotation axis, and one might designate each of the six groups of molecules about the axis as a "subfilament." One particular arrangement within each subfilament that produces a compact structure is supercoiling (which may be considered a special kind of tilting). Thus, each of the six subfilaments could consist of supercoiled groups of myosin molecules with the bridges in a row every 400 Å. Packing these cable-like subfilaments would then generate a structure in which each molecule was related by a sixfold screw (Lowey and Cohen, 1962). In all of these structures, the filament center, which is the location of the symmetry axis, would be "empty" or might be occupied by another protein. The size of this central core would depend on the specific mode of packing of the myosin molecules. It could be one α-helical coiled coil in diameter, or the size of a subfilament in some cable models.

The factors limiting the length of the myosin filament depend, of course, on the exact nature of its construction. If the myosin filament were built with each unit (either one or a group of monomers) having the same bonding to every other unit, as in any regular helical lattice, then it is likely that some kind of second component would be cocrystallized in the structure to fix its linear dimension. In tobacco mosaic virus, for example, the length of the nucleic acid limits the length of the particle. Similarly, synthetic actin filaments appear to vary in length, but in striated muscles the length of the actin filaments is fixed. Thus, a second component may be involved. (One may note, however, that a relatively narrow limit may be set on the length of a helical aggregate to produce a lowest-energy state [Caspar, 1963]). If, however, the myosin filament is built so that each molecule or group of molecules is not in an identical environment, then a pattern of contacts may be established so that there is a self-termination mechanism. For example, if the angle that each molecule makes with the axis of the filament decreases as more units are added, then a point would be reached where further growth is unstable.

These considerations are quite general, since at present we do not have ⌐ough detailed structural information on vertebrate myosin filaments, or ⌐ed on myosin, to test models rigorously. Estimates of muscle myosin ⌐nt give a figure between one and two molecules per "bridge," thus making the exact structure unit uncertain. Striated muscle yields a series of meridional spacings with a period of 435 Å (Huxley, 1953; Worthington, 1959) that must come from part of the myosin structure, but some of these reflections are precluded by an exact screw symmetry. Dried paracrystals of LMM have a period close to 435 Å (429 Å $\pm$ 5 Å) (Szent-Györgyi *et al.*, 1960). This fact indicates that the period of the myosin filament is determined primarily by LMM, or that the length of the myosin molecule may be approximately a multiple of this period. Although a hollow core or differentiated center has been shown in the filaments of insect muscle (Hodge, 1955) and in the larger filaments of crayfish muscle (Gilev, 1964), no evidence for this kind of structure has been obtained for vertebrate myosin filaments, with the exception of one report on developing amphibian muscle (Hay, 1963). An interesting feature noted by various investigators, however, is the occasional triangular appearance of vertebrate filaments in the electron microscope (Sjöstrand and Andersson-Cedergren, 1957). Collapse of a group of six subfilaments will lead to this shape. Thus far, the growth of the vertebrate myosin filament appears to take place by an aggregation of single molecules (Huxley, 1963), and no indications of cable-like subfilaments as an intermediate in the assembly have been found.

In surveying various myosin filaments from a variety of animals, we note a strikingly wide range of filament lengths and diameters. In vertebrate smooth muscle such as uterus, the filaments may be as small as 50 Å or less in diameter (Shoenberg, 1958). (Thus, although all "thick" filaments contain myosin, all myosin filaments need not be "thick.") At the other extreme in size are the myosin-containing filaments of molluscan catch muscles, which may be as large as 1,500 Å in diameter. These structures contain another protein, paramyosin, in addition to myosin. The fundamental similarity in design assumed to exist in all myosin-containing filaments is the location of the ordered array of enzymatic sites at the surface of the filament. This objective would be readily achieved in the "thin" filaments of vertebrate smooth muscle. There may be a maximum diameter for a filament built on this scheme. To build larger filaments, a grouping of subfilaments about a symmetry axis may take place, resulting in a core that is hollow or contains a second protein component. In the filaments of very large diameter, such as those in molluscan catch muscle, the nonenzymatic protein forms the core, and the myosin appears to form some kind of surface lattice (see Hanson and Lowy, 1962). In terms of evolution, a protein component that may have a structural role in some animals might assume a functional one in others, as paramyosin in molluscan catch muscle.

Although it has not yet been demonstrated that all muscles function by a "sliding filament" mechanism, it appears that in systems as diverse as vertebrate striated muscle (Huxley, 1957; Page and Huxley, 1963), insect flight muscle (Hanson, 1956; Huxley and Hanson, 1957), and molluscan catch muscle (Hanson and Lowy, 1962), the myosin filaments maintain their constancy of length during contraction. The significant aspect of this scheme is that shortening occurs, not by a folding of the polypeptide chains, but by the relative motion of "rigid" filaments. The wide-angle X-ray evidence that showed the presence of the α diagram in both rest-length and contracted muscle is thus a manifestation of the role played by the α-helical coiled coil in the muscle filament. This role is not, as once thought, to change conformation, but rather to maintain conformation. The interaction of the coiled-coil regions would be significant in determining the packing of the molecules, so that the globular parts containing the active sites could be ordered on the surface. On the basis of this picture, conformation changes, the folding and unfolding of polypeptide chains, would take place in the bridge portion of the molecules — regions which do not contribute to the wide-angle α diagram.

## Fibrinogen-Fibrin

The fibrinogen-fibrin system illustrates another kind of assembly problem in the α-proteins. Fibrinogen is present in the plasma as a soluble euglobulin in concentrations of about 0.3%. At the site of an injury, a series of pro-enzyme-enzyme conversions takes place (so-called clotting factors), resulting in the explosive production of thrombin. Fibrinogen is then acted upon proteolytically by thrombin, and aggregates to form an insoluble fibrin clot. In the course of physiological coagulation, "fibrinase" (or the Laki-Lorand factor [Laki and Lorand, 1948; Loewy et al., 1961]) stabilizes the fibrin clot, which retracts soon after formation. The critical step in this series of reactions is the conversion of fibrinogen to fibrin by the action of thrombin, and this part of the system can be analyzed in vitro.

We can only speculate at present on the precise structure of the fibrinogen monomer. The molecular weight is 340,000 (Katz et al., 1952; Shulman, 1953), and the intrinsic viscosity of 0.25 g/dl indicates an asymmetric shape (Shulman, 1953). Early electron microscope studies of fibrinogen revealed filamentous particles having a nodose appearance like a string of beads (Hall, 1949a, b; Siegel et al., 1953), A more recent study by Hall and Slayter (1959) gives as the best model for fibrinogen three globular units that are connected by a thin strand (see Fig. 3). The length of the molecule was estimated at about 475 Å ± 25 Å. Such a picture is in reasonable agreement with the hydrodynamic and light-scattering data. (One must stress that without direct visualization of the molecule, leading to a knowledge of mass distribution, one cannot interpret the physicochemical data in an unambiguous way.) This model is also in agreement with the optical rotatory dispersion data which give an estimate of helix content of 30% (Cohen and Szent-Györgyi, 1957), indicating large nonhelical regions. As mentioned above, one may hypothesize that the part of the model that would give rise to the wide-angle diagram would be the thin rod connecting the globular units.

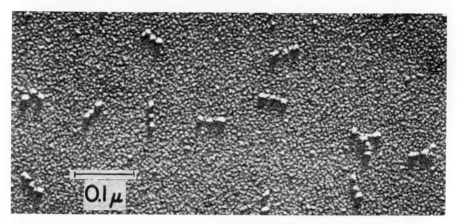

**Fig. 3.** Electron micrograph of fibrinogen molecules. Shadow-cast technique. (Courtesy, C. Hall and H. Slayter.)

It is important to emphasize, however, that a variety of molecular structures is seen in the electron micrographs of fibrinogen preparations and that, although the model selected appears with greatest frequency, one cannot be certain at present of its validity, either in terms of length or in terms of the distribution of mass. For example, the length of the monomer has been reported to vary with $p$H (Hall and Slayter, 1962), and on occasion strings of five rather than three spherical subunits have been observed (Hall and Slayter, personal communication). Changing parameters on the size of the subunits could lead to a reasonable fit with the hydrodynamic data.

In the conversion to fibrin, thrombin releases two pairs of highly negatively charged peptides amounting to only 3% of the weight of fibrinogen (Bethelheim and Bailey, 1952; Lorand and Middlebrook, 1952; Blomback and Sjöquist, 1960; Laki et al., 1960). The molecule then undergoes a dramatic change in interaction properties, and an insoluble but highly ordered aggregate results. The periodicity of fibrin fibers in the electron microscope was first demonstrated by Hawn and Porter (1947) and studied in more detail by Hall (1949a, b). The fibers stain readily with phosphotungstic acid (PTA), showing a 230-Å period and a distinctive banding pattern (see Fig. 4 A).

Two explanations are possible for the relatively short period in fibrin compared to the longer length estimated for the fibrinogen monomer. It has been postulated that a large-scale change may occur in the structure of the monomer when acted upon by thrombin and that fibrin may represent a simple end-to-end polymerization of the altered fibrinogen monomers. Thus the 230-Å period in fibrin would represent the length of one monomer (Hall and Slayter, 1959). Alternatively, the fibrinogen molecule may maintain its structure after proteolysis and may aggregate in such a way that the period observed represents some fraction of the length of the molecule.

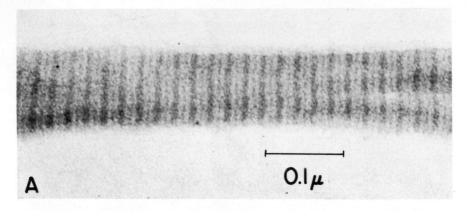

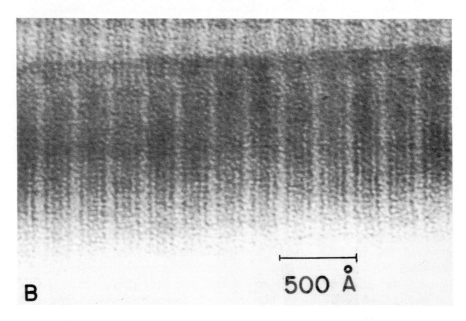

**Fig. 4.** A: fibrin stained with phosphotungstic acid. B: fibrinogen tactoid stained with uranyl acetate. (Courtesy, C. Hall and H. Slayter.)

In effect, the question raised by the fibrinogen-fibrin conversion is a classical one relating to the changes in state occurring in the fibrous α-proteins. As described above, the contraction of muscle was at one time viewed as some kind of folding of the polypeptide chains in myosin. Only relatively recently has the concept arisen of a rigid array of myosin filaments that maintain their structure during contraction. Thus, if the linkage between the globular units in fibrinogen is considered a flexible single chain, then one might well picture possible conformation changes in fibrinogen leading to the period observed in fibrin. If, on the other hand, it is postulated, by analogy with the other fibrous $\alpha$-proteins, that the coiled coil is the rod linking the globular subunits, then one may view the monomer as a stable, rigid unit whose interaction properties only are affected by the loss of the peptides upon the action of thrombin.

An early attempt to answer this question was the wide-angle X-ray diffraction study of Astbury and coworkers (Bailey *et al.*, 1943). Fibrinogen and fibrin were shown to give $\alpha$ X-ray diagrams. These authors therefore concluded that no large-scale change in the structure of fibrinogen occurred in the conversion to fibrin. This experiment is similar to the study on rest-length and contracted muscle, but we recognize now that at the most only 30% of the fibrinogen molecule was contributing to the $\alpha$-helical diagram. One does not have information on the conformation changes of the parts of the molecule that do not have the coiled-coil conformation.

A more recent approach has been the investigation of the ordered aggregates formed by fibrinogen, by small-angle X-ray diffraction and electron microscopy. In the first stages of this work, birefringent gels of fibrinogen prepared by ultracentrifugation were shown to yield a diagram consisting of four meridional orders of a 226-Å period. Wet fibrin gives a similar X-ray diagram (Stryer *et al.*, 1963). This evidence is the first clear-cut proof that fibrinogen can form a paracrystalline state similar to fibrin.

It was then shown that certain preparations of fibrinogen may produce ordered structures when precipitated from solution (Cohen *et al.*, 1963). These needle-shaped tactoids or fibrous masses may show a period of 226 Å — identical to that found in fibrin. The paracrystals stain with difficulty with PTA, but show a regular structure with uranyl acetate (UA) (see Fig. 4 B, where the banding is contrasted with that found in fibrin stained with PTA). When fibrin is stained with UA, a similar but not so clearly resolved structure as that found in the paracrystals is observed.

It appears, moreover, that fibrinogen may form more than one kind of ordered aggregate. Thus, tactoids from cold-insoluble fibrinogen (or so-called cryofibrinogens) tend to show the fibrin-like electron microscope picture described above. More soluble "native" fibrinogen preparations may give apparently "aperiodic" tactoids in the electron microscope and yield an X-ray diagram with the same period as that of fibrin but a different intensity distribution. (Furthermore, electron microscope studies of fibrinogen tactoids have on one occasion revealed a structure with a 460-Å period; this has not, however, been obtained in a reproducible manner.) It seems likely, therefore, that modifications of the fibrinogen monomer may lead to a variety of ordered structures — of which fibrin is but one (Cohen, Slayter, Kucera, and Hall, in preparation). The important point is that the only large period so far observed reproducibly is 230 Å. This fact argues strongly for the rigidity of the fibrinogen monomer.

We may note that the paracrystals of fibrinogen are particularly suitable for high-resolution electron microscopy. Relatively thin sheets of molecules may sometimes be obtained, perhaps only a few molecules (or one molecule?) thick. Because of the size of the globular subunits in fibrinogen (about 50 Å), it may be possible to identify the monomeric unit or some of its significant features in these pictures. Thus, in Fig. 4 B one can see clusters of units in regular packing. In contrast, high resolution of fibrin specimens is not easy to achieve, because of preparative difficulties. One should recognize, also, that the marked difference in appearance between PTA- and UA-stained fibrin indicates that one must be cautious in identifying specific areas with protein or stain; i.e., both positive and negative staining may be occurring in this sytem.

In principle, the electron density of fibrin to a resolution of about 40 Å may be deduced from the small-angle X-ray diagrams. The significant feature in diagrams of wet fibrin is the strong first- and third-order diffraction. This set of intensities indicates an approximately cosinusoidal variation in electron density along the fiber; that is, about half the period has greater than average electron density, and half the period has less than average. Since the structure is not polar, the amplitudes of the reflections are either positive or negative, and the diagram may be "phased" by standard methods. This procedure allows the projected electron-density distribution to be determined. A practical difficulty in carrying out these procedures, at present, is the variation in intensities on the fibrin X-ray diagrams: although the first and third orders are strong, the ratio of their intensities varies. This variation must be examined in detail before selection of any one electron-density distribution.

For purely *illustrative* purposes, we may describe a structure for fibrin based on the mass distribution of the Hall–Slayter fibrinogen model with a length of 460 Å for the monomer. End-to-end polymerization, and a half-staggered lateral aggregation, yields a close-packed structure with a period of 230 Å. One should emphasize, however, that this model without modification gives only fair agreement with the X-ray intensities, since the first order calculated from the structure is considerably stronger than that generally found experimentally (Stryer, Langridge, and Cohen, unpublished observation).

This model is heuristic but illustrates certain possible features of the fibrinogen-fibrin aggregation. Each molecule is in an equivalent environment, and the structure can build indefinitely, in contrast to the myosin filament, whose size is defined. Furthermore, the globular parts of the molecule, rather than the coiled-coil regions, dictate the interaction properties. But, similarly to myosin, the coiled-coil part of the structure confers rigidity to the monomer, whose length remains intact in the fibrin structure. Here the vital function of the protein is the self-assembly process. In myosin, the formation of the filaments occurs in the course of development; in the fibrinogen-fibrin system, the assembly takes place each time blood clots.

The coiled coil has thus been shown to be the characteristic feature of a class of proteins whose role is not merely structural, but whose condition for functioning depends on the maintenance of a high degree of order.

## ACKNOWLEDGMENT

I thank Dr. D. L. D. Caspar for valuable discussions, particularly on the assembly of the myosin filament; Dr. Susan Lowey for useful criticism and for Fig. 2; Dr. Betty Twarog for discussions on molluscan muscle; and Dr. A. G. Szent-Györgyi for continued advice.

## REFERENCES

Abram, D., and H. Koffler. 1964. *J. Mol. Biol.* 9: 168.

Ada, G. L., G. J. V. Nossal, J. Pye, and A. Abbot. 1963. *Nature* 199: 1257.

Astbury, W. T. 1945. *Nature* 155: 501.

Astbury, W. T. 1947. *Proc. Roy Soc. (London) Ser. B* 134: 303.

Astbury, W. T., and C. Weibull. 1949. *Nature* 163: 280.

Astbury, W. T., E. Beighton, and C. Weibull. 1955. In *Fibrous Proteins and Their Biological Significance*, ed. R. Brown and J. F. Danielli. *Symp. Soc. Exptl. Biol.* No. 9. New York: Academic Press, Inc. P. 282.

Bailey, K. 1948. *Biochem. J.* 43: 271.

Bailey, K., W. T. Astbury, and K. M. Rudall. 1943. *Nature* 151: 716.

Bear, R. S. 1944. *J. Am. Chem. Soc.* 66: 2043.

Bear, R. S. 1945. *J. Am. Chem. Soc.* 67: 1625.

Bear, R. S. 1956. *J. Biophys. Biochem. Cytol.* 2: 363.

Bethelheim, F. R., and K. Bailey. 1952. *Biochim. Biophys. Acta* 9: 578.

Blomback, B. and J. Sjöquist. 1960. *Acta Chem. Scand.* 14: 493.

Blout, E. R., C. de Lozé, S. M. Bloom, and G. D. Fasman. 1960. *J. Am. Chem. Soc.* 82: 3787.

Bragg, W. L., J. C. Kendrew, and M. F. Perutz. 1950. *Proc. Roy. Soc. (London) Ser. A* 203: 321.

Caspar, D. L. D. 1963. *Advan. Protein Chem.* 18: 37.

Cochran, W., F. H. C. Crick, and V. Vand. 1952. *Acta Cryst.* 5: 581.

Cohen, C. 1961. *J. Polymer Sci.* 151: 144.

Cohen, C., and R. S. Bear. 1953. *J. Am. Chem. Soc.* 75: 2783.

Cohen, C., and K. C. Holmes. 1963. *J. Mol. Biol.* 6: 423.

Cohen, C., and A. G. Szent-Györgyi. 1957. *J. Am. Chem. Soc.* 79: 248.

Cohen, C., J. P. Revel, and J. Kucera. 1963. *Science* 141: 436.

Cowan, P. M., S. McGavin, and A. C. T. North. 1955. *Nature* 176: 1062.

Cowan, P. M., A. C. T. North, and J. T. Randall. 1953. In *The Nature and Structure of Collagen*, ed. J. T. Randall. London: Butterworth & Co., Ltd. P. 241.

Crick, F. H. C. 1953. *Acta Cryst.* 6: 689.

Edmundson, A. B., and C. H. W. Hirs, 1961. *Nature* 190: 663.

Erlander, S. R., H. Koffler, and J. Foster. 1960. *Arch. Biochem. Biophys.* 90: 139.

Gilev, V. P. 1964. *Biochim. Biophys. Acta* 79: 364.

Hall, C. E. 1949a. *J. Am. Chem. Soc.* 71: 1138.

Hall, C. E. 1949b. *J. Biol. Chem.* 179: 857.

Hall, C. E., and H. S. Slayter. 1959. *J. Biophys. Biochem. Cytol.* 5: 11.

Hall, C. E., and H. S. Slayter. 1962. In *Proc. Intern. Conf. Electron Microscopy, 5th, Philadelphia, 1961*, Vol. 2, ed. S. R. Breese, Jr. New York: Academic Press, Inc. Pp. 0–3.

Hanson, J. 1956. *J. Biophys. Biochem. Cytol.* 2: 691.

Hanson, J., and H. E. Huxley. 1955. *Symp. Soc. Exptl. Biol.* 9: 228.

Hanson, J., and J. Lowy. 1962. *Physiol. Rev.* 42, Suppl. 5: 34.

Hanson, J., and J. Lowy. 1963. *J. Mol. Biol.* 6: 46.

Hawn, C. Z. V., and K. R. Porter. 1947. *J. Exptl. Med.* 86: 285.

Hay, E. D. 1963. *Z. Zellforsch. Mikroskop. Anat.* 59: 6.

Hodge, A. J. 1955. *J. Biophys. Biochem. Cytol.* 1: 361.

Holtzer, A., S. Lowey, and T. M. Schuster. 1962. *Symp. Fundamental Cancer Res., 15th, Houston, 1961*. Austin, Texas: Univ. of Texas Press. P. 259.

Huxley, A. F., and R. Niedergerke. 1954. *Nature* 173: 971.

Huxley, H. E. 1953. *Proc. Roy. Soc. (London) Ser. B* 141: 59.

Huxley, H. E. 1957. *J. Biophys. Biochem. Cytol.* 3: 631.

Huxley, H. E. 1960. In *The Cell*, Vol. IV, ed. J. Brachet and A. E. Mirsky. New York: Academic Press, Inc. P. 365.

Huxley, H. E. 1963. *J. Mol. Biol.* 7: 281.

Huxley, H. E. 1965. *Proc. Edmonton Meeting on Muscle, 1964*, ed. W. M. Paul, E. E. Daniel, G. Monckton. New York: Pergamon Press Inc. P. 3.

Huxley, H. E., and J. Hanson. 1954. *Nature* 173: 973.

Huxley, H. E., and J. Hanson. 1957. In *Electron Microscopy, Proc. Stockholm Conf., 1956*. New York: Academic Press, Inc. P. 202.

Jakus, M. A., and C. E. Hall. 1947. *J. Biol. Chem.* 167: 705.

Katz, S., K. Gutfreund, S. Shulman, and J. D. Ferry. 1952. *J. Am. Chem. Soc.* 74: 5706.

Kerridge, D., R. W. Horne, and A. M. Glauert. 1962. *J. Mol. Biol.* 4: 227.

Kielley, W. W., and W. F. Harrington. 1960. *Biochim. Biophys. Acta* 41: 401.

Kobayashi, T., J. N. Rinker, and H. Koffler. 1959. *Arch. Biochem. Biophys.* 84: 342.

Laki, K., and L. Lorand. 1948. *Science* 108: 280.

Laki, K., J. A. Gladner, and J. E. Falk. 1960. *Nature* 187: 758.

Loewy, A. G., K. Dunathan, R. Kriel, and H. L. Wolfinger. 1961. *J. Biol. Chem.* 236: 2625.

Lorand, L., and W. R. Middlebrook. 1952. *Biochem. J.* 52: 196.

Lowey, S., and C. Cohen. 1962. *J. Mol. Biol.* 4: 293.

Lowey, S., J. Kucera, and A. Holtzer. 1963. *J. Mol. Biol.* 7: 234.

Lowy, J., and J. Hanson. 1964. *Nature* 202: 538.

Matoltsy, A. G. 1964. *Nature* 201: 1130.

Moffitt, W., and J. T. Yang. 1956. *Proc. Natl. Acad. Sci. U.S.* 42: 597.

Mueller, H. 1964. *J. Biol. Chem.* 239: 797.

Page, S. G., and H. E. Huxley. 1963. *J. Cell. Biol.* 19: 369.

Pauling, L., and R. B. Corey. 1953a. *Proc. Natl. Acad. Sci. U.S.* 39: 253.

Pauling, L., and R. B. Corey. 1953b. *Nature* 171: 59.

Pauling, L., R. B. Corey, and H. R. Branson. 1951. *Proc. Natl. Acad. Sci. U.S.* 37: 205.

Perutz, M. F. 1951. *Nature* 167: 1053.

Phelps, R. A., and F. W. Putnam. 1960. In *The Plasma Proteins*, Vol. I, ed. F. W. Putnam. New York: Academic Press, Inc. P. 143.

Ramachandran, G. N., and G. Kartha. 1955. *Nature* 176: 593.

Rice, R. V. 1961a. *Biochim. Biophys. Acta* 52: 602.

Rice, R. V. 1961b. *Biochim. Biophys. Acta* 53: 29.

Rice, R. V. 1964. In *Biochemistry of Muscle Contraction*, ed. J. Gergely. Dedham Conference, 1962. Boston: Little, Brown and Company. P. 41.

Rich, A., and F. H. C. Crick. 1955. *Nature* 176: 915.

Shoenberg, C. G. 1958. *J. Biophys. Biochem. Cytol.* 4: 609.

Shulman, S. 1953. *J. Am. Chem. Soc.* 75: 5845.

Siegel, B. M., J. P. Mernan, and H. A. Scheraga. 1953. *Biochim. Biophys. Acta* 11: 329.

Sjöstrand, F. S., and E. Andersson-Cedergren. 1957. *J. Ultrastruct. Res.* 1: 74.

Stryer, L., C. Cohen, and R. Langridge. 1963. *Nature* 197: 793.

Szent-Györgyi, A. G., and C. Cohen. 1957. *Science* 126: 697.

Szent-Györgyi, A. G., C. Cohen, and D. E. Philpott. 1960. *J. Mol. Biol.* 2: 133.

Waugh, D. F. 1954. *Advan. Protein Chem.* 9: 325.

Weibull, C. 1948. *Biochim. Biophys. Acta* 2: 351.

Weibull, C. 1951. *Acta Chem. Scand.* 5: 529.

Worthington, C. R. 1959. *J. Mol. Biol.* 1: 398.

Yaguchi, M., J. Foster, and H. Koffler. 1964. *Abstr. Intern. Congr. Biochem., 6th, New York, 1964.* II: 210.

Zobel, C. R., and F. D. Carlson. 1963. *J. Mol. Biol.* 7: 78.

# Design and Assembly of Organized Biological Structures[1]

**D. L. D. Caspar**

*Children's Cancer Research Foundation*
*The Children's Hospital Medical Center*
*and*
*The Harvard Medical School*
*Boston, Massachusetts*

## Introduction

Organized biological structures are built up of smaller structures arranged in a definite pattern. This is simply the definition of any kind of organized structure. The distinctive feature of biological structures is that they have been selected for specific functions in dynamic self-reproducing systems. The component parts can be synthesized separately by a subassembly process and then associated, following definite rules, to form the organized structure. Different types of control mechanisms are used at the various stages of synthesis and assembly. The advantage of such a process is that biological control can be exercised at each level of organization, and even if mistakes occur at the various stages, the defective components can be rejected. The net result is that very complex systems can be built up with high efficiency.

The synthesis of specific small molecules such as amino acids, nucleotides, and lipids can be controlled by coupled enzymatic reactions. The energy to drive these reactions is generally provided by phosphorylated compounds, such as ATP, which are themselves enzymatically synthesized, using either the

[1] This investigation was supported by Public Health Service Research Grant CA-04696 from the National Cancer Institute.

191

energy released by degradation of food molecules or that provided by photo-synthesis. The synthesis of macromolecules that are relatively simple homo-polymers, such as polysaccharides, can also be directly controlled by enzymes.

The synthesis of specific macromolecules, as the enzymes themselves and structural proteins, cannot, however, be controlled efficiently by enzymes. The basic control mechanisms in protein synthesis are now quite clear. The order of amino acid residues in proteins is determined by messenger RNA molecules (m-RNA), which in general are synthesized on a DNA template that also serves as the template for its own reduplication. (In the special case of RNA viruses, the RNA is its own template.) The maximum size polypeptide chain that can be synthesized in this way is limited not only by the amount of information that can be contained in a nucleic acid molecule, but, more signif-icantly, by the accuracy with which this information can be translated into a polypeptide chain.

It appears likely, as we shall see, that the maximum size polypeptide chain that can be accurately synthesized on a nucleic acid template probably con-sists of less than 1,000 amino acid residues. To form a large protein structure requires additional control mechanisms at a higher level of organization. A very large covalently bonded molecule could be built up of several different smaller chain segments that are linked together by specific enzymes. Because of the specificity of enzymes, such a subassembly process could be carried out with high accuracy, but a considerable amount of genetic information would be required to specify the sequences of all the chain segments and all the enzymes. Since the amount of genetic information required would increase much more rapidly than the number of residues in the structure, economical use of the nucleic acid coding capacity would very likely limit the maximum size of such a protein to only several times greater than that which could be directly synthesized.

Large organized biological structures can be formed with high efficiency — that is, both accurately and economically — by making use of the specificity of the noncovalent-bond interactions that are possible between macromole-cules. It is clear that specific noncovalent interactions play a significant role at all levels of biological organization. These interactions determine the specific association of enzymes with their substrates and of antibodies with antigens. A number of proteins can be reversibly denatured, which demon-strates that their stable configuration is determined by the specific pattern of intrachain interactions allowed by the amino acid sequence under particular environmental conditions. Moreover, many different protein molecules can reversibly associate in definite structures held together by specific noncovalent bonds between the units. The most significant feature of organized structures built in this way is that their design and stability can be determined completely by the bonding properties of their constituent units. Thus, once the compo-nent parts are made, they may assemble themselves without a template or other specific external genetic control.

A biological advantage of a self-assembly design for any large structure is that it can be completely specified by the genetic information required to direct the synthesis of the component molecules. Economical use of the genetic information that can be carried by the nucleic acid will require that identical copies of some basic molecule or group of molecules be used to build any large structure. Organized structures, such as ribosome particles, may be built by self-assembly of different subunits, but the maximum size structure that can be built of units, all of which are different, is limited by the available genetic information. Large protein-containing structures such as the protein coats of virus particles, muscle filaments, tendons, cell membranes, etc., will necessarily consist of a large number of subunits, and the number of different types of subunits will, in general, be small. In many protein structures there may be only one type of subunit. Examples of some highly organized biological structures that can be dissociated into subunits that are, or at least appear to be, identical are the protein coat of tobacco mosaic virus, the actin and myosin filaments of muscle, collagen fibers, and the hemocyanin aggregates of invertebrates. In all these, the dissociated components can be reassembled under appropriate conditions *in vitro* to produce structures that appear the same as, or at least very similar to, the organized structures assembled *in vivo*.

It is clear then that many biological structures are built of identical structure units by a self-assembly process. The nature of possible designs for such structures is limited by the principles that govern their construction. Additional control mechanisms can operate in structures built by self-assembly of two or more different components, but the same general principles will apply to their construction.

The nature of biological organization, in both its static structural aspect and its dynamic functional aspect, is governed by two broad general principles: the physical principle of minimum energy embodied in the laws of thermodynamics, and the biological principle of natural selection that is the foundation of the theory of evolution. The operation of these principles is evident at all levels of biological organization. All chemical reactions in living cells proceed in the direction that leads to a decrease in free energy. Enzymes can enormously speed up the rates of reaction, but they cannot change the energy levels of substrate or product. Thus, the only reactions that can occur are those which are thermodynamically possible. The operation of natural selection has picked out those reactions from the multitude of possible reactions that meet the functional requirements of each living system. It might seem, at first sight, considering the complexity of even the simplest biological systems and the extreme generality of the fundamental principles that govern their organization, that these principles could not serve as the basis for making any significant predictions regarding the nature of any aspect of biological organization. However, this is not the case. Two general aspects of biological organization will be considered here from the point of view of how certain functional requirements can be realized energetically. The first is the accuracy of the construction processes used in living systems that establishes limitations on the size of structures that can be built efficiently by different processes. The second is the nature of the possible designs and control mechanisms that may be selected for self-assembly structures.

## Size of Protein Subunits

The molecular weights of the polypeptide chains of well-characterized globular proteins are roughly in the range 10,000–70,000, with values in the range 15,000–40,000 occurring most frequently. Many protein structures have much higher molecular weights, but in all cases that have been carefully investigated there is, at least, an indication that they are built up of smaller chain segments. The lower limit for the size of protein molecules is undoubtedly determined by the minimum size chain that can form a stable functional structure. The upper limit, as already suggested, may be determined by the accuracy of the synthetic process.

The sequence of amino acids is determined by an m-RNA template, and the amino acids are added sequentially to build the chain. The accuracy of the over-all reaction will be determined by the precision of the individual steps. If the mean probability of a mistake (e.g., a wrong amino acid being added) at each step is $\delta$, then the probability of correctly synthesizing a polypeptide chain of $n$ amino acids is $P = (1 - \delta)^n$. Since protein synthesis proceeds with reasonable efficiency, $\delta$ must be very small; thus $(1 - \delta)^n$ is effectively equal to $e^{-\delta n}$. Judging from studies on the amino acid sequence of small proteins, it appears that an accuracy at least 99% or better may be achieved in their synthesis. For an error level of less than 1% in the synthesis of a polypeptide consisting of 100 amino acids and with a molecular weight $ca.$ 10,000, $\delta$ would have to be less than $10^{-4}$; similarly for $n = 1,000$, $\delta < 10^{-5}$.

Many amino acid substitutions may not produce a defective protein, and mistakes that prevent the normal folding of the polypeptide could be rejected if they are sensitive to proteolytic digestion. The serious mistakes would be those which compete or interfere with the normal function of the correctly synthesized protein. It is obviously difficult to decide, as yet, from available experimental evidence what is the maximum size of polypeptide chains directly synthesized on an RNA template and what is the maximum level of error that can be tolerated in their synthesis. Nevertheless, it does appear likely that this maximum size comprises less than 1,000 amino acids, and the normal error level may not be greater than 1%. This suggests that the mean probability of a mistake at each amino acid addition is not greater than one in 10,000, and may be at least an order of magnitude smaller.

The probability of a wrong amino acid residue being added at a particular step in synthesis can also be estimated from the degree of specificity possible in the processes involved in incorporation. The basic processes are, first, the linking of the amino acids to specific adapter molecules (s-RNA) by activating enzymes that are specific for each amino acid and each adapter and, second, the alignment of the amino acid at the growing end of the peptide chain by binding the appropriate aminoacyl-s-RNA molecule to a specific site on the m-RNA–ribosome complex. Before the actual discovery of specific adapter molecules, the need for them to align the amino acid properly on the template was predicted by Crick, on the grounds that there was no energetically feasible mechanism by which an RNA template could directly distinguish amino acids with similar side chains. The precision of the distinction, at the level of amino acid activation, depends on the ability of the enzyme to discriminate among different side chains. The probability of mistakes at this level will depend on the specificity of association of particular amino acids with their activating enzymes and on the reaction rate for forming the aminoacyl-adapter bond.

There are three pairs of amino acids whose side chains differ only by a single methyl group: glycine-alanine, valine-isoleucine, and serine-threonine. It is sterically possible for the smaller amino acid of each pair to bind to the enzyme specific for the larger; e.g., glycine may bind to the alanine-activating enzyme. The relative specificity of the enzyme for the larger amino acid of each pair must be determined by the interactions with the additional methyl group. If this methyl group fits compactly in a nonpolar cavity in the enzyme surface, the maximum energy from van der Waals interaction (i.e., transient dipole-induced dipole interaction) would be the order of $-1$ kcal/mole. Similarly, the maximum contribution of hydrophobic bonding (i.e., the change in free energy on removing the methyl group from an aqueous to a hydrocarbon environment) would also be the order of $-1$ kcal/mole. Since there are no other physically significant interactions probable for the methyl group, the maximum difference in free energy for glycine bound to the alanine enzyme, or for the other two corresponding mistakes, would be the order of $+2$ kcal/mole. The concentration ratio of enzyme associated with the wrong amino acid compared to the correct combination is $e^{-\Delta F/RT}$ (assuming equal concentration for the free amino acids). Thus, there is about a 3% chance that the wrong amino acid is bound. It is physically unlikely that any non-covalent association mechanism could distinguish with a specificity much better than this between any pair of molecules that differ by a single methyl group. On the other hand, the ability of the activating enzymes to distinguish different s-RNA molecules may be quite high, since even a difference of a single nucleotide could lead to a large change in the binding energy.

The probability that the wrong amino acid is covalently linked to the s-RNA adapter depends not only on the chance of forming the wrong enzyme-substrate complex, but, in addition, on the enzyme-catalyzed reaction rate. Even if the presence or absence of the methyl group in the substrate did not influence the reaction rate, the chance of forming the wrong link is not simply the same as the chance of forming the wrong complex. If the reaction rate is slow compared to the mean time the substrate remains associated with the enzyme, the probability of a reaction occurring would be proportional to this time, which is, in turn, dependent on the equilibrium constant. Under these conditions, the probability of linking the wrong amino acid would be proportional to the square of the equilibrium constant for forming the noncovalently bonded complex, e.g., about one chance in 1,000 that glycine would be linked in place of alanine to the alanine adapter RNA. The specificity could be higher than this if the additional methyl group of alanine were involved in catalyzing the reaction. Moreover, the discrimination between amino acids with more distinctive side chains could obviously be better than this. These calculations indicate that at the level of amino acid activation the probability of mistakes involving amino acids with similar side chains could be less than $10^{-4}$, but it is unlikely to be a great deal less.

The adapter RNA presumably attaches to m-RNA using the same kind of noncovalent base-pairing as occurs in DNA. Thus the specificity of this combination may be comparable to that in which nucleotides are incorporated in DNA synthesis. The probability that at any nucleotide addition a wrong base is incorporated in a DNA chain can be estimated from the energy of the nucleotide-pairing interactions and also from the frequency of gene mutation together with an estimate of the number of nucleotide pairs per gene. Both estimates suggest that the probability of a mistake at each addition is the order of $10^{-8}$ or less. This very low error level in nucleotide incorporation implies that polynucleotide chains consisting of the order of $10^6$ residues and a molecular weight of $6 \times 10^8$ for a double-helical DNA molecule can be replicated with a high degree of accuracy. There are undoubtedly differences in the nucleotide interactions involved in amino acid incorporation and those involved in nucleic acid synthesis. For example, the nature of the ribosome structure plays a part in the specificity of the adapter-messenger interaction, since mutations in the ribosome structure can lead to significant errors in the way in which the messenger is read. Nevertheless, the probability of reading mistakes may not generally be greater than that of errors in amino acid activation.

It is thus physically plausible that the mean probability of a mistake at each amino acid addition in protein synthesis is less than $10^{-4}$. We have already seen that a precision of this order of magnitude would be required for accurate synthesis of polypeptide chains of the sizes that are produced by cells. Therefore it appears that the specificity that may be realized in the individual steps of protein synthesis corresponds to the limit determined by the physically possible specificity of the molecular interactions involved. In other words, the adapter-coupling and the template-control mechanisms have generally evolved to operate as efficiently as possible. The numerical estimates of the precision given here are necessarily approximate. Moreover, the sensitivity of the functional properties of all proteins to mistakes in synthesis is not the same, and for any particular protein, mistakes at certain positions in the sequence will be much more critical than at others. Nevertheless, it is clear that there will be some finite error in the synthesis of any protein, and the over-all accuracy will decrease approximately exponentially with the length of the chain being made. Any plausible estimate of the possible specificity of the steps in protein synthesis indicates that the maximum size chain that can be made accurately is considerably smaller than the coding capacity of cellular DNA molecules. In contrast, the physically possible accuracy of the DNA-copying mechanism is several orders of magnitude greater than that of protein synthesis. Thus, the maximum size DNA molecule that can be efficiently copied may code for a thousand or more different proteins of optimum size.

## Size of Self-Assembly Structures

Unlike a template-controlled synthesis, the maximum size of a self-assembly structure that is held together by noncovalent bonds is not intrinsically limited by the probability of mistakes at the individual steps in the construction. The reason for this is that noncovalent bonding is normally spontaneously reversible, whereas enzymes are generally required to make or break the covalent bonds of biological molecules. Mistakes in protein synthesis could only be corrected by digesting the defective molecules and reutilizing the component amino acids for new synthesis. In contrast, mistakes in self-assembly can be corrected during the construction process. The correct bonding will necessarily be that which leads to a state of lowest realizable free energy for the system — if this were not the case, a stable structure could not exist. Incorrect bonding may occur frequently during assembly if the difference in free energy between different bonding states is small, but through dissociation and reassociation the most stable bonding patterns can be continued. Irreversible mistakes could be produced by covalent cross-linking or incorporation of abnormal units that bind firmly and block normal growth. However, natural selection will tend to reject any system in which such irreversible mistakes are common.

The ordered self-assembly structures that have been most intensively studied are the regular crystal lattices. The maximum possible size of a crystal is in principle unlimited — at least to a scale where macroscopic forces do not affect the mechanical stability. Under optimum conditions a crystal can grow indefinitely as long as there is a supply of the constituent molecules. A characteristic of many biological structures is that they have well-determined dimensions, and it is evident that the regular crystal lattices, which are capable of indefinite extension without change in their local properties, are generally unsuited for the functional requirements of a living system. The limited size of biological self-assembly structures is not a consequence of any physical limitation in the accuracy of the construction process; rather, designs have been selected for specific functions that are intrinsically self-limited. Self-limitation may result from the coordinated interactions between two or more different types of components, or it may be an essential property of the stable bonding pattern of a single type of subunit. Before discussing the nature of the possible designs for organized biological structures of finite extent, it will be relevant to consider some general aspects of the thermodynamics of the self-assembly process that are independent of design.

## Thermodynamics of Self-Assembly

An essential characteristic of any self-assembly structure consisting of a large number of units is that its construction is a cooperative process. Examples are the condensation of a gas into a liquid and the growth of crystals. The stability of any particular condensed state of matter is determined by the sum of the differences in free energy of each unit in that state compared to all other possible states. Molecules can crystallize even though the free energy per molecule in the lattice is only a fraction of $k$T lower than the free energy in solution. Similarly, even if the difference in free energy per molecule in different possible lattices is quite small, all the molecules may crystallize in the most stable form. As the number of units that can be combined in a condensed state increases, the smaller is the specificity required in the molecular interactions to determine a unique stable state for the system.

Since the stability of any condensed state consisting of a large number of units is a very sensitive function of the relative free energy of the units, the transitions between different possible states will take place almost discontinuously at critical environmental conditions. The cooperative nature of the molecular interactions in solids and liquids is indicated by their sharply defined melting and boiling points. Similarly, the helix-coil transition of polymer molecules that corresponds to a melting process becomes more sharply defined as the length of the polymer increases. The same general thermodynamic considerations also apply to intermolecular self-assembly of proteins in organized structures: the greater the number of units in the structure, the more critical the conditions for its formation.

We have seen that a selective advantage of self-assembly in the construction of any biological structure is the economical use of genetic information. Another advantage, particularly for any dynamic biological system, is the capacity of such structures to undergo controlled reversible changes in state in response to environmental changes. The changes in state can be from one organized structure to another as, for example, the transitions between different lattice forms that occur in crystals or the transition involved in the contraction of the bacteriophage tail sheath; alternatively, the change can be from an organized to a disorganized state as in a dissociation or melting process. The conformational stability of a protein molecule is determined by the cooperative interactions between the amino acid residues. Many proteins may have only a single stable functional state, but others undoubtedly can exist in different conformations with distinctive functional properties. The conformational changes postulated for allosteric enzymes may be triggered by binding the substrate through a cooperative process even though the differences in free energy for the individual side chains in the two conformations are very small. Similarly, the state of association of intermolecular aggregates, such as virus particles, chromosomes, etc., can respond to small changes in environmental conditions. A change in state of organization may be coupled to an energy-yielding reaction such as the splitting of ATP — this occurs in muscle contraction and in other systems that do mechanical work — but the process may still be a cooperative response to an external stimulus that is intrinsically determined by the bonding properties of the constituent units.

Even though the design of a self-assembly structure is determined by the properties of its component parts, it does not necessarily follow that the assembly of the energetically favored structure will occur spontaneously. The crystallization process provides a clear illustration of this point. Pure liquids can be cooled below their freezing point (more exactly, their equilibrium crystallization temperature) without crystallizing. Since crystallization is a cooperative process, the activation energy for initiating the process is relatively high; that is, the relative free energy of a molecule in a lattice increases as the size of the crystal decreases. Thus, the initiation of crystal growth requires a nucleation process to overcome this energy barrier. Although the details of this process are not well understood, it generally involves "impurities" which serve to catalyze the crystallization. The rate of crystal growth and the final size of the crystal depend on the number of nucleating centers initially present. Moreover, some molecules can crystallize in different lattices with comparable free energy, and in such situations the nature of the nucleation process may determine the design.

The cooperative assembly of biological structures may be subject to the same general type of kinetic control, but the nucleating agent may itself be a gene product. Such control could be described as enzymatic if it accelerates the rate of assembly or as a template if it selects a unique design from a number of possibilities. It might be deemed inappropriate to apply the term self-assembly to a construction process that involves some type of catalytic rate or template control. However, the point to be emphasized is the essential control step in construction. All biological synthesis, in general, requires some combination of self-assembly, template, and enzymatic control. Protein synthesis involves enzyme-substrate association and other self-assembly processes, as well as enzyme-catalyzed bond formation. The importance of the template is that there is no way in which the amino acids and enzymes alone can determine a unique sequence for a growing polypeptide chain. In contrast, the design of intermolecular aggregates such as virus particles or muscle filaments is essentially controlled by the specific bonding between their component parts, whether or not additional controls are applied in the assembly.

The free energy of any persisting assembly must be at a minimum that is separated by energy barriers from other potentially stable states. A structure that does not represent the lowest possible state of free energy for the components is said to be metastable if the activation energy is large enough to prevent the spontaneous transition to a more stable state. The design of any stable or metastable structure is necessarily such that any small change in its coordinate parameters leads to an increase in free energy. The simplest designs for ordered structures are those that result from the specific association of identical structure units. The structure unit is defined as the smallest functionally equivalent subdivision, and may be a single molecule, a group of molecules, or even a part of a molecule that has regular substructure. The possible minimum-energy designs for such ordered structures can be systematically analyzed by considering the ways in which identical units can be equivalently or quasi-equivalently related in space. The designs of more highly differentiated structures can often be described as ordered assemblies of regular substructures. The organization of any self-assembly structure will be determined by the bonding properties of its parts and the control mechanisms that are applied in its construction.

## Design of Self-Assembly Structures

Any ordered structure built of identical units must have some type of well-defined symmetry. Specific bonding between the units necessarily leads to a symmetrical structure, since there will be only a limited number of ways in which each unit can be connected to its neighbors to form the maximum number of most stable bonds. Spatial symmetry relations can be represented by geometrical models, and all the possible symmetry relations can be mathematically enumerated. However, the epistemological relevance of these mathematical abstractions to the design of real structures is often misunderstood. The fact that a geometrical model illustrates the appearance of a physical structure may be fortuitous unless the model also represents the energetically significant spatial relations in the real structure.

The view that the harmony of the real world can be deduced from the properties of abstract models without attempting to relate the postulates on which the models are constructed to the nature of our empirical knowledge is the essential basis of Platonic mysticism. This type of mysticism is evident in many of the attempts to construct models to account for the molecular morphology of organized biological structures, but mysticism is, of course, not restricted to this field. An elegant illustration of the fundamental irrelevance of Platonic geometrical concepts of problems of physical design is provided by Kepler's *Mysterium Cosmographicum*. In this work Kepler tried to account for the ratio of the radii of the orbits of the known planets in terms of the ratio of the radii of spheres that consecutively inscribe and cirumscribe the five regular polyhedra, as shown in Fig. 1. This model is wrong, not because it is in disagreement with experimental observations, but, more fundamentally, because the symmetry relations on which it is based are unrelated to the energetically significant interactions that have determined the structure of the solar system.

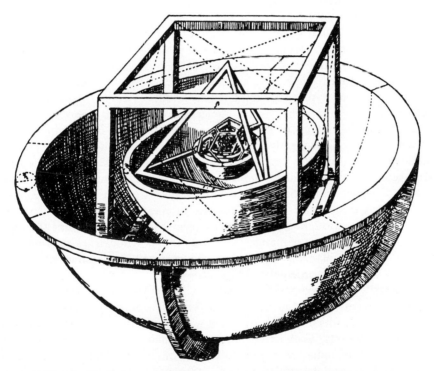

**Fig. 1.** Kepler's model of the solar system, from his *Mysterium Cosmographicum,* published, in 1596, was based on symmetry relations among the five regular polyhedra (in the order, octahedron, icosahedron, dodecahedron, tetrahedron, and cube, from the center of this model). These mystical relations, however, have no intrinsic physical relation to the structure they are designed to represent.

Models can be classified as empirical or theoretical. An empirical model is an effective way of summarizing the results of a particular set of observations, but it is hazardous to generalize from such a model or to regard its properties as intrinsically significant beyond the point of representing the observations. A theoretical model, on the other hand, is a logical consequence of an abstraction. In fundamental theories, the basic abstractions are statements of the nature of the knowledge that can be obtained from particular types of observations, rather than generalizations from the observations themselves. The test of a theory is not only that its predictions agree with observations but, moreover, that the postulates are epistemologically sound and that the conclusions follow logically from these postulates. There is a regrettable tendency in science to regard as theory any sort of calculation or model-building — or, for that matter, anything that is not empirical observation. However, scientific theory consists fundamentally of abstracting the general rules that govern the behavior of real systems.

The basic rule that governs the design of any stable physical structure is the condition that the system be in a state of minimum free energy. Any condensed state of matter must have some type of order, and the nature of this order is determined by the interactions between its parts. The two general types of order are typified by crystals and liquids: a crystal has a uniquely determined structure, whereas the molecules of a liquid are only locally ordered. Random states of matter occur only when the interaction energy between the parts is negligibly small, as in a gas or dilute solution. The perfect order of a crystal lattice results because there is only one type of packing arrangement of the constituent molecules that leads to a state of minimum free energy. The long-range disorder of a liquid is a consequence of the increase in entropy that compensates for the increase in energy resulting from the departures from optimum packing of the molecules. Crystals are not the only regularly ordered states of matter. Any array that is symmetric about a point, along a line, in a plane, as well as in space, represents a possible minimum-energy design for an ordered structure.

The types of ordered structures that are simplest to describe are those built up of equivalently related identical units. The concept of equivalence is illustrated in Fig. 2, which represents a shell with icosahedral symmetry built up of 60 identical units. Each unit is bonded to its neighbors in exactly the same way; thus all the units are in equivalent environments. Fixing the bond distances and the angles between them is sufficient to determine the structure. Any structure built of equivalently related units is necessarily symmetric, and the description of the symmetry defines all the structurally significant spatial relations among the parts. The only possible spatial symmetry operations are reflection, inversion, rotation, and translation. All the combinations of these operations have been mathematically enumerated and are represented by the regular point-, line-, plane-, and space-groups. The epistemological relevance of these abstract geometrical constructs to the design of physical structures is

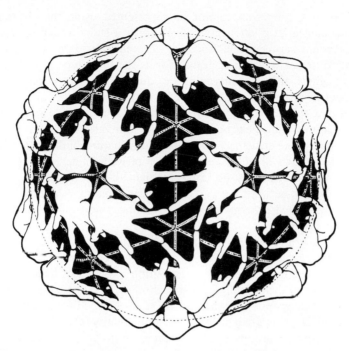

**Fig. 2.** A model illustrating strict equivalence in a shell with
icosahedral symmetry constructed from 60 identical enantiomorphic structure units. The symmetry relations in this shell are
indicated by the underlying triangular surface lattice. Models
for biological structures in which symmetrical objects are used
to represent the subunits do not bring out the point that the
structure units are enantiomorphic and have specific bond sites.
This drawing has been constructed to emphasize the fact that
the design of any ordered structure is determined by the bonding
between its parts.

that they represent all the ways in which identical units can be bonded together so that all the units are in equivalent environments. Since biological
structures are built of enantiomorphic molecules of one hand only — as indicated by the left hands in Fig. 2 — mirror or inversion symmetry is not possible at the molecular level of organization. This restricts the regular designs
that can be selected for biological structures to the possible combinations of
rotational and translational symmetry.

It is evident that any symmetry group represents a possible minimum-
energy design for an ordered structure. The necessary energetic relations
between the structure units in such regular systems can be implicitly represented by the geometrical formalism of strict equivalence. However, many
minimum-energy designs for ordered structures built of equal units with

specific bonding properties cannot be represented using the abstraction of strict equivalence. It is often possible to form a stable ordered structure in which the bonds between equal units are systematically deformed in a number of slightly different ways. If each unit forms the same type of bonds with its neighbors, then all the units will be quasi-equivalently related. Quasi-equivalence in ordered structures can be defined as any small, nonrandom variation in a regular bonding pattern that leads to a more stable structure than does strictly equivalent bonding. A random variation in bonding would lead to a liquid-like structure. Any ordered structure built of quasi-equivalently related units will still have some type of well-defined symmetry. However, the over-all symmetry no longer defines all the structurally significant bonding relations between the parts. All these bonding relations can, nevertheless, be described in terms of all the symmetry and quasi-symmetry relations in the structure.

A clear illustration of quasi-equivalent bonding is provided by the coiled-coil structure of the fibrous proteins that can be represented by two or three $\alpha$-helical chains supercoiled about a common axis. Strict helical symmetry, as in the regular $\alpha$-helix, requires a straight axis, and the equivalent relation of all the peptide groups is defined by the screw axis. However, if the helix is bent, then all the groups can no longer be equivalently related. In the $\alpha$-helical coiled coil, peptide groups occur in seven symmetrically distinct environments, and the over-all symmetry of the structure can be represented by equivalently related segments of seven peptides. However, since the departures from the regular $\alpha$-helix are small, all the peptide groups are quasi-equivalently related. The coiled-coil structure is very stable, since the increase in free energy required to deform the $\alpha$-helical chains periodically is more than offset by the decrease in free energy resulting from the interhelix bonding.

Possible designs for ordered structures built of quasi-equivalently related units can be analyzed by considering the energetically plausible systematic modifications of strictly regular designs. Since quasi-equivalence cannot be expressed in absolute mathematical terms, the decision as to what constitutes quasi-equivalence depends on the physical analysis of the energetically allowable variation in the bonding of particular systems. Thus, a comprehensive description of all possible designs for structures built of quasi-equivalently related units cannot be obtained by the rigorous enumeration that has been applied to strict symmetry groups. Nevertheless, the plausible minimum-energy designs for many different types of structures can be systematically described. Quasi-equivalent bonding is a topological necessity in the design of closed shells constructed from a large number of identical units, and here all the designs that maintain a regular pattern of local connection can be enumerated. Quasi-equivalent bonding will occur in any structure in which all the interactions between neighboring units are not compatible with the same repeating pattern. For example, if a set of units designed to form a linear aggregate has two sets of bond sites that require different axial separation for optimum bonding, these units could not form a regularly periodic aggregate in which all the optimum bonds are made. Such structure units could form a quasi-periodic linear aggregate of determined length. As more units are combined, progressively greater deformations of the units would be required to form both sets of bonds. Thus a point would be reached where further association would be thermodynamically unstable. This type of quasi-periodic axial bonding can account for the stable two- and three-turn aggregates of tobacco mosaic virus protein that form under certain solvent conditions, and could also account for the stable three-turn aggregates of cephalopod hemocyanin and the six-turn aggregates of gastropod hemocyanin. Moreover, quasi-periodic bonding could also provide a mechanism for size limitation of two- and three-dimensional lattice aggregates.

The design of some biological structures may be based on three-dimensional lattices — for example, in the packing of collagen molecules in tendon and in the polymerization of fibrin. The size of such aggregates is likely to be determined by the kinetics of their formation. However, the occurrence of regular crystalline inclusions in cells often reflects a pathological condition. Most globular proteins can be crystallized in vitro, but they generally have the property that they remain soluble in vivo either as monomers or as small aggregates. Hemoglobin, for example, is soluble at very high concentrations under physiological conditions, but the mutated sickle-cell hemoglobin that can associate more readily does so with grave consequences. The well-determined size of many multienzyme complexes and other small protein aggregates indicates that the designs selected are such that the specific bonding potential of the parts is saturated in some closed configuration. If such aggregates consist of identical molecules or groups of molecules, they will necessarily have some type of point-group symmetry, and their design can be represented by a closed-surface lattice. Helical structures, or, more generally, all linearly periodic assemblies have some type of line-group symmetry, and these designs can be represented by open-ended, tubular-surface lattices.

The enumeration of possible designs for surface lattices can be carried out by considering the ways in which regular plane lattices can be connected to form cylinders or closed shells so that each structure unit can form the same pattern of contacts with its neighbors. Describing the design of helical or polyhedral intermolecular aggregates in terms of surface lattices has the advantage that the local bonding relations that determine the over-all symmetry can be recognized easily. Moreover, it is possible to represent in this way many types of physically significant quasi-equivalent bonding arrangements that could not be described in terms of strict symmetry concepts.

Buckminster Fuller first recognized the general relevance of surface lattices in the analysis of energetically favorable designs for closed containers. His geodesic domes (see Fig. 3) can be described as icosahedral surface lattices

**Fig. 3.** A Fuller geodesic radome. The surface is made up of quasi-equivalent triangles grouped in hexamers and pentamers about the small rings of the dome. This design can be derived by a triangulation of the surface lattice underlying the model in Fig. 2 and leads to the addition of points with quasi-hexagonal symmetry in the surface.

derived from the plane equilateral triangular net (i.e., the hexagonal lattice), and they represent optimum designs for closed containers. It is not surprising that the same type of design has been selected in the construction of the protein coats of many isometric virus particles. However, the design problem is not exactly the same for molecular shells and man-made domes. Geodesic domes are obviously not self-assembly structures, nor are all the component parts identical. The fact that the solutions to different physical problems have the same mathematical form may mislead one into believing that the mathematical model itself has some intrinsic or occult significance. Kepler's model shown in Fig. 1 includes polyhedra with icosahedral symmetry, but the relations between this model and the icosahedral structures shown in Figs. 2 and 3 do not imply any meaningful physical relation. The possible types of spatial symmetry are restricted by the nature of space, but the physical relevance of these abstractions is to be found, not in the designs themselves, but in their relation to the physical interactions that determine the properties of real structures.

Icosahedral surface lattices represent the optimum designs for highly subdivided closed containers. However, considering only the interactions between the parts in the surface, they are not the only possible designs for such structures. The stability of the protein coat of a virus particle, for example, will depend on both the bonding between its structure units and their bonding with the contents of the particle (e.g., the nucleic acid). The occurrence of icosahedral designs for many different virus particles indicates that the bonding properties of their coat proteins have played a predominant role in the selection. However, if there are specific interactions with other components, a design for the coat may be selected that is not intrinsically the most stable bonding arrangement for its structure units alone. Nevertheless, any design that is selected must, itself, be physically plausible; that is, a possible minimum-energy state for the structure with regard to small changes in its coordinate parameters must exist. The nature of such designs can be predicted *a priori*, but the decision as to which design is actually selected can only be established by experimental observation.

The ultimate objective of biomolecular structural studies is the determination of the physically significant molecular anatomy. The realization of this objective requires accurate morphological observations. However, these observations cannot be interpreted nor even be accurately described without a clear understanding of the nature of the forces that determine the morphology. D'Arcy W. Thompson has shown in *On Growth and Form*[2] that the morphology of even complex organisms can be described in a way that relates the appearance to the physical forces that determine the appearance. For the molecular structures, the important forces are the bonds between the component parts. Organized biological structures are built of enantiomorphic molecules with specific bonding properties. Any structure consisting of identical parts must have some regularity, and the possible designs are restricted by the nature of the assembly process. The designs selected are those suited for specific functions.

## REFERENCES

The design principles described here are of a general nature. Specific experimental observations have, however, played an important role in the development of these concepts. Some systems whose design and assembly can be analyzed in terms of these principles have been described by Dr. Cohen and Dr. Van Holde at this symposium, and Professor Katchalsky has provided an illuminating discussion of the thermodynamics of structural transitions. A more detailed analysis of the design of surface lattices and their relation to virus particle structure is given in the paper by D. L. D. Caspar and A. Klug, 1962, *Cold Spring Harbor Symp. Quant. Biol.* 27: 1, and that paper includes references to the relevant literature.

[2] 2nd ed. (Cambridge, England: Cambridge Univ. Press, 1942).

# Deoxyribonucleic Acid Arrangement in Living Sperm[1]

**Shinya Inoué** and **Hidemi Sato**

*Department of Cytology*

*Dartmouth Medical School*

*Hanover, New Hampshire*

## Birefringence of the Sperm Head

During the last decade much has been learned about the structure of deoxyribonucleic acid (DNA) molecules (Watson and Crick, 1953; Crick and Watson, 1954; Wilkins, 1963) and their genetic role in protein synthesis. In spite of the remarkable advances at the chemical level, we still know very little about the precise arrangement of DNA molecules within the chromosomes (Kaufman *et al.*, 1960; Ris, 1963). The problem was therefore to devise means to study and measure the arrangement of DNA in chromosomes in a living cell.

In order to undertake such a study, we have selected certain sperm cells in which the molecular arrangement of DNA is reflected in a measurable physical parameter (Inoué and Sato, 1962).

Figure 1 (figures follow text) depicts several stages in the process of sperm maturation in a living squid testis smear as observed through the phase contrast microscope. During spermiogenesis the chromosomes gradually become condensed and aligned as the nucleus decreases in volume. In the mature sperm the chromosomes are very dense and packed together so tightly that they can no longer be resolved as separate strands (Sato and Inoué, 1964).

[1] Supported in part by grants from the National Science Foundation (G 19487) and National Cancer Institute, United States Public Health Service (CA 04552).

209

When the same process is studied through the polarizing microscope, one sees a gradual increase in contrast of the nucleus during sperm maturation (Fig. 2). The contrast is caused by the negative birefringence of DNA molecules in the chromosomes, and the increase in contrast reflects the increased alignment and packing of the DNA molecules as the sperm matures (Seeds and Wilkins, 1950; Wilkins and Bataglia, 1953; Wilkins and Randall, 1953; Sato and Inoué, 1964).

The alignment of DNA in the mature squid sperm is nearly perfect or virtually crystalline, for an X-ray diffraction pattern of DNA in the B form (Fig. 3) was demonstrated in a bundle of fresh squid sperm by Wilkins and Randall (1953) and Wilkins (1963).

Figure 4 shows the needle-shaped heads and portions of the tails of sperm of the cave cricket *Ceuthophilus nigricans* Scudder as observed under the polarizing microscope. The head appears bright in one orientation and dark in the other, while the tail shows the reverse contrast. The contrast and the orientation of the compensator axes show that the head exhibits a negative birefringence while the tail and the acrosome exhibit a positive birefringence with respect to the length of the individual sperm (Pattri, 1932; Schmidt, 1937). The negative birefringence is intrinsic. It is caused, not by the texture of submicroscopic structures, but by the optical character of the constituent DNA molecules (Wilkins, 1951; Inoué and Sato, 1962). The coefficient of birefringence of the head measures $-2 \times 10^{-2}$, the same order of magnitude as that found for stretched gels of pure DNA (Wilkins, 1951; Seeds, 1953; Beaven *et al.*, 1955; Ruch, 1956). Protein fibers in general exhibit a positive birefringence (Schmidt, 1937).

### Effect of Polarized Ultraviolet Irradiation

We have found that irradiation of a small part of a living sperm with a beam of ultraviolet light (UV) results in the disappearance, in visible light, of the birefringence from that part (Inoué and Sato, 1962) (Fig. 5). This signifies that the molecules responsible for the birefringence could be changed structurally, destroyed, or lost. However, the last possibility can be excluded, for the dry mass of the irradiated area, as observed with the phase contrast microscope, does not change (Fig. 6).

As we have earlier stated, the oriented DNA molecules are mainly responsible for the sperm birefringence (Schmidt, 1937; Wilkins, 1951; Wilkins and Randall, 1953; Inoué and Sato, 1962; Sato and Inoué, 1964). Disappearance of sperm-head birefringence induced by irradiation in the 2,500–3,000-Å range suggests that DNA is directly absorbing the UV and losing its birefringence.

As seen in Fig. 7 (Crick and Watson, 1954; Feughelman *et al.*, 1955), the purine and pyrimidine bases in the B-form DNA lie in planes at 90° to the backbone of the molecule and form the steps of a spiral staircase. This is the form of DNA that Wilkins and his coworkers found in the fresh squid sperm by X-ray diffraction analysis (Wilkins and Bataglia, 1953; Wilkins and Randall, 1953). These bases are responsible for the greater refractive index measured at right angles to the backbone of the molecule compared with that measured along the long axis (Seeds and Wilkins, 1950; Thorell and Ruch, 1951; Seeds, 1953; Beaven *et al.*, 1955). In other words, the arrangement of the bases is responsible for the negative birefringence of DNA. The bases also absorb more light energy when UV vibrates parallel to their planes than when it vibrates perpendicular to them (Kasha, 1961). The arrangement of the bases, therefore, gives rise to a negative dichroism of DNA in UV in addition to the negative birefringence that is seen with visible light. Figure 8 shows the UV dichroism of stretched DNA films measured by Seeds and Wilkins (1950) and Seeds (1953). At 90% relative humidity, the condition giving the B-form X-ray pattern for sodium DNA, the dichroic ratio is 3.5 to 4 throughout the wavelength range 2,400 Å to 3,000 Å.

Thus, irradiation of cave-cricket sperm with the UV ray polarized with its electric vector (E-vector: indicated in figures by double arrow) vibrating parallel to the base planes should remove the birefringence more effectively than should irradiation with the UV ray polarized with its E-vector perpendicular to the base planes. This is found to be true, as shown in Fig. 9. (See Fig. 10 for a schematic diagram of the polarized-UV microbeam system.) Induction of the same degree of birefringence loss takes three to four times longer with the UV E-vector parallel to the sperm axis than with it perpendicular. This is in agreement with the UV dichroism of a pure DNA fiber that loses its birefringence two to three times faster with the UV E-vector perpendicular to the fiber axis than with it parallel (Fig. 11). Again, little loss of dry mass is observed with the phase contrast microscope. Further, Seeds (1953) has shown that the parallel absorption of UV in an irradiated DNA fiber *rises* to offset the drop of perpendicular absorption at 260 m$\mu$, which indicates, not that the bases are being destroyed, but rather that their orientations are becoming randomized. The evidence is therefore strong that the UV-induced birefringence change directly reflects disorientation of DNA bases in the sperm head.

The UV-induced change in birefringence can be used to study the detailed arrangement of DNA molecules in the living sperm head. Figure 9 shows the internal structure of the cave-cricket sperm that can be discerned under polarized light. The pictures in this figure were taken under the rectified polarizing microscope, which was designed to give a highly corrected image of weakly birefringent specimens at the maximum resolution obtainable with a light microscope (Inoué and Hyde, 1957; Inoué and Kubota, 1958; Inoué, 1961). This structure that is seen with polarized light, but which is not visible with the phase contrast microscope, gives the impression of a helical configuration of birefringent regions. Rotation of the specimen on the microscope stage shows that the alternate bright and dark regions reflect minute domains where the crystalline axes are not exactly parallel to the long axis of the sperm but slightly tilted to the left and to the right. In other words, although on the average the sperm head shows a negative birefringence as if the backbone of the DNA molecules were precisely parallel to the sperm long axis, in detail the molecules are tilted slightly and form zigzag microdomains.

## Response of Sperm to Irradiation by UV Ray Polarized at 45°

When the irradiating UV ray is polarized perpendicular to the sperm axis, the UV E-vector is nearly parallel to the DNA bases in all of the microdomains, and absorption of UV and loss of birefringence are uniform and maximum. Contrastingly, with the UV E-vector parallel to the sperm axis, the DNA bases are all nearly perpendicular to the E-vector, and absorption and birefringence loss are low. These effects are shown in Fig. 9.

When the UV is polarized with its E-vector tilted 45° to the sperm axis, microdomains with bases tilted in the same direction lose their birefringence faster than those with base planes tilted in the opposite direction. After appropriate exposure, the former microdomains lose their birefringence but the latter microdomains retain some of their birefringence. Therefore the *average* axis of birefringence, which before irradiation was parallel to the sperm axis, is now rotated toward the E-vector of the irradiating UV, as shown schematically in Fig. 12 and in the composite photograph in Fig. 13. Each pair of pictures in Fig. 13 was taken with the compensator set for reversed contrast (Köhler, 1921; Swann and Mitchison, 1950; Hartshorne and Stuart, 1960). As shown in the middle set, where the sperm axes lie parallel to the polarizer axis, the unirradiated regions show alternate black-white stripes representing the zigzag tilt of the intact microdomain axes. After irradiation with a UV beam polarized at 45° with respect to the sperm axis, as indicated by the double arrow, all microdomains in this region appear either white and gray or black and gray, showing the elimination of birefringence in individual microdomains with one direction of tilt.

The tilt angle or azimuth of the microdomains can be determined from the extinction angle of the irradiated region. As shown in Fig. 13, the contrast of the irradiated region is minimum when the sperm axis is turned 15° *counterclockwise*. Thus the rotation *clockwise* of the optical axis due to irradiation must be approximately 15°, for in this position the altered optic axis of the irradiated region is nearly parallel with the polarizer axis. Alternatively, if the sperm axis is turned 15° *clockwise*, the average axis of the irradiated region will now be 15° + 15°, or 30°, off from the polarizer axis, that is, near the angle providing maximum contrast. This experiment again supports the view that the individual DNA bases directly absorb polarized UV and lose their birefringence according to their submolecular orientation relative to the UV E-vector.

Some of the microdomains are as small as 0.2 $\mu$ in width. The arrangement of DNA bases can be shown to exist in zigzag array even when the microdomains are not resolved, for their arrangement manifests itself as a rotation of the average birefringence axis following irradiation with UV polarized at 45°. For example, the sperm head of the fruit fly (*Drosophila busckii*) is only 8 $\mu$ long and too small to reveal microdomains even under the highest resolution of the rectified polarizing microscope. However, irradiation of this sperm head with UV at 45° from the sperm axis brings about a measurable rotation (9°) of the average birefringence axis, indicating a similar zigzag arrangement of the DNA. Figure 14 shows the loss of birefringence in such an irradiated sperm head.

We have thus far shown the presence of zigzag microdomains that suggests a helical structure. However, a packing problem arises regarding the arrangement of the DNA molecules within such a structure, because it is known that the length of such molecules is of the order of at least a few hundred micra (Cairns, 1961, 1963; Kleinschmidt et al., 1962; Hershey et al., 1963).

## Photographic Microdensitometry

To ascertain the arrangement of DNA molecules within each microdomain, it is necessary to measure the birefringence and tilt angle of individual microdomains, and for this purpose we have devised the following method of photographic microdensitometry.

A set of photographic negatives of a cave-cricket sperm is taken at a particular orientation with respect to the axis of the polarizer and with the compensator (Köhler, 1921; Swann and Mitchison, 1950) set to various angles (Fig. 15). As the compensator is turned, the background intensity changes from bright to dark and back again to bright. The oriented microdomains also change contrast but reach darkness at different settings of the compensator (e.g., see point $V$, Fig. 15). It is important that such sets of photographic negatives be processed simultaneously.

Each image and its background are then scanned with a Joyce-Loebel microdensitometer (Fig. 16). The densities of the negatives are translated into densitometer readings, and the heights of the readings for each microdomain and its background are recorded (Fig. 17). When these readings are plotted against compensator settings (Fig. 18), two similar "parabolic" curves are obtained, one for the microdomain and one for the background. The lateral displacement of these two curves gives the orientation of the compensator providing maximum extinction, or the compensation angle of the specimen. It should be noted that the reading of the compensation angle ($\beta$) is directly in degrees. The method relies on the consistency of both the photographic processing and the densitometer tracings and does not require any further assumptions regarding the linearity of the gamma curve or of the densitometer readings *per se*.

This procedure is repeated several times for the same microdomain with the sperm axis oriented in several different directions with respect to the axis of the polarizer. For one microdomain we thus obtain a set of angles relating sperm orientation $\theta$ (in degrees of stage angles) to compensation angle $\beta$ for each orientation (Fig. 18). If each microdomain has acted optically as though it were a single crystalline body, then $\theta$ and $\beta$ must be related by the following equation:

$$\sin \frac{\Delta x}{2} \sin 2(\theta + \alpha) = -\sin \frac{\Gamma_{comp}}{2} \sin 2\beta \qquad (1)$$

where $\Delta x$ is the retardation (coefficient of birefringence $\times$ thickness) of the specimen, $\alpha$ is the angle by which the microdomain axis deviates from the average sperm axis, and $\Gamma_{comp}$ is the retardation of the compensator, which is known.

The equation is solved graphically (Fig. 19) by first plotting $\sin \theta$ against $\sin 2\beta$, giving rise to a curve (an ellipse) as indicated by the +'s. The intercept of the tangent to this curve near the origin with the $\sin \theta$ axis provides a tentative value for $\alpha$, since from Eq. (1) at $\beta = 0$,

$$\theta = -\alpha \qquad (2)$$

$\alpha$ is then introduced into Eq. (1), and $\sin 2(\theta + \alpha)$ plotted against $\sin 2\beta$ The correct $\alpha$ is found by successive approximation until the plotted points fit a straight line passing through the origin. This straight line is in fact the long axis of the ellipse. Naturally, no value for $\alpha$ can be found to fit this criterion unless Eq. (1) is valid, or in other words, unless the assumptions concerning the use of the equation as well as the measurements themselves are accurate. The graphic solution then provides a built-in test for the validity of both the measurements and the assumptions. The final $\alpha$ is the deviation angle, the retardation of the particular microdomain.

The deviation angles and retardations for some 50 microdomains along a 4-$\mu$ length of a cave-cricket sperm are plotted in Fig. 20. As determined from the extinction axis of the irradiated region (Fig. 13), the average axis of that region measures $-15°$ from the axis of the nonirradiated area. The azimuth or tilt angles in the nonirradiated microdomains do not oscillate $\pm 15°$, but only $\pm 10°$. However, the azimuth angles of the irradiated region oscillate with extreme angles at $-25°$ and $-5°$. These observations conflict with the assumption that all the bases of DNA molecules in each microdomain are parallel.

The observation can, however, be explained if the DNA bases within each microdomain were tilted $\pm 15°$ from the average domain axis, which in turn is tilted $\pm 10°$ from the over-all sperm axis. This is explained schematically in Fig. 21. Before irradiation, the DNA backbones in one set of microdomains are tilted $+10° \pm 15°$, or $+25°$ and $-5°$, to the over-all axis; those in the other set are tilted $-10° \pm 15°$, or $+5°$ and $-25°$. Upon exposure to UV polarized at $-45°$, those bases making less of an angle with the UV E-vector, namely, those in DNA regions tilted $+25°$ and $+5°$ absorb greater energy and lose birefringence faster than do those in regions tilted $-5°$ and $-25°$.[2] The result should be a rotation of all microdomain axes toward the UV E-vector, but to a different final angle; hence oscillation of azimuths within the irradiated area. The axes of the irradiated microdomains then change from $+10°$ and $-10°$ to $-5°$ and $-25°$. These are, in fact, the values observed, as shown in Fig. 20.

The same model predicts the azimuth changes upon irradiation with UV polarized perpendicular to the sperm axis (Fig. 22). Here, the bases tilted least ($\pm 5°$) absorb UV energy maximally, and the residual birefringence should be that due to bases tilted to the extreme, namely $+25°$ and $-25°$. This is found to be so (Fig. 23).

With UV polarized parallel to the sperm axis, most of the bases absorb little UV energy, but those with extreme tilts should absorb more, and the residual birefringence would be due to those bases tilted least, or $\pm 5°$ (Fig. 24). Figure 25 shows this expectation verified also.

It is therefore concluded that within each microdomain the axes of the DNA molecules themselves tilt by approximately 15° to the microdomain axes.

## Suggested Model

A preliminary model of the DNA arrangement in cave-cricket sperm (elaborated in the legend of Fig. 26) now emerges as a coiled coil in which the bulk of the DNA backbone is still parallel to the long axis of the sperm. However, the measured distribution of the azimuth angles and the retardation can only be satisfied by two overlapping double helices as shown in Fig. 27. In addition, if the whole helices are somewhat compressed as shown in Fig. 27, *b*

---

[2] According to the cosine square law, each group of bases would absorb UV polarized at $-45°$ by:

| Base azimuth (b) | Fraction absorbed $\cos^2(-45° - b)$ |
| --- | --- |
| $+25°$ | 0.12 |
| $-5°$ | 0.59 |
| $+5°$ | 0.41 |
| $-25°$ | 0.88 |

so that the cross-section is elliptical rather than circular (as in Fig. 27, *a*), more of the DNA backbones would fit the average tilt angles required, and the tilt of all of the microdomains would fit the measured azimuth angles without distorting the helices locally.

Taking into account the azimuth distribution across the width of the sperm, the model can be fitted to the data without locally distorting the gyres only if the double helices were interrupted at specific loci where the ends of the adjoining breaks would then lie parallel to each other. This yielded a re-synthesized image of the DNA-containing structure as shown in Fig. 28. The notion that the "breaks" may represent chromosome ends and that the chromosomes in certain insect sperm may be arranged in tandem (also see Cooper, 1952; Nakanishi, 1957; Reitberger, 1964) as illustrated is strengthened by the tritiated-thymidine labeling experiment by Taylor (1964). He finds that grasshopper sperm labeled during meiosis often show a section that lacks labeling yet shows a Feulgen-positive reaction. He interprets this as the locus of the X-chromosome, which has been demonstrated to incorporate thymidine into DNA later than do the other chromosomes in grasshopper cells.

We find that in the three sperm heads thoroughly analyzed, the breaks all occur in the same position, shorter segments and long segments always appearing respectively in the same positions. This suggests that the chromosomes are arranged not only in tandem but with a sequence that is nonrandom and unique. The average length between breaks is 3.4 $\mu$. This is in reasonably good agreement with the length of the sperm head ($41\mu$) divided by the chromosome numbers 18 and 19.

The arrangement of DNA proposed in the model apparently does not conform to published electron micrographs of other sperm (Ris, 1959; Sotelo and Cenóz, 1960). This is not too disturbing, for we found that immersion of cave-cricket sperm in dimethylsulfoxide (DMSO) does not change the magnitude or distribution of birefringence (Fig. 29), and that the DMSO-treated sperm can be embedded in plastic and sectioned for electron microscopy without further dehydration or alteration of birefringence. Dr. R. E. Kane, Department of Cytology, Dartmouth Medical School, has taken electron micrographs of such sections, shown in Fig. 30. A structural organization of DNA not inconsistent with our model is then demonstrable in the sperm nucleus with the electron microscope.

## Concluding Remarks

We have developed a new method for fine structure analysis that can reveal with high precision the distribution and orientation of dichroic molecules in living cells. Several new techniques, which may find application in related fields of study, have been introduced in this paper. The biological findings may be significant in understanding UV-induced mutations as well as the arrangement of DNA in chromosomes generally.

The probable nonrandom sequence found in the living needle-shaped sperm head should provide exceptional opportunities for controlled modifications and analyses of chromosomes and genes.

## ADDENDUM

Recently, Maestre and Kilkson (1965) computed the intrinsic birefringence of multiple-coiled DNA and proposed a valuable equation. They applied their theoretical formula to our model and measurements of cave-cricket sperm and calculated that the azimuth oscillation of each micro-domain should be $\pm 9°$ and the angle of coiling of the secondary helix 15.3°, agreeing quantitatively with our experimental results.

## REFERENCES

Beaven, G. H., R. R. Holiday, and E. A. Johnson. 1955. Optical properties of nucleic acids and their components. In *The Nucleic Acids, Chemistry and Biology*, Vol. 1, ed. E. Chargaff and J. N. Davidson. New York: Academic Press, Inc. Pp. 493–553.

Cairns, J. 1961. An estimate of the length of the DNA molecule of $T_2$ bacteriophage by autoradiography. *J. Mol. Biol.* 3: 756–761.

Cairns, J. 1963. The bacterial chromosome and its manner of replication as seen by autoradiography. *J. Mol. Biol.* 6: 208–213.

Cooper, K. W. 1952. Studies on spermatogenesis in *Drosophila*. *Trans. Am. Phil. Soc.* 1951: 146–147.

Crick, F. H. C., and J. D. Watson. 1954. The complementary structure of deoxyribose nucleic acid. *Proc. Roy. Soc. (London) Ser. B* 223: 80–96.

Feughelman, M., R. Langridge, W. E. Seeds, A. R. Stokes, H. R. Wilson, C. W. Hooper, M. H. F. Wilkins, R. K. Barclay, and L. D. Hamilton. 1955. Molecular structure of deoxyribose nucleic acid and nucleoprotein. *Nature* 175: 834–838.

Hartshorne, N. H., and A. Stuart. 1960. *Crystals and the Polarizing Microscope*, 3rd ed. London: Edward Arnold Ltd.

Hershey, A. D., E. Burge, and L. Ingraham. 1963. Cohesion of DNA molecules isolated from phage lambda. *Proc. Natl. Acad. Sci. U.S.* 49: 748–755.

Inoué, S. 1961. Polarizing microscope: design for maximum sensitivity. In *The Encyclopedia of Microscopy*, ed. G. L. Clark. New York: Reinhold Publishing Corp. Pp. 480–485.

Inoué, S., and W. L. Hyde. 1957. Studies on depolarization of light at microscope lens surfaces. II. The simultaneous realization of high resolution and high sensitivity with the polarizing microscope. *J. Biophys. Biochem. Cytol.* 3: 831–838.

Inoué, S., and H. Kubota. 1958. Diffraction anomaly in polarizing microscopes. *Nature* 182: 1725–1726.

Inoué, S., and H. Sato. 1962. Arrangement of DNA in living sperm: a biophysical analysis. *Science* 136: 1122–1124.

Kasha, M. 1961. The nature and significance of $n \to \pi^*$ transition. In *A Symposium on Light and Life*, ed. W. D. McElroy and B. Glass. Baltimore: The Johns Hopkins Press. Pp. 31–38.

Kaufmann, B. P., H. Gay, and M. McDonald. 1960. Organizational patterns within chromosomes. *Intern. Rev. Cytol.* 9: 77–127.

Kleinschmidt, A. K., D. Lang, D. Jacherts, and R. K. Zahn. 1962. Darstellung und Längenmessungen des gesaten Desoxyribonucleinsäure-Inhaltes von $T_2$-Bacteriophagen. *Biochim. Biophys. Acta* 61: 857–864.

Köhler, A. 1921. Ein G. Glimmerplätchen Grau. I. Ordnung zur Untersuchung sehr Schwach doppelbrechender Präparate. *Z. Wiss. Mikroskopie* 38: 29–42.

Maestre, M. F., and R. Kilkson. 1965. Intrinsic birefringence of multiple-coiled DNA, theory and applications. *Biophys. J.* 5: 275–287.

Nakanishi, Y. H. 1957. Some observations on the internal structure of the sperm head of the grasshopper, *Oxya yezoensis*, after dehydration and hydration treatments. *J. Fac. Sci. Hokkaido Univ.* Ser. VI. 13: 276–280.

Pattri, H. O. E. 1932. Über die Doppelbrechung der Spermien. *Z. Zellforsch. Mikroskop. Anat.* 16: 723–744.

Reitberger, A. 1964. Lineare Anordnung der Chromosomen im Kern des Spermatozoids des Lebermooses *Sphaerocarpus donnellii*. *Naturwiss.* 51: 395–396.

Ris, H. 1959. Die Feinstruktur des Kerns während der Spermiogenese. In *Chemie der Genetik*. Berlin: Springer-Verlag. Pp. 1–30.

Ris, H. 1963. Ultrastructure of the cell nucleus. In *Funktionelle und Morphologische Organization der Zelle*. Berlin: Springer-Verlag. Pp. 1–14.

Ruch, F. 1956. Birefringence and dichroism of cells and tissues. In *Physical Techniques in Biological Research*, Vol. 3, ed. G. Oster and A. W. Pollister. New York: Academic Press, Inc. Pp. 149–176.

Sato, H., and S. Inoué. 1964. Condensation of the sperm nucleus and alignment of DNA molecules during spermiogenesis in *Loligo pealii*. *Biol. Bull.* 127: 357.

Schmidt, W. J. 1937. Die Doppelbrechung von Karyoplasma, Zytoplasma und Metaplasma. *Protoplasma Monogr.* 11. Berlin: Gebrüder Borntraeger Verlag.

Seeds, W. E. 1953. Polarized ultraviolet microspectrography and molecular structure. *Progr. Biophys. Biophys. Chem.* 3: 27–46.

Seeds, W. E., and M. H. F. Wilkins. 1950. Ultraviolet microspectrographic studies of nucleoproteins and crystals of biological interest. *Discussions Faraday Soc.* 9: 417–423.

Sotelo, J. R., and O. Trujillo Cenóz. 1960. Electron microscope study on spermatogenesis. Chromosome morphogenesis at the onset of meiosis (cyte 1) and nuclear structure of early and late spermatids. *Z. Zellforsch. Mikroskop. Anat.* 51: 243–277.

Swann, M. M., and J. M. Mitchison. 1950. Refinements in polarized light microscopy. *J. Exptl. Biol.* 27: 226–237.

Taylor, J. H. 1964. The arrangement of chromosomes in the mature sperm of the grasshopper. *J. Cell Biol.* 21: 286–289.

Thorell, B., and F. Ruch. 1951. Molecular orientation and light absorption. *Nature* 167: 815.

Watson, J. D., and F. H. C. Crick. 1953. A structure for deoxyribose nucleic acids. *Nature* 171: 737–738.

Wilkins, M. H. F. 1951. I. Ultraviolet dichroism and molecular structure in living cells. II. Electron microscopy of nuclear membrane. *Pubbl. Staz. Zool. Napoli* 23: Suppl. 104–114.

Wilkins, M. H. F. 1963. Molecular configuration of nucleic acids. *Science* 140: 941–950.

Wilkins, M. H. F., and B. Bataglia. 1953. Note on the preparation of specimens of oriented sperm heads for X-ray diffraction and infra-red absorption studies and on some pseudo-molecular behavior of sperm. *Biochim. Biophys. Acta* 11: 412–415.

Wilkins, M. H. F., and J. T. Randall. 1953. Crystallinity in sperm heads, molecular structure of nucleoprotein *in vivo*. *Biochim. Biophys. Acta* 10: 192–194.

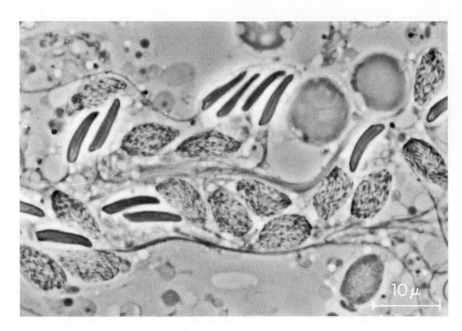

**Fig. 1.** Photograph through phase contrast microscope of spermatid nuclei of the squid *L. pealii*, at various stages of sperm maturation. Teased fresh testis imbibed in nontoxic Kel F-10 oil to reduce Brownian movement and improve image quality.

During spermiogenesis, nucleus of young spermatid goes directly from "telophase" to "prophase." In this stage, many coils of chromonemata are arranged more or less longitudinally in the sperm head. The oriented chromonemata shorten and become more compact and more densely packed as the sperm approaches maturity. No structure in the mature sperm head is resolvable. Nucleus gradually condenses laterally but does not change in length (*ca.* 7.8 $\mu$) during maturation process.

**Fig. 2.** Photograph through polarizing microscope of fresh smear of squid testis imbibed in Kel F-10 oil, as for Fig. 1. Compare weak birefringence (almost zero) in young spermatid nuclei, increasing birefringence of nuclei in developing sperm, and strong ($-30$ m$\mu$) birefringence in mature sperm. Since the width of the mature sperm is 1.4 $\mu$, the coefficient of birefringence reaches $-2 \times 10^{-2}$. A negative coefficient of birefringence is characteristic of well-oriented DNA gels.